Whoosh Goes the Market

Whoosh Goes the Market

Algorithms, Automation, and Alienation

Daniel Scott Souleles

The University of Chicago Press

Chicago and London

The University of Chicago Press, Chicago 60637
The University of Chicago Press, Ltd., London
© 2024 by The University of Chicago
Published 2024
Printed in the United States of America

33 32 31 30 29 28 27 26 25 24   1 2 3 4 5

ISBN-13: 978-0-226-83377-4 (cloth)
ISBN-13: 978-0-226-83379-8 (paper)
ISBN-13: 978-0-226-83378-1 (e-book)
DOI: https://doi.org/10.7208/chicago/9780226833781.001.0001

Library of Congress Cataloging-in-Publication Data

Names: Souleles, Daniel Scott, author.
Title: Whoosh goes the market : algorithms, automation, and alienation /
    Daniel Scott Souleles.
Description: Chicago ; London : The University of Chicago Press, 2024. |
    Includes bibliographical references and index.
Identifiers: LCCN 2023048028 | ISBN 9780226833774 (cloth) | ISBN
    9780226833798 (paperback) | ISBN 9780226833781 (ebook)
Subjects: LCSH: Stockbrokers. | Online stockbrokers. | Electronic trading
    of securities—Social aspects—United States. | Stock exchanges—Social
    aspects—United States. | Capital market—Social aspects—United States. |
    Technology—Social aspects—United States. | Algorithms—Social aspects. |
    Alienation (Social psychology) | BISAC: SOCIAL SCIENCE / Anthropology /
    Cultural & Social | COMPUTERS / Data Science / Machine Learning
Classification: LCC HG4621 .S68 2024 | DDC 332.640973—dc23/eng/20231212
LC record available at https://lccn.loc.gov/2023048028

♾ This paper meets the requirements of ANSI/NISO Z39.48-1992
(Permanence of Paper).

To Amanda Lee Shapiro with love.
Thank you for coming north with me.

Contents

Preface: Five Times a Day? ix

1. Whooshing Up 1
2. Everything Is Down Again 15
3. The Greatest Trader in the World 36
4. On Markets: Rallies and Flows 51
5. Eternal Optimizers 64
6. A Nice Chianti for Our Trading Partner, the Target Bomber 79
7. They Don't Tell You That There's No Price 96
8. Why Would You Buy an Electric Car on Jet Ski Friday? 113
9. The Economy Will Be Open by Easter 127

Acknowledgments 137
Appendix A. Note-Taking Summary 141
Appendix B. Profanity Distribution 143
Appendix C. AlgoFinance Project Informants 147
Appendix D. How Exchange Professionals Use the Word Market 159
Appendix E. How Quants Use the Word Stem Algo 165
Glossary of Some Trading Words 173
Notes 183
References 195
Index 205

Table 1. Members of the options market making group at TradeCo

Pseudonym	Approximate age	Gender	Racial/ ethnic identity	Education[1]	Job function
Jeff Miller	40	M	White, Euro-American	Bachelor's in a humanities discipline	Team Leader
Walt Bennett	55	M	White, Euro-American		Supervising Partner
Aaron Meyers	23	M	White, Euro-American	Bachelor's in physics and economics	Junior team member, coding, analytic work, apprentice trading work
Tony Ellis	29	M	White, Euro-American		Options Trader, monitoring group market-making positions, occasional pit trading
Brandon Price	35	M	Asian, Chinese American	Master's in financial mathematics	Options Trader, Monitoring group market-making positions
Rob Ortiz	40	M	Latino, Mexican American		Options Trader, trading on yield curve spreads
Lee Foster	35	M	White, Euro-American		Options Trader, Pit Trader
Kyle Hughes	30	M	Asian, Chinese American		Options Trader, monitoring some market making trading, programming
Zach Bauer	50	M	White, Euro-American		Chief Information Officer

1. At one point, Tony noted that just about everyone on the team had come through the financial mathematics master's program at a local, elite university. I'm fairly certain that Kyle, Rob, and Tony, at least, have a master's in financial mathematics.

Five Times a Day?

Despite the fact that they seemed to perform an essential service for financial markets, it wasn't immediately obvious to me that Jeff Miller[1] and his group of six traders were good at making money. The seven of them worked as a team of "market makers" or middlemen (all seven of them are, in fact, men—see table 1 for a demographic chart). They both bought and sold stocks, stock options, and other derivative financial products via both computer terminals and on a trading floor across a variety of American markets, all for a company we'll call TradeCo. TradeCo is a large, privately owned capital-management firm with a number of teams and divisions in cities around the world. As market makers, and as just one group within the much larger TradeCo organization, Jeff and his team simply wanted to make their money by buying low and selling the same thing high, collecting the "spread," or the money in between those two prices, over and over again, as often as they could. They didn't want to invest, they simply wanted to trade, to provide the service of "liquidity," or the presence of an always willing buyer and an always eager seller to various markets and their sundry participants. Markets always need middlemen. Given that, it should be a reliable way to make money as one small part of TradeCo's larger portfolio. So far, so essential.

As to the specifics of what exactly they're trading, what a "stock option" or a "derivative" is, don't worry, we'll get to that in due course. For now, suffice it to say that Jeff and his team are middlemen; they're traders, and they feel they're providing present-day capital markets a fairly basic functional service. After all, so the thinking goes, if there were no middlemen, you might encounter a situation where you wanted to sell some stock and couldn't find a buyer or wanted to buy some stock and couldn't find a willing seller. Carrying on this thought experiment, without market makers or some mechanism for providing liquidity on financial markets, capitalism would stop working. A financial crisis, when you get down to it, is precisely this: the absence of liquidity, the evaporation of buyers and sellers, the consequent devaluation of assets and an inability to make good on debt obligations, and the panicked halt to the circulation of money—the borrowing and lending lifeblood of a monetized, financialized, capitalist society. Given the importance of this kind of liquidity, you'd think, provided that you had some start-up money, the correct licensing, dense social networks in finance, a large organization within which to work, and a long history trading on various financial markets, that it might be fairly easy to make money as a market maker. Despite having all of those seemingly essential prerequisites, Jeff and his team would often vacillate between rage, cynical despair, and boredom—as well as their opposites: glee, satisfaction, and triumphalism—all at their ability to make (or lose) money and at the slim prospect of their group's long-term survival. Take one typical after-market-hours discussion as an example.

As part of a much larger, multiyear research project, I spent a month (two weeks in February 2019 and two weeks in May 2019) observing Jeff and his team. What this amounted to was me sitting with their group at their office listening, watching, and asking questions, writing up everything everyone said, all leading to just shy of one thousand pages of typed-out conversation and observation notes (see app. A for a summary of the volume of notes I took). One day, an hour or two after market hours had closed, I was left with three members of Jeff's team: Rob, Kyle, and Aaron. Aaron, at twenty-three, was the most junior member of the team, and he was just out of college. I was curious whether he planned on being a trader for the rest of his career. It turned out his answer depended on the length of his life.

Aaron. Well, that's a complicated question, given that I could die on the way home. I mean, if that happened, then yeah, I'd be a trader for the rest of my life.
Daniel Souleles. [*Laughs*]
A. I could die.
D. That's pretty morbid.
Rob. Can't you tell we're all pretty morbid around here? Brandon [another trader] says that he hopes his tongue is pulled out and his hand is chopped off so he can't trade anymore.

D. [*Laughs*]

A. I've downloaded this app that reminds me five times a day that I'm going to die.

D. Oh, is this that app that is supposed to help with depression? Like showing you how absurd the depression is?

A. That sounds about right. Five times a day. It's based on a saying from Bhutan that says that you need to be reminded of death five times a day to enjoy life, or something.

D. Is the app working?

A. Eh [*shrugs*]. I'm pretty anxious.

D. Do you figure you'll be a trader in the next five to ten years?

A. Actually, we've been talking about this a lot lately. We worry that the big guys like the Citadels of the world are coming for us. If they start taking equity options volume, we'd be in trouble. We're worried all the time.

Kyle. I have a friend who works at Citadel. They're not worried at all. They just run a program and it adds to PnL [profit and loss] all day. They never have down days.

Aaron, Rob, and Kyle had no shortage of gallows humor. Aaron has death on his mind. Rob admires Brandon's prodismemberment exit strategy. And Kyle compares their angst to the placid profitability of another firm that does market making, the algorithmically, and therefore, to his mind, automatically profitable Citadel. The comparison to Citadel is instructive as it points to massive changes that have occurred on financial markets over the last few decades, of which Jeff's team at TradeCo worried they were on the losing end.

In 1975 the US Congress passed an amendment to the Securities and Exchange Act of 1934 that would allow the Securities and Exchange Commission to establish a "national market system" (Public Law 94-29, 94th Congress). In 2005 the US Securities and Exchange Commission (SEC), the main body responsible for the regulation of most, though not all, financial markets in the US, made good on this authority and passed "Reg NMS," or a series of regulatory rules and changes that were designed to create a truly "national market system" (NMS). The core of the National Market System was the idea that if one were on a US financial market, individual exchanges would guarantee the best prices for buying and selling that were on offer at any exchange in the United States (or at least route you to another exchange that could meet such prices), all within some minimal quantum of time. No longer would the SEC tolerate local variations in pricing. Naturally this would entail a networking of exchanges and a consolidated account of prices for buying and selling securities across all exchanges (see Bhupathi 2010; MacKenzie et al. 2012; Lewis 2015; Pardo-Guerra 2019, 248–301; MacKenzie 2021).

Not too long ago the majority of United States stock trading occurred in two places: in person on the New York Stock Exchange or electronically via NASDAQ's automated brokerage network. When I started drafting this book, there were twenty-three official National Securities Exchanges (United State Securities and Exchange Commission n.d.a), as well as thirty-three alternative trading systems (many of which are known as "dark pools") (United States Securities and Exchange Commission n.d.b). It's not just the quantity of trading venues that have increased, it's the complexity of the market system and the sheer volume of trades. Each of those exchanges has its own data feeds, its own order types, and its own peculiarities, of which traders, particularly market makers, need to be aware.[2]

Moreover, electronic access to exchanges has freed trading from the in-person pits and granted access to anyone with a subscription and an internet connection. The history of the Chicago Mercantile Exchange (CME), the largest futures trading venue in the world, is an illustration of this volume increase. In 1992 the CME launched an electronic trading platform, Globex. In the year 2000, there were roughly five hundred thousand contracts traded on the CME, and about 10 percent of those were electronic. By 2016 nearly four billion contracts were traded per year (around fourteen million per day), of which 90 percent were electronic (Blythe 2018). Imagine this manner of increase across most financial markets and then having to reckon with this scalar increase as a trader like Aaron, Rob, and Kyle.

Part of this mini–Industrial Revolution's consequences has pushed old-school, in-person traders out of in-person, exchange-housed trading pits (Zaloom 2006; Pardo-Guerra 2010; see also Preda 2017). Jeff and Brandon both started as human, in-person, shouting, pit trader, market makers in options and have transitioned to mostly being screen traders, both managing automated market making and hedging systems and taking some trades over the phone. As Jeff and Brandon (mostly) moved out of the pits, large, technologically sophisticated, automatic, high-speed traders have moved into various markets, often as market makers. The Citadel that Kyle is referring to is one such firm. To Kyle's mind, it's basically impossible to compete with firms like Citadel—they're too advanced, too rich, and too fast. Jeff's team survives in part, in their mind at least, because Citadel hasn't come after the types of trades they work—equity options or VIX (volatility index) products.

If Citadel chose to, theoretically, it could end Jeff's team's run. That Citadel hasn't confuses them, and that came up next in the same conversation:

Rob. We actually get some people to interview here from Citadel from time to time. They get frustrated by being a cog in a big machine. They might make [US$]500,000 a year on [US$]20 million for the firm. So, they see relatively little upside to making these big amounts of money.

Kyle. What you see across the board with us here is we are the people who feel comfortable making a bet on ourselves. Ultimately, this is the niche that we have. Once you're market making with options, you're making a bet on a direction and you are taking a lot of risk given the way that options multiply risk.

Aaron. For whatever reason, the big boys haven't gotten into it yet. There isn't really anything stopping them.

K. There is also a real chance we could blow up.

Periodically, traders will look for a little more autonomy or a change of professional scenery and will interview with Jeff and his team. These interviews offer an opportunity for reflection. The pay per person seems to be a bit lower at Citadel than on Jeff's team at TradeCo, but the work seems much more reliable—no "down days," after all. It's also a bit nerve wracking to Aaron—why hasn't Citadel come for us? From his point of view, there should be nothing stopping them. Perhaps it's just a matter of time. However, Kyle isn't sure that it would happen, that Citadel would outcompete them before they blow themselves up. Options are volatile, after all—they magnify risk. All this background led to an interesting reflection from their leader, Jeff.

Toward the end of my time with TradeCo, Jeff was getting ready to move to another city in another time zone and work in an office, probably by himself, telecommuting to join the rest of his team. This seemed to make him reflective and led to a bit more evaluation on the part of the group than would perhaps be normal. One afternoon, as he surveyed the mostly empty office in which his team sat in the middle among rows of abandoned trading stations and listless office chairs, he pondered his group's fortune and fate as he chatted:

Aaron. What about [that trader]?

Jeff. Oh, he's oh for three; he is oh for treasuries, oh for copper, oh for grains [different futures contracts one could trade].

Rob. Did he last on all?

J. All were short term scratched. [Another trader was] oh for two. [Runs through thirteen other names of failed traders in rapid succession.]

Tony. Did they all lose or not make money?

J. [More names], all big losers.

A. [That one guy]?

J. . . . Lost one million bucks . . . [two other guys] lost fifteen million in eighteen months—just an astonishing amount.

Kyle. Challenge accepted.

[Long conversation about specific losers and specific trades]

J. It's amazing we've survived. This shit is really hard. Only a few people in TradeCo consistently make money. Everyone else comes and goes, comes and goes. Would you believe that sixteen, seventeen groups have come and gone here? It's even more remarkable, this office has gone one and seventeen over a decade . . . unbelievable.

By Jeff's count, in the last decade, from roughly 2009 to 2019, sixteen different trading groups with sixteen (or more) different strategies have blown up in one way or another in his office. Put another way, seventeen groups of financiers and traders and speculators and investors in "Hub City's" TradeCo office have attempted to make money on financial markets under the auspices of TradeCo and with TradeCo's capital. All but Jeff's group have failed. Moreover, as Aaron, Kyle, and Rob point out, this is an odd occurrence, as it's not entirely clear why Citadel hasn't competed them out of the market already too. And, to Jeff's point, well, this shit is hard.

This book, then, is about how Jeff and his team think, feel, and act while they do the day-to-day work necessary to stay afloat on contemporary capital markets. It's about how they manage and develop their trading technology, how they understand the markets they trade on and the news that moves them, how they understand their trading opponents and colleagues, and what they think of each other. It's also specifically about a constant stream of agitated swearing and yelling and joking, of which the above fatalism is just a taste, that attends all of the work that they do. What I'll suggest is that Jeff and his team's specific struggles and triumphs offer a good vantage point for understanding and criticizing how present-day capital markets, and capitalism more generally, are working. To be a bit more specific, Jeff and his team's attempts at trading—the work that keeps them riled up, anxious, and agitated—shows some of the persistent alienating features that come with technological change and wage labor in a capitalist context regardless of what exactly your job is. Moreover, paying attention to this sort of estrangement and alienation is a good way to understand why financial markets behave the way they do in the shadow of their digitization and automation.

Some explanation may help. When I say capitalism, I basically follow anthropologist Hadas Weiss (2019, 26–27) in seeing capitalism as a largely unplanned process of surplus value accumulation. What this means is that, in a capitalist system, in a centrally *uncoordinated* way, capitalists hire workers who create productive capacity, and those workers, in turn, make all manner of services and goods. These workers, goods, and services are meant to respond to some idea of market demand and are sold to generate surplus wealth that accrues to capitalists. Over the last two centuries, much effort across the social sciences writ large has been given to understanding how and why capitalism works the way it does and how and why capitalism affects people the way that it does (e.g., Marx [1867] 1992).

This widespread, diffuse, and ongoing effort has led to a number of generalizations about what comes with being a worker in a capitalist context. One such thoroughgoing fact of capitalist wage labor seems to be some form of alienation and estrangement felt on the part of individual workers and workers as a class of people. Again, following Hadas Weiss's (2021) recent work on "Elusive Adulthood" in Spain, I'll suggest that the precise dynamics of how and why alienation and estrangement occur helps to explain and give some context as to why exactly Jeff and his team worry that the wolves are at the door and are simultaneously confused that, as of yet, TradeCo's team remains uneaten.

Alienation and estrangement are difficult ideas to get our heads around. In plain language they suggest feeling separate or distant from something that one perhaps should be close to. The words also connote that this is not a happy separation but rather one that is unfortunate and upsetting. If we start thinking about wage labor and how wealth is generated in a capitalist context, we can see how estrangement describes an essential part of the work process and much of what Jeff's team is going through.

Again, capitalism is all about the uncoordinated accumulation of surplus wealth. Part of the way this accumulation occurs is by paying a worker for their labor (i.e., renting a worker out and buying their time), having that worker generate more wealth than they are paid for in the course of doing their job, and then keeping that extra wealth as capitalist profit. Very basically, a worker is kept separate from and unpaid for a part of what they produce. This fundamental estrangement is one basis for the accumulation of wealth in a capitalist economic system. There is a bit more to how estrangement works, though, that changes it from a static descriptive fact about wage labor into a diagnosis of the sort of trajectory labor tends to take in a capitalist context. Explaining a bit more about alienation and estrangement helps describe how technology, that is, productive capacity, develops and changes the experience of being a worker.

Before writing *Capital*, Marx kept a series of journals and manuscripts in which he prefaced and prefigured much of his later thinking about capitalism. One essay in 1844 spoke to the dynamics of estranged labor as follows:

> The worker becomes all the poorer the more wealth he produces, the more his production increases in power and range. The worker becomes an ever-cheaper commodity the more commodities he creates. With the increasing value of the world of things proceeds in direct proportion the devaluation of the world of man. (1978, 71)

> All these consequences are contained in the definition that the worker is related to the *product of his labour* as to an *alien* object. For on this premise, it is clear that the more the worker spends himself, the more powerful the alien objective world becomes which he creates over-against himself, the poorer he himself—his inner world—becomes, the less belongs to him as his own. (1978, 72)

What Marx is suggesting here is that there is a dynamic in which estrangement is part and parcel of wage labor and that, generally speaking, estrangement increases as capitalist production advances. Again, in plain language, what this means is that workers, in the normal course of their jobs, by virtue of accumulating wealth, create the technology and capacity that allows the production of ever more goods and services with ever less human labor. Workers make the efficient factories and the automated computer systems that produce more goods and services with fewer people. Simply put, increased productive capacity tends to mean fewer people employed per thing produced.

This process should start to sound familiar: humans creating the means of their own obsolescence is the core of some of our recent anxieties around the ever-advancing development of "intelligent" automated computers that are capable of "learning" coupled with worries around increased efficiency in industrial processes leading to declining amounts of factory work in North Atlantic countries. Economic historian and social theorist Aaron Benanav (2020) suggests that deindustrialization, automation, and the end of work make up no small amount of our anxiety about how the future is going, and that we might understand these anxieties as in part being due to capitalism's inherent capacity to overproduce and accumulate surpluses. As we create more manufacturing capacity globally, as we automate previously manual job tasks, as production writ large requires fewer and fewer people, we are faced with increasing numbers of people either working jobs in which their scope for action and agency is diminished or increasing numbers of surplus people who are alienated from productive work altogether, all against the backdrop of an ever more productive economic system (see also Chiang 2023b).

Jeff and his team seem to be just on the cusp of this sort of alienation and estrangement. They're not exactly sure which way their own work will go. They still trade, but their day-to-day life is marked with frustration at their ability to do their job on increasingly automated markets. They're not sure whether they'll blow themselves up, whether Citadel will knock them out, or whether they'll get to keep doing their work indefinitely (though on that last count they are not terribly confident). Given all this, they also don't quite know what the future will bring, so they speculate, and swear, and joke, sometimes wildly.

A look at some of the work on wage labor and estrangement also illustrates that Jeff and his team are in good or at least common company. Work in anthropology and economic history suggests that wage labor and its alienation have the capacity to dramatically change what people's work and lives look like. Anthropologist Michael Taussig (1977) observed that as capitalists forced people to become landless wage laborers on sugar plantations in the Cauca Valley of Columbia, those laborers came to understand and even pursue increases in their own productivity as compacts with the devil. Cultural historian E. P. Thompson (1967) observed how, as capitalist wage labor spread in Europe, precise factory and industrial clock time came to displace local ideas of time that were anchored to specific places and noncapitalist social arrangements such as agricultural time, solar time, or church time. More recently, no small amount of alienation, anxiety, and rage among destitute women in Manhattan (Waterston 1999), the "white working class" in the US (Sample 2018), and the professional managerial class, again in the US (Ehrenreich 1989), have all been in part attributed to society steadily needing fewer and fewer people to keep its economic system going. It's worth noting, too, that despite being wealthy and talented, estrangement comes for TradeCo all the same (see also Stein 2018; compare to DiFruscia 2012).

Weiss (2021) suggests that this sort of structured capitalist alienation has made it so that increasing numbers of adults in Spain are both no longer capable of achieving conventional milestones for becoming adults and, due to the way that alienation and estrangement work, "productivity, progress, and autonomy appear like personal accomplishments, and their absence like personal failures" (4). Weiss's observation that people tend to internalize these larger structural capitalist processes at the expense of making systemic diagnoses of their problems is helpful to understand the everyday way that Jeff and his team preserve their own agency and dignity by relating to the markets they work on in terms of their *individual* actions, their *individual* capabilities, their *individual* relationships, and crucially, the *specific* actions of others. Understanding this individualization and everyday enaction of alienation is part of the promise of this book and of paying attention to TradeCo.

Given their uneasy relationship with the present and their relatively minor, interstitial place on capital markets, some might say that Jeff and his team are unusual protagonists for the sort of narrative I'm suggesting. After all, they're not big central market participants, and their future, though not necessarily forgone, does not seem guaranteed. They're also not yet categorically down and out. All this, though, is what makes them interesting—they offer the ability to see the uncertain process of workplace alienation and estrangement unfold for relatively wealthy and at least somewhat powerful market actors, and they also offer the ability to see how this sort of estrangement changes how financial markets behave.

I'll suggest, too, that TradeCo's liminal status has a bit to offer wider social science work on finance and markets. Over the past few decades, social scientists have paid a lot of attention to the electrification and automation of markets and what those twin changes have done to the act of trading. Jeff and his team, though, don't fit neatly into these narratives, either. Given that, it'd probably be helpful to hear a bit about why TradeCo is useful to study vis-à-vis the social studies of finance and how Jeff and his team can help connect scholarship on finance to larger questions about the distribution of wealth in society.

So, across a number of academic studies, a neat directional history of the last half century of financial markets has partially emerged, and it goes something like this. Before electrification and automation, trading was in person or over the phone and was built on relationships and market feeling. While never altruistic, professional norms structured trading activity and led to somewhat intelligible market outcomes occurring on a human scale (Baker 1984; Abolafia 1996; Zaloom 2006). Engineers and market designers, in turn, kicked off processes of electrification and automation, which removed traders from adversarial pits, put them on trading desks in their own firms, and consigned them to life behind the screen (Pardo-Guerra 2019). In our academic telling, these changes had three primary, nonreversible effects.

First, traders had to imaginatively recreate and often quantitatively model the markets that they used to experience in person using the signs and signals coming through their screens (Cetina and Bruegger 2002; Beunza and Stark 2004; Cetina and Preda 2007; Borch, Hansen, and Lange 2015). Second, traders had to contend with myriad new limitations on their activities: ignorance mushroomed and it became increasingly difficult to know why other market actors were behaving the way they were (Lange 2016; Lang, Lenglet, and Seyfert 2019; Souleles 2019a); algorithmic and automated trading led to increasingly confusing, dramatic, and or rapid changes in aggregate market prices (Borch 2016; MacKenzie 2018b; MacKenzie 2021; Hansen and Borch 2021; see also Seyfert 2016); and finally, trading consolidated into fewer larger firms—either happening at huge market-making proprietary-trading firms, hedge funds, or large investment bank/financial service firms (e.g., Beunza 2019). One further upshot of the electrification, automation, and consolidation of trading is that there is increasingly a professional extinction, diminution, and replacement occurring across markets—old-school, gregarious, networked market guys are forced out of finance by far fewer people with backgrounds in physics, mathematics, data science, and engineering (Zaloom 2006; Derman 2004; Pardo-Guerra 2019; Zuckerman 2019).[3]

This literature is great in a lot of ways, and I'll return to it periodically over the course of this book. But for all its merits, Jeff and his team, despite being active, profitable market participants, fit awkwardly into it. Though their work is partially automated, they still do pit and phone trading. They haven't been displaced by larger firms (yet), and they still employ people with conventional trading backgrounds (though perhaps not as new hires). Also, unlike many of the traders who emerge from the above scholarship, Jeff and his team are outspoken, politically opinionated critics of the basic structure and governance of the markets they trade on and the way those markets allocate wealth. Jeff and his team, in some ways at least, surf the steady chaotic accretion of varying forms of market technology and infrastructure (as described in Pardo-Guerra 2019, 6; MacKenzie 2018b, 2019).

For Jeff and his team, the recent history of trading isn't so much linear and unequivocal as it is patchy and partial, with its final terminus, though heavily foreshadowed, not yet come and still worth yelling about. It seems that alienation and dispossession of a sort is partially here, but it's not clear how, when, and even if it will terminally degrade work life at TradeCo. Moreover, understanding what's happening at TradeCo from the standpoint of their technology or the networks and infrastructures they build misses the larger story of how people cope with alienation in the workplace and just how sharp and insightful critique can be when it comes from people being ground up by the advancement of certain forms of automation.

The way I'm navigating the specialist scholarship on finance and financial markets also speaks to a larger distinction in what I hope to explain by studying finance people. My basic anthropological interests have to do with how humans identify that which is valuable, turn it into some form of wealth, and then allocate that wealth to create abundance and poverty. Finance then, is a site to watch this sort of thing happen on a global scale (see, e.g., Souleles 2020a). Keith Hart and Horacio Ortiz (2014) have suggested that in studying finance, one is able to track how and why money flows the way it does around the world. Horacio Ortiz (2020; see also 2021) has further suggested that by showing how financiers "imagine and experience themselves" (5), we can understand how it is that financiers contribute to global hierarchies of wealth. This is a different scale of analysis than a more organizationally focused account of, say, the development of a stock exchange (Pardo-Guerra 2019), or even a more technologically focused account that is curious about how wealth, power, and capacity relate *within* and *among* financial industry participants (MacKenzie 2021). Instead, I hope to follow Ortiz and Hart and use an account of Jeff and his team's estranged relationships to their own work as traders to illustrate how wealth flows on and through an increasingly depopulated world of financial markets.

What we'll see is that these markets are heavily automated, politically managed, confusingly regulated, fiendishly complex, ruthlessly competitive, and constantly changing. All this constrains who is able to give and receive money in American society, structuring a world in which winners accumulate vast wealth, and most have precious little opportunity to compete to begin with.

If we extrapolate further, we might suggest that Jeff and his team's struggle to live in and with complex automated systems can also stand as an allegory for one aspect of the present human condition. After all, these sorts of systems seem to be encroaching on all aspects of our lives—everything from health care to finding love to becoming an adult to going shopping to listening to music to answering questions and expressing ourselves and even to enforcing laws and catching criminals—all are increasingly bound and constrained by similarly complex, largely autonomous computer systems and the alienated work lives to which they lead. While many readers may find it difficult to empathize with a few specialized, relatively wealthy traders, I'd like to suggest that if even Jeff and his team are feeling the crunch, I don't imagine the rest of us will be able to avoid automation and estrangement in our own worlds. There is something in their struggle that we may find useful and perhaps even relatable (or at least cathartic). But I'll leave the final judgment to the reader.

So, what exactly is it, in and on financial markets, that makes Jeff, Tony, Kyle, Rob, Brandon, Lee, and Walt confounded, agitated, and angry so often and all to the point of obscenity?

I

Whooshing Up

Toward the end of my second stay with Jeff and his group, I realized I was missing something basic—I did not have a succinct explanation for how they made money. So, in the course of a fairly typical stream of conversation they had with each other—commenting on the news, the market environment, and their positions—I interjected.

Daniel. I don't know how you guys make money.
Kyle. [*Laughs*]
Rob. We make money.
Jeff. Sometimes.
[ongoing exchanges about current market conditions]
J. Really, the way we make money is that we sell VIX options that are too rich and buy equity options that are too cheap. People pay too much money for VIX options and sell their options too cheap—they over pay for portfolio insurance; that's VIX. There is this mindset for the two groups of people: VIX buyers are fund managers insuring against losses from market corrections; equity options buyers are more retail and guys who are more specialized in a single name [a specific stock]. We also see give-ups, banks and stuff trading with us—we never know who is behind the curtain.

Jeff says it's very simple: people reliably pay too much money for VIX products, and, just as reliably, people sell their stock options too cheap. Stock options are, as the name would suggest, a contract that allows the holder to either buy or sell a certain quantity of stock at any point over a set period of time for a specific price.[1] Stock options are a way for people to speculate and insure themselves against future price changes in a stock. Let's say I'm convinced that GM's stock price is going to double in the next year because they've finally embraced electric vehicles, which are clearly the way of the future. If other people on the market don't think this is the case and they think that the price won't change much, I should be able to buy options contracts that would allow me to either buy (a call option) or sell (a put option) GM stock at the present price. If I were correct in my speculation, at some point before the option contract ended and GM's stock doubled I could use the option to make a profit reflecting that double by buying at the lower option price and selling at the higher market price. If I were wrong, the option would simply expire as a worthless bet, "out of the money," and a market maker, someone who writes options contracts like TradeCo, would pocket my purchase.

Options exist on a calendar, too, with different prices and different times to expiration, generally running about two years into the future at daily, then weekly, then monthly, then yearly intervals. Jeff says that people have a tendency to sell their options too quickly and, consequently, too cheaply without realizing the most profit they might generate.

VIX-related contracts are a bit more complicated. A few years after the 1987 stock market crash, the Chicago Board Options Exchange (CBOE), started displaying a "volatility index," or the "VIX." Volatility is simply a relative measure of how much the price of a stock or an option or some other financial thing moves around. Lots of price swings in a short amount of time would probably mean high volatility. VIX, then, is a numerical heuristic for the implied volatility of financial markets and has been constructed in a few different ways by aggregating call and put options from a fairly common representative sample of stocks called the S&P 500 stock index over some indicative period of time. Roughly speaking, the lower VIX goes, the more call (to buy) than put (to sell) options there are, and the more stable prices are (and it's never gone much lower than 8). In turn, the higher VIX goes, the more put to call options there are, and the more unstable market prices likely are (it's rarely gone above the thirties, and has only done so in spikes, such as the spike to the eighties around the COVID-19 pandemic). Another, somewhat circular, way to think about this is that as volatility goes up, options become more valuable (as a sort of insurance). Given that, there is a way to reason backward from the price of options, infer some expectations about volatility, and produce a metric like the VIX (see also MacKenzie 2018c). So far, and this is the confusing bit, the VIX is just a numerical abstraction of stability or volatility. How might people trade it if it's just a number?

Financial institutions, then, make contracts that are based on the VIX index—contracts that are reliant on the VIX hitting a particular number on a particular date and thereby leading to a payout or expiring worthless. Investors buy either side of these contracts, making wagers on the likelihood that VIX will change, in part, as Jeff says, as portfolio insurance. You might expect the VIX index to go up in times of disruption; as such, a contract that pays out in such an occurrence could be a countermeasure, a way to hedge a portfolio against the loss of value that would come with a financial crisis, depression, or act of God. If you're ever curious to see how finance people are feeling about current events and their effect on capitalism, it's worth doing a quick web search for the "VIX Index" (see also the VIX chart [fig. 3] in the last chapter of this book).[2] Jeff observes that people tend to overpay for portfolio insurance, or VIX-based contracts. That is, people pay too much for the peace of mind they might bring their portfolio.

That's it. A million dollars a day is now yours. Just go and sell VIX contracts to people who need insurance. You can also go and buy options that are too cheap, wait a while, and sell them back at a higher price or exercise them at a profit. Simple as that. However, there are some practicalities you may want to keep in mind.

The first has to do with determining the price of the options or the VIX contracts. Collectively, these instruments are known as "derivatives" in that they theoretically derive their price from an underlying asset—that is, as the underlying assets, say a stock relative to a stock option changes, the prices of the derivatives should change too.[3] Traders commonly use some version of the Black Scholes Merton equation, a calculus-based transformation[4] of a formula in physics used to describe Brownian particle motion, in order to determine a price[5] (see MacKenzie 2006). In addition, it's worth noting that because the present and future volatility of financial instruments can't be measured (whereas past volatility can), the value of an option going forward is never an incontrovertible fact; there will always be some manner of judgment in coming up with options prices, some inference to "implied" volatility.

Given that, if the market deviates from some predicted price, you might have an investment opportunity, an expectation of reversion to the mean, and a chance to buy or sell. This, though, is further complicated, again, as options exist in chains on into the future. Not only do you need to figure out a price of a given option but also the prices of other options in the chain, setting up a whole string of related calculations. Even if you have the ability to calculate the chain to your own satisfaction and can explain any discrepancies between your calculations and the market, you need to act on your calculations before whatever opportunity you've found goes away. Put another way, you have to execute your order faster than other people watching the same data and making the same sorts of calculations. So, the second consideration has to do with speed.

As markets have computerized and automated, the speed with which people respond to changes in prices has also accelerated. Michael Lewis (2015; see also MacKenzie 2018b; MacKenzie 2021) described precisely this sort of phenomenon in his book *Flash Boys*. He noted that with Reg NMS came a data feed (the SIP [Securities Information Processor]) that aggregated trading activity from all equities exchanges and produced a best bid to buy and offer to sell reference that all other exchanges were meant to post, match, or route orders based on. The problem was that this aggregated data feed was slower than the data that traders could get directly from exchanges. In turn, this allowed traders to anticipate market moves before those market moves could show up on the SIP. A trader might be able to see a large order hit one exchange, shift price levels, and adjust their quotes on another exchange before the rest of the market could find out about it. This sort of race happens all the time on financial markets and is exacerbated the more fragmented markets become. One could imagine, too, that this would become amplified across an option chain where the change in one stock's price or volume or velocity of trade would affect the entire chain. And in a delightful, frustrating bit of looping, every once in a while, someone on Jeff's team would look at their orders and say they were getting "flashboyed," suggesting that some big player, a Citadel say, had beat them to an order at a previously posted price or removed an order before Jeff and his team could hit a given price level.

Accounting for the speed of present-day markets as well as the difficulty in pricing assets leads to a third set of concerns, and that is doing all this at scale or systematically. To do this, not only do you need fast market data, a systematic way to both figure and change the prices of your investments, and extremely fast market connections, you also have to make sense of the larger market environment to price in news (say, the release of employment statistics or changes in interest rates) and events (say US military aggression in the Middle East, or labor unrest in France, or the development of a vaccine in a pandemic). Doing all this requires the ability to turn intangible events into specific bets on portfolio positions and adjust accordingly and at pace.

What I suggest is that for Jeff and his team, addressing these practicalities involves real-time analysis and action that occurs in a sort of never-ending conversation with topics coming and going and taking up most of their day. Finding pattern and meaning in this never-ending conversation illustrates how they can survive in this extremely complex, competitive environment, and it is the descriptive task of this book. A look at a typical bit of conversation from May 15, 2019, will help explain this. This early in the chapters, it will probably read as a bit confusing. Please, bear with it, and trust that clarity will come; and, perhaps, enjoy the color commentary.

How Are Things on the Market?

Jeff. Weeklies are thirty-one—pretty messed up. We were up forty-two yesterday, then dropped twenty and twenty. [The position is] basically unched [unchanged]—thirty-four, thirty-three, thirty-two, thirty-four, thirty-three, thirty-one—one and a half percent.

Tony. How aggressive do you want us to buy or sell stuff?

J. Probably get off some scalps.

T. Bought 1.5 million banks so far. Bought a million on the open. I'm just buying more. Fuck this shit. Buy three million on the open right now—basically a third of it. So fucking much [inaudible]. Also, up to two.

J. Want to sell fucking Microsoft puts.

T. Whoosh up; fucking hell. Can't even get a minute to goddamn buy anything.

J. I was going to blast a bunch of fucking Microsoft puts, but holy shit.

T. Whoosh down B-A-C vol.

J. Microsoft vol up a lot.

T. Pulling B-A-C. Selling us options. I'm done.

J. Not pulling anything.

T. Fuck that shit.

J. Got a little bit.

T. Crazy mark in E-W-Z marking us down.

J. Google, Microsoft, Square, Twitter, Baba up.

T. We're up no money now. That's sad. None.

J. Big fucking rally—five handles so far.

T. Just as planned—print up the VIX to fuck us.

J. Massive rally. What's going in rates?

Rob. Lower interest rates.

J. Might be too early to rally rally.

T. I would watch your CITI stuff; I would not buy anything.

J. Vol down on the day.

T. Lyft is crazy strong.

J. You long?

T. Like three thousand, not much. Did you read into that naked short? Seem like a huge—just fucking their client.

J. What did you read?

T. I read that they sold short into the IPO . . .

J. . . . knowing they'd get raked.

There are a few things worth noting in the above bit of conversation. First, the traders spend a lot of time relaying basic information about markets to each other. At any given time, they're trading options on perhaps sixty stocks (specific "names"), as well as other derivative products, such as those based on the VIX, or S&P 500 futures (for a specific list, see table 2 in the next chapter). Each of these products, in turn, entails both positions on a full options calendar as well as things to hedge these positions (generally "delta hedging" or buying and/or selling equities to offset the risk of an options position turning severely unprofitable). While they do have automated systems to flag trades that have become money losers, they generally need to make a human judgment about how they will adjust the risk profile of a given position. This work is far too much for any individual to pay attention to all at once, so Jeff and his team help each other out.

After Jeff makes some observations about the weekly version of something they are trading, reflecting on its change, Tony asks for guidance on how aggressively the team should be trading. Jeff suggests some trades of opportunity (some "scalps"), Tony notes what he's done, and they start cycling observations and narrating their responses to the market via their trade decisions, back and forth. Jeff points out that a number of the tech stocks they trade—Google, Microsoft, Square, Twitter, and [Ali] Baba—are all up. Jeff and Tony also point out to each other that a "rally" is occurring, or that some things are "whooshing" up some number of handles.

A handle is the whole number value of a price or an index. When things move by handles instead of decimals, in dollars instead of pennies, markets are moving quickly. If they're talking about a market-wide whoosh up as opposed to a specific name, they're often referring to a whole exchange, such as NASDAQ or NYSE, or a specific index, such as the S&P 500 stock average, or futures based on the S&P 500 (which expire quarterly and are called Spooz). Talking about these "handle whooshes" is a way to talk about market direction. Again, market direction is important because it can lead to a realignment of the whole portfolio or at least evaluation of whether this is necessary (when to pull or post "shit"). Some amount of whether they would like to market-make in specific options has to do with bets on market direction and how much trading will happen in that circumstance.

In addition to simply presenting each other information, Jeff and Tony also offer commentary, suggestions, and advice. Rob notes that there are lower interest rates, and Jeff is wondering whether the timing is right for a real rally, a "rally rally." Tony feels like the change in the VIX is inexplicable and bad for their position. Jeff feels like this much market movement might allow for some quick trades and profits, some "scalps." And toward the end of the exchange, Jeff and Tony are talking about the recent Uber initial public offering (IPO) of stock. Tony read something that suggests that insiders sold Uber stock short because they knew its price was going to go down after the IPO. This would be something a market maker would want to know about while they plan their positions (in addition to being a terrible way for Uber to treat their own investors). This also seems to be making Lyft, another ride-sharing company, look good by comparison. All this was very loosely in response to Tony's question about how aggressive Jeff wanted them to trade, which set the path for this chunk of conversation.

All told, TradeCo's division of talk between observation and commentary seems to reflect a pattern Koenraad Kuiper (1996) observed in his study of auctioneers and sportscasters. Kuiper noted that both auctioneers and sportscasters have occasion to verbally comment on quick-moving, quick-changing phenomena, such as, say, a horse race or an auction that lasts perhaps only a number of seconds. Both types of callers need to respond fluidly and in time and give some account of what they see. Kuiper's insight into this form of conversation is that both auctioneers and sportscasters need to be "smooth talkers," that is to say, "rapid time pressures to speak produce increasingly formulaic oral performances" (7). Management scholar Daniel Beunza (2019, 61–63), drawing on work about situated, context-specific cognition (e.g., Hutchins 1995; Heath et al. 1994), noted similar patterns of talk and thinking in his work on a much larger mixed-strategy trading room at a large financial firm.

We can see formulaic talk when Jeff starts listing off prices and spreads in some weekly contract and Tony and Jeff talk about aggregate directional "whooshes," or more basically and more sparely when things are described as up or down relative to a period of time. This sort of formulaic play-by-play accounting is one thoroughgoing structuring feature of Jeff's team's work. However, their play-by-play reporting is broken up by another genre of speaking: commentary (see Kuiper 21ff.).

Jeff and Tony make use of each other's real-time, compressed, formulaic reporting of market events that they think are important and in turn interpret them via a less (though not entirely un-) formulaic "commentary" genre of speech. Tony suggests that Uber short sellers are "fucking their clients." Tony is also frustrated ("fucking hell") at the market whooshes not leaving him enough time to buy what he wants. Jeff emphasizes a "big fucking rally"; and, at another point, he wants to (emphatically) sell some "fucking Microsoft puts."

Not everything is fucked: interspersed among the exclamations, verbs, and modifiers, Jeff and Tony also use milder language to talk about pulling back on some of their proposed sales as well as to speculate on the timing of the rally. This commentary genre of speaking blends with Jeff and Tony's play-by-play genre to give a real-time glimpse of how Jeff and his team do their work. As anthropologist and folklorist Richard Bauman notes, "each genre will be distinguished by its thematic or referential capacities, as a routinized vehicle for encoding and expressing particular orders of knowledge and experience" (2000, 85). For Jeff and his team, play-by-play and commentary each have different capabilities and functions related to the high volume of information they need to process and understand in the course of their job.

Dirty and Clean

One thing that may also be apparent from the above bit of dialogue from the trading room is that Jeff and his team swear a lot. In this one stretch of dialogue, over barely a page and a half, there are nine "fucks": four modifiers with a noun (e.g., "fucking Microsoft puts"); two transitive uses of the verb (e.g., "just as planned—print up the VIX to fuck us"); one phrasal use of the verb with "this"; and one phrasal use of the verb with "that" ("fuck this [and or] that")—all of which inflect a snippet of conversation in which Jeff and Tony are describing market conditions and how to act given those conditions.

Across the one thousand or so pages of notes that I collected, I found 694 *fucks* scattered across 387 *fuck*-bearing conversation chunks (see app. B for a table summarizing the *fucks'* morphological distribution). These chunks approximate a discrete burst of conversation around the topic covered by the *fuck*.[6] These chunks allow us to follow Jeff and his team's commentary on their market activity and see to what they draw attention.[7]

However, before we can appreciate that, it'd be helpful for me to explain how exactly I'm understanding their use of the word *fuck*, and why I think it's a good index for tracking what they're thinking about. To do this we should proceed in two steps: first to explore what it means to be a group of people who swear, and second to understand specifically what that group is doing with their blue streak.

Let's start with the sheer fact of swearing. In a basic way, how a group of people uses a given language distinguishes themselves as compared to other groups that use the same language. We might call these distinct ways of talking, of using a common language, "registers." Groups—doctors, cops, Reddit trolls, and so forth—all have registers of language that distinguish them from other groups of people (Agha 2000, 2015b). Put another way, a group of people is in part a distinct entity because of the specific register within a larger language community that they use. Swearing, here, is part of the register of being a trader; and the register of "trader" is in turn a subdivision of American English. The particular use of profanity that traders employ as one bit of the repertoire of language that makes up their professional register both allows them to communicate internally (via play-by-play and commentary genres) and marks them as a distinct group. Swearing, though, isn't as innocent as having a specialized medical jargon for, say, protein binding or for, say, a court officer categorizing motor vehicle violations.

Asif Agha (2015a), in theorizing "slang," makes this point. For Agha slang is a "framework for reasoning about language that defines a class of deviant registers of language" (306). People categorize some registers as slang and then make judgments about not only the members of a group but what their quality and worth is. "To say that some utterance is slang, or contains slang expression, is to inhabit a metapragmatic stance that evaluates its speaker as deviating from a presumed standard" (307). It's not just that Jeff and his team have a professional register (they do) but that they have a register that many in the larger language community might see as a deviant form because of the prominent place of swearing. What does it mean, then, that swearing is a part of their argot?

Swearing does particularly interesting things for group formation and distinction. To start at least, it's worth noting that Jeff and co. do a very specific type of swearing, one that we might characterize as "obscenity" and "profanity" (for more on this distinction, see McIntosh 2021). Sitting with them, you'll hear all manner of *fucks*, *shits*, *asses*, and so on. You will also hear plenty of blasphemy: "Goddamnit," "Jesus Christ," and so forth. You will not, however, hear many racial epithets. Once in a while there will be teasing about people in the group's ethnic heritage or racial identity that may involve some midrange epithets. However, I don't recall hearing particularly taboo racial epithets or racial epithets spoken in anger. They didn't use, for example, the N-word, or use racial slurs to express anger at each other. That said, one class of categorical epithet that did come up a few times were epithets for women (e.g., b—— and c——). While these did come up from time to time (c—— twice from one trader; b—— as a noun five times from two traders; b—— or b——ing as a verb and mode of complaining: around sixteen times from most of the traders), the vast majority of their swearing was in the form of obscenity and profanity.[8]

What's interesting, too, about their use of obscenity is that it's almost never literal (see further Mohr 2013, 7ff.; Seizer 2011). Across all instances of the word, I found only two *fucks* that were literal (out of nearly seven hundred instances), and both were related to stories about athletes and their sex lives. Rather, the traders use their *fucks* mostly metaphorically, figuratively, and idiomatically.[9] This general, all-purpose usage helps constitute the commentary genre that Kuiper identifies and what Agha might see as part of a group register that could qualify as a slang.

Susan Seizer's (2011) work on live stand-up comedy in the US Midwest helps explain a bit what this *fuck*-full register might mean. Seizer explains that one distinction running through stand-up comedy is whether or not a comedian is "dirty" or "clean" (212). She goes on to note that, "the register of dirty words . . . plays a large part in orienting audiences to the kind of playful communicative relationship that constitutes live stand-up comedy . . . [and is] linked to the fact that the majority of performance venues on the comedy club circuit are also bars, in which one rightly expects to encounter looser-than-usual behavior" (211). Put another way, "Audiences attending live stand-up in such night spots expect to hear speech onstage that would be otherwise and elsewhere, unmentionable, and road comics know this" (212). For the comics, dirty comedy, the use of swearing points toward adult spaces and spaces where relaxed or intimate social behavior is acceptable.

Seizer further suggests that this sort of swearing, "may make us feel, somewhat paradoxically, that the comedian speaks to us 'from the heart'" (214). "Obscenity in these performances serves to heighten and intensify the expression of the speaker's perspective, affect, and experience. . . . Such use puts audiences at ease and makes the dialogic performance event feel like colloquial, quotidian talk" (230). For road comics, then, swearing both points to an adult, relaxed space, and, because of taboos elsewhere in society, a sort of shared transgression that allows for swearing to index authentic, intimate talk. This two-step helps piece together Jeff and his group.

As Seizer notes, swearing is a generally taboo behavior in US society, and sites that allow swearing are demarcated, set aside, and probably adult. Moreover, communities that are comfortable swearing with each other probably have access to a range of emotional and seemingly authentic expression that may not be present in more mixed and restricted public social contexts (see also Adams 2016 and Byrne 2018). This is basically what is going on with Jeff and his traders. Their swearing forms a part of their professional speech register, a slang that sharply delineates them from other groups in the larger society (see also Preda 2012, 160). Two small examples indicate the specific role that swearing plays in defining them as a group—despite swearing constantly, I never saw them swear with or at the administrative assistants in their office or on the phone with their families (with them, they were basically calm, respectful, and polite). Swearing was mostly a part of their workplace and the group of people with whom they collaborate. Moreover, they use their swearing, as the above extract points out, to evaluate and comment on their ongoing trading and the circumstances that allow or frustrate it.

Often the *fucks* are used to modify nouns, verbs, or adjectives in an incidental way. Linguists might see these as "discourse markers," or bits of language that functionally bracket or organize "units of talk" (Schiffrin 1987, 31; see also Mendoza-Denton 2008, 265ff.). At one point, Jeff notes a "big fucking rally." In this sentence, we might wonder what's the "fucking" doing there? If we take it away, it's still a "big rally." The "fucking," though, emphasizes the observation and suggests that Jeff thinks it's an extra noteworthy observation and draws Tony's attention. In Seizer's terms it "heightens" and "intensifies" Jeff's take on the market and invites Tony to a similar level of general observation.

At another point, after pulling some trades, that is, canceling some orders, Tony says, "fuck that shit," to indicate his frustration and disgust at both market conditions and TradeCo's ability to make money thereon. "Fuck that shit" doesn't add any new overt information, but it does allow Tony to add an affective tag to this sequence of conversation and show to Jeff how he is feeling about the trading day. It also makes a small, tacit argument for Tony's decisions to pull trades: something happened that got him to object, "fuck that shit"; under those conditions, sure, pull your trades. Jeff accepts Tony's gloss and actions as an appropriate comment on and response to markets, and the conversation and trading continues alternating between observation and mostly frustrated commentary.

Again, all these instances of swearing happen in the repetitive language of observation and commentary that makes up the trading group's daily round. I suggest that paying attention to the topics that Jeff and his team swear about provides a fairly good inventory of what they are concerned with on markets, what they feel it's important to pay attention to, and how they're dealing with their alienated moment in financial history. Given this assumption on my part, I took the 387 *fuck*-bearing conversation extracts I created when tracking their use of the word and coded them according to conversation subject (NB: some fragments have multiple topics, so the total will sum to more than 387). Table 2 breaks down what they're swearing about.

All told, this inventory of what Jeff and his group swear about offers a good window into how it is that they, as a group constantly communicating with each other, actually make money in an ongoing way. They have to manage their own proprietary technological infrastructure. They have to evaluate markets and the news. They have to hone trading strategies around specific stocks and against their perceived partners (though as Jeff points out and as will be made apparent below, they never really get to get "behind the curtain" and see whom they're trading against). And they have to understand each other and the world they operate in. These topics, then, will make up the rest of the book—technology, markets, trading, and floating above it all, their worldview. Taken together, understanding and following what they swear about points toward what they think is important to note, comment on, and manage in the course of their professional lives. Taken in aggregate the fact that there is so much to swear about gestures toward a bit of what made being a human trader on financial markets so complicated and frustrating and ultimately alienating in 2019. One more thing, though, is necessary to understand the significance of what Jeff and co. do: comparison.

Table 2. Fuck topics

Topic	Frequency
A specific financial instrument	124
General market conditions	101
The state of their trading technology	62
Their trading partners	50
Their trading strategies	45
News and politics	37
Describing people and things	19
Describing themselves	16
Sports	14
Calculating their profit and loss statements	8
Specific trades	3
Regulations	3
Hiring	2
Exchanges/trading venues	2
Miscellaneous	10

Onward, Comparatively

The larger project that saw me spend a month with Jeff and his team produced a huge amount of research on the larger financial world, work that I will use to give context and comparison to the guys at TradeCo. After all, it wouldn't do to take one trading room for the entirety of the financial world. Given that, an overview is of use.

The AlgoFinance project was led by Christian Borch, was run at the Copenhagen Business School in Denmark from 2017 to 2021, and was funded by the European Research Council. Its goal was to understand how the rise of computerized and algorithmic trading has changed financial markets. It wanted to do so by combining ethnographic (context-specific social science fieldwork on specific people) and computer simulation approaches to studying markets and the people on them. In practice this meant that Christian Borch, Bo Hee Min, Kristian Bondo Hansen, and I, social scientists all, conducted fieldwork, mostly interviews and observations in financial hubs, with regulators, exchange operators, traders, data scientists, and investors to create as broad picture as possible of typical market behavior. All told this led to 184 interviews in New York, Chicago, Los Angeles, San Francisco, Washington, DC, London, Amsterdam, Copenhagen, Stockholm, and Frankfurt as well as observational work in two trading firms and a few expert workshops to check our findings. I conducted sixty-nine of these interviews and worked (almost) exclusively in the United States. For a digest of all of this, see appendix C.

On the simulation side of things, Nicholas Skar-Gislinge, Zachary David, and Pankaj Kumar designed an agent-based modeling platform to simulate different market environments with different blends of traders and structuring conditions. The idea with the simulation was that there is a point beyond which humans can't actually see what is going on in markets. There are too many trades between too many partners across too many exchanges. Even if one were to be able to see the trades, you wouldn't be able to see the algorithms behind the trades or the strategies various traders were employing to do their trading. Given that, we hoped to create an approximation of that activity in an agent-based modeling simulation. Agent-based models are simulations in which individual actors are programmed with a set of parameters and then are allowed to interact with each other according to their pre-programmed logics. Often these simulations produce some aggregate complex behavior that is not necessarily a given based on their parameters. In the case of financial markets this could be sudden crashes or overwhelming herding behavior. Overall, our ethnographic work structured the parameters of our simulation work. And our simulation work led to further questions for our ethnographic work.

As I describe how Jeff and his team see technology, markets, trading, and the world, I'll draw on data from the wider project as well as secondary and theoretical sources, as is more conventional in ethnographic reporting and anthropological writing, to offer a glimpse into the financial universe with which TradeCo traders are reckoning. Specifically, I'll pair each chapter on TradeCo with a broader comparative chapter making use of primary data from the AlgoFinance project. I'll also show, occasionally, how Jeff and his team might miss certain things or excel at other things because of the particularity of their professional predicament and the biases they carry. For now, though, we'll start basic and look at a frequent object of their frustration—their technology.

2

Everything Is Down Again

I suppose it was telling that on the first day I sat with Jeff and his group at TradeCo on February 4, 2019, the first obscenity I noted had to do with their computer system's ability to communicate with one of the exchanges they traded on, "NYSE Arca." Arca, short for "Archipelago," is a formerly independent stock exchange that is now owned by the New York Stock Exchange (hence, NYSE Arca). On Arca you can trade equities (stocks), options, and products made of up of lots of different equities (ETFs, or exchange traded funds). Arca also offers incentives or "rebates" to get market makers like Jeff's team at TradeCo to operate on their exchange—a few pennies to offer stocks for others to buy, and a fee of a few pennies for removing stocks by buying them yourself. This is meant to encourage liquidity providers or "makers" and discourage liquidity buyers or "takers" (see MacKenzie 2018a), leaving lots of inventory posted on the market for trading. That said, and we'll return to this, TradeCo traders didn't feel they made money buying or selling equities; the Citadels of the world beat them to that possibility. Rather, they bought equities in order to hedge the risk of their options positions and occasionally made a bit of profit on them from rebates like Arca's. This morning, though, things weren't going smoothly.

There was a bit of confusion, specifically about receiving messages from Arca. Given that it was my first day, I was still taking hand notes and typing them up over two or three hours in the evening, and I had not yet started taking real-time pseudo-stenographic notes on my laptop (that came on day three). This, then, is the first note of a leitmotif that cuts across just about everything Jeff and his team did (and probably undercounts the obscenities present):

> In the early morning they had trouble communicating with Arca. Apparently, their tech people had put some patches in to deal with new messages that Arca was going to be sending. However, it didn't seem to work. They [Jeff and his team] kept saying things like, "What the fuck is going on?" and, "I leave the office for two days [the weekend] and everything goes to shit."

Welcome to the field.

Several things are worth noting in this account. First, their tech people, whom we'll meet shortly, are not in the office with Jeff and his team (see Pardo-Guerra 2019, 132–33). They work remotely, and in this case over the weekend, on some tasks for them. Second, with a bit more context, this problem with Arca illustrates how complex their systems are. On any given day, Jeff and his team will place "buy" or "sell" orders on every exchange in the United States. They do so via a variety of techniques—sometimes they have a collocated server in the exchange's building. Other times they go through a third-party execution router with a company like ITG (more on them below). What this means is that TradeCo has to be capable of sending and receiving messages to and from all exchanges. Moreover, they have to be able to receive and interpret data feeds from all of the exchanges. As Arca illustrates, the exchanges are liable to change the way they communicate or the format of their data. Consequently, it's up to the people who trade on their exchanges to keep up. It's worth noting, too, that this sort of basic communication, sending and receiving of information, comes before any sort of trading or investing or making or losing of money. Once Jeff and his team and their off-site tech people manage to get communication settled, there is still the issue of managing their positions.

While I was there, they had around seventy-five symbols or names of financial instruments that they were trading (see table 3 for an approximation). The exact number and distribution of names they traded changed day to day. Moreover, the amount they traded in each name could vary dramatically, too, depending on market opportunities they saw. If they saw trading opportunities as options market makers and then actively traded, they could take up as much as 15 to 20 percent of options trading volume in a specific

Table 3. TradeCo tradable names

Count	Symbol	Name	Description
1	1VXX	Same as symbol	A future "exchange traded note" based on the VIX
2	1VXXB	Same as symbol	A future exchange traded note based on the VIX
3	AA	Alcoa Corporation	American industrial corporation, known for producing aluminum
4	AAL	American Airlines Group	American air travel company
5	AAPL	Apple Incorporated	American technology company
6	AMD	Advanced Micro Devices	American technology company
7	AMZN	Amazon.com Inc.	American e-commerce and technology company
8	BABA	Alibaba Group Holding Ltd. ADR[1]	Chinese technology and e-commerce company
9	BAC	Bank of American Corp.	American financial services company
10	BMY	Bristol-Myers Squibb Co.	American pharmaceutical company
11	C	Citigroup Inc.	American financial services company
12	CELG	Celgene Corp.	Swiss pharmaceutical company (now a part of Bristol-Myers Squibb)
13	CGC	Canopy Growth Corp.	American cannabis company
14	CRON	Cronos Group Inc.	American cannabis company
15	DAL	Delta Air Lines Inc.	American air travel company
16	DB	Deustche Bank AG	German financial services company
17	DDD	3D Systems Corp.	American 3D printer company

(continued)

Table 3. (*continued*)

Count	Symbol	Name	Description
18	DE	Deere & Co.	American farm equipment company
19	DIS	Walt Disney Co.	American entertainment company
20	DWDP	DowDuPont	American chemical company
21	EBAY	eBay Inc.	American e-commerce and auction company
22	EEM	iShares MSCI Emerging Markets ETF	Exchange traded fund built up of a basket of over 800 stocks from emerging markets[2]
23	EFA	iShares MSCI EAFE ETF	Exchange traded fund built up of over 900 stocks in Europe, Australia, Asia, and the Far East[3]
24	EWZ	iShares MSCI Brazil ETF	Exchange traded fund built up of Brazilian companies
25	F	Ford Motor Co.	American car company
26	FR	First Industrial Realty Trust Inc.	American industrial real estate developer
27	GE	General Electric Co.	American technology and manufacturing company
28	GLNG	Golar LNG Ltd.	American ocean-based natural gas company
29	GS	Goldman Sachs Group Inc.	American financial services company
30	HAL	Haliburton C.	American oil field service company
31	HSBC	HSBC Holdings PLC ADR	UK-based financial services company
32	I	Intelsat S.A.	American satellite communication company
33	INTC	Intel Corp.	American technology company

Count	Symbol	Name	Description
34	IWM	iShares Russell 2000 ETF	Exchange traded fund built up of 2,000 small-cap American companies
35	JD	JD.com Inc. ADR	Chinese e-commerce company
36	JPM	JPMorgan Chase & Co.	American financial services company
37	MJ	ETFMG Alternative Harvest ETF	Exchange traded fund built up of thirty-seven cannabis companies
38	MOMO	Momo Inc. ADR	Chinese mobile-based social and entertainment company
39	MSFT	Microsoft Corp.	American technology company
40	MU	Micron Technology Inc.	American technology company
41	NBEV	New Age Beverage Corp.	American health drink company
42	NBR	Nabors Industries Ltd.	American oil and gas company
43	NFLX	Netflix Inc.	American entertainment company
44	NIO	NIO Inc. ADR	Chinese car company
45	NSC	Norfolk Southern Corp.	American train transport company
46	NVDA	NVIDIA Corp.	American technology company
47	OSTK	Overstock.com Inc.	American e-commerce company
48	PBR	Petroleo Brasileiro S/A ADR	Brazilian oil and gas company
49	PCG	PG&E Corp.	American electricity and gas provider
50	PDD	Pinduoduo Inc. ADR	Chinese mobile internet company

(continued)

Table 3. (*continued*)

Count	Symbol	Name	Description
51	QQQ	Invesco QQQ Trust Series I	Exchange traded fund built up of large technology companies
52	RIG	Transocean Ltd.	Swiss offshore drilling company
53	SCHW	Charles Schwab Corp.	American investment management company
54	SMH	VanEck Vectors Semiconductor ETF	Exchange trade fund built up of semiconductor companies
55	SNAP	Snap Inc.	American social media company
56	SPX	S&P 500 Index	Index of five hundred large American companies
57	SPY	SPDR S&P 500 ETF Trust	Exchange traded fund built up of S&P 500 companies
58	SQ	Block Inc. (formerly Square Inc.)	American technology conglomerate historically concerned with financial services and payment processing, though now with a number of additional lines of business including media streaming and web hosting
59	SVXY	ProShares Short VIX Short-Term Futures ETF	Exchange traded fund meant to trade in the opposite direction of the S&P 500
60	T	AT&T Inc.	American telecommunication company
61	TLRY	Tilray Inc. Cl 2	American medical cannabis company
62	TLT	iShares 20+ Year Treasury Bond ETF	Exchange trade fund built up of twenty-year US treasury bonds
63	TSLA	Tesla Inc.	American electric car and battery company
64	TWTR	Twitter Inc.	American social media company
65	UAL	United Airlines Holdings Inc.	American air travel company

Count	Symbol	Name	Description
66	UVXY	ProShares Ultra VIX Short-Term Futures ETF	Exchange traded fund meant to match a multiple of the S7P 500 VIX short-term futures index
67	VALE	Vale S.A. ADR	Brazilian metal company
68	VIPS	Vipshop Holdings Ltd. ADR	Chinese e-commerce company
69	VIX	CBOE Volatility Index	Monthly VIX options expirations
70	VIXW	CBOE Volatility Index	Weekly VIX options expirations
71	VXXB	iPath Series B S&P 500 VIX Short-Term Futures ETN	Exchange traded note meant to mimic the behavior of short-term VIX futures
72	VXZ	iPath Series B S&P 500 VIX Mid-Term Futures ETN	Exchange traded note meant to mimic the behavior of mid-term VIX futures
73	WFC	Wells Fargo & Co.	American financial services company
74	XCF	KTMG Ltd.	Singapore-based textile and clothing company
75	XOP	SPDR S&P Oil & Gas Exploration & Production ETF	Exchange trade fund meant to match the performance of oil and gas companies in the S&P 500 index

Note: For the symbols I didn't know, I looked them up at marketwatch.com on March 1, 2020. If I did not know what the symbol was or did, I did a Google search to check either Wikipedia or the symbol's website.

1. ADR stands for American Depository Receipt and indicates that a foreign company has deposited shares with an American bank. Those are the shares, then, that trade on US exchanges.

2. This one is fascinating—ishares.com breaks down this specific ETF's portfolio by country and percent exposure as follows: China 36.23%; Taiwan 11.84%; Korea (South) 11.55%; India 9.12%; Brazil 6.59%; South Africa 4.37%; Russian Federation 3.77%; Saudi Arabia 2.51%; Mexico 2.29%; Thailand 2.28%; Indonesia 1.82%; Malaysia 1.79%. According to iShares, then, this is the "emerging market" and the appropriate level of exposure to each country an investor should have.

3. According to ishares.com, Europe, Australia, Asia, and the Far East are broken down as follows: Japan 24.2%; United Kingdom 15.61%; France 11.28%; Switzerland 9.73%; Germany 8.55%; Australia 6.88%; Netherlands 4.04%; Hong Kong 3.63%; Spain 2.85%; Sweden 2.74%; Italy 2.4%; Denmark 1.96%.

name. If they were just hanging out in a name, though, and thought there wouldn't be much trading activity, they could post and trade at less than one percent.

More than any given direction of a stock or any given news (though they both did matter a bit), they liked to trade names that were traded a lot, since, as market makers, they make money from a large volume of trade by posting liquidity. Really, just about any sort of volume could work, too—everything from impending company mergers leading to flurries of speculative special-ist buying and selling to hyped meme stocks on Reddit leading to a churn of retail money. Given that, the names they chose to pay attention to reflected their sense that there would be reasonable activity in a given instrument or a given sector. As such, table 3 is a snapshot of their varied interests and where they thought activity would occur in the spring of 2019.

Recall, too, that Jeff and his team are options market makers. What this means is that for each name they follow, they're tracking an options calendar that extends out a few days, two weeks, three weeks, four weeks, five weeks, six weeks, seven weeks, three months, six months, nine months, one year, and two years, and they're making markets across this calendar, exploiting price discrepancies across the various expiration dates. Within their mon-itoring system each of these expiration dates in turn generates a number of statistics that they use to track positions, evaluate future positions, and initiate automated buying, selling, and hedging. The specific statistics their interface develops follow (they won't make much sense at first, but bear with me): EXP (expiration date), $Delta, Delta, Gamma, Vega, Theta, PremovrPty, OmktPnL, DMK, PnL, Mktpnl, OtheoPnL, DTheoPnL, TheoPnL.

A few things are worth noting about this list. First, all the Greek letters—delta, gamma, vega, theta, and so on—are variables in the Black Scholes Merton equation used to price options, and they become, in this statistical form, heuristics for understanding how a given option is performing. Delta speaks to the relationship of an option to its underlying stock or instrument. Gamma speaks to how an option's price and that of its underlying stock relate to and change with one another. Vega speaks to the relationship between an options price and the volatility of its underlying stock. And theta represents the way that time changes an option's prices. Taken together, these "Greeks" give the language through which options traders analyze their positions.

The second thing worth noting is how many of these tabs have PnL in them. This stands for profit and loss and reflects different ways the trad-ers can imagine profit and loss and see how various positions make or lose money given a set of buy and sell parameters. Finally, you'll note that Theo is appended to a few of these tabs. This is short for theoretical and is a projection of a given number, given some set of assumptions. Again, this may seem a bit esoteric, but these are the sorts of things Jeff and his team pay attention to and seek to automate as they trade and, as we'll see here and there, the terms that make up much of their formulaic language as they track their portfolio.

Now that we have a sort of baseline of Jeff and his team's activity, and perhaps now that we are still pondering the parable of the faulty relationship with Arca, it'd be helpful to see what other technology got the team agitated (spoiler alert: all of it, at one point or another). Once I present this, I'll be able to explain a bit about the specific historical circumstances that have put Jeff and his team in a situation in which they're almost always frustrated by some aspect of their system. Moreover, I'll be situated, too, to explain a bit why I think their technology leads to rage as often as it does. It's worth remembering, too, that the work conditions that Jeff's team occupy are, at least from a historical perspective, basically new. Jeff and Brandon, again, were both able to start their careers as in-person pit traders (and still trade in pits occasionally, when Lee is away from the office), and they have transitioned (mostly) to screens as digitalization and automation have changed working conditions and the composition of the workforce in finance. But first, the litany.

On Latency

Latency is a word to describe the lag between intended action and consummation on financial markets. It's the amount of time between clicking buy, and your order actually executing in a server in New Jersey or in Illinois. As noted above, TradeCo often can't compete on speed, particularly in equities markets. This is a potential problem because TradeCo needs to buy equities at specific prices to hedge their options positions. One morning Tony couldn't get his hedges off and complained to no one in particular, "Fucking hell. Stop missing hedges. Piece of shit."

ICE Chat

At any given time, the traders would have half a dozen windows and applications open across their four to six stacked computer monitors on their workstation. Some windows contained market feeds; other windows contained a real-time reporting of their automated buying and selling; other windows summarized their various options positions and liabilities; other windows allowed them to change the parameters of their automated trading; and still other windows allowed them to manually trade through third-party interfaces. Periodically they would open web browsers to do a bit of research, read *Zero Hedge*, or play YouTube videos. In addition to all these windows, they would have ICE chat open. ICE chat is an instant messaging service for financial market participants that allowed Jeff and his team to talk with each other, other traders, and brokers and to occasionally make and take orders. However, it seemed that ICE chat didn't always integrate well with the blend of other applications open on the traders' computers and would periodically lead to oddly timed screen refreshes:

[Tony and Kyle's screens blacked out and reloaded leading them to say, "what the fuck."]

Tony. You may call the upside offer if you want it. I don't think you want to buy it; it's at May—don't think you want to buy it.

Brandon. Agreed.

T. Fuck ICE chat. ICE chat is fucking up our computer.

Kyle. If you leave your rush running past a certain time.

T. It's really hard to sell Wells—trying to get like a thousand. I get a couple hundred. Ah. There's a good fill—twenty thousand Wells through strike. Whoosh down Apple; whoosh up banks. Whoosh down energy.

In the course of a blend of fairly normal play-by-play and commentary, Kyle and Tony's screens go out. They reckon it has to do with ICE chat screwing up their system, and it makes it hard for them to get the fills they would like initially.

The Trade Tape

One function TradeCo's system served was to track all the trades the team made. One way this sort of record is useful is in the team's ability to audit what their automated systems are doing and check whether they're trading correctly. An error in this tape could lead to large problems in the management of their portfolio.

Tony. How much edge do I need to trade Jan of 2021 SNP? I just want to see the best price so far.

Jeff. Does three thousand, four thousand, most recent, anything bigger than fifty? I see a dollar fifty versus eight-nine-seven.

T. Do you know where it started? This trade tape is impossible to use.

J. There are a lot of bugs in it. 3,500 contracts—they've traded. They started at a dollar and a quarter versus eight-seven-three. Now, he's a dollar twenty versus eight-nine-five. I'm going to toss out that first one. That's a fuck up. One twenty is his top. Lots of people are happy to sell at one twenty right now.

T. Send a vol order. Fuck. Could you show me how the trade tape works?

J. I think time and scale is easier. Select it: trades only. I had this issue too—it bugged out and showed a weird time. Once I selected, "filter by quantity," this time, too—drag over to see most recent. If you don't drag it and it's two, you're going to miss the most recent. It doesn't look like it's done yet.

T. This sucks.

Tony is trying to figure out what sort of profit he needs to make to be able to trade January 2021 expirations of Snapchat options. He's trying to do so, in part, by consulting TradeCo's trade tape. However, he's discovering that it is both riddled with errors and difficult to use correctly. In short, it sucks.

The Scanner

The scanner was an automated tool the team used to identify good trades that they might otherwise miss. It was always operating in the background and could lead to the manual entry of both trades on the part of Jeff and his team and changes in the parameters of their automated-trading software (and a significant portion of their automated trading had to do with automatically hedging their portfolio's position to make sure their positions weren't too risky). However, for the scanner to be effective it had to produce up-to-date quotes.

Jeff. I had the opposite view. The only thing we could do is go down progressively.

Tony. Snapchat—one day its earnings came in one hundred points.

J. 350 clean points on thousand vega—that shit happens.

T. I disagree with you.

J. Showed it to you.

T. Those options expired.

J. Next week was also being run at four hundred for a brief period of time. Tony kept saying, "not true," but I keep seeing it. Shit moves a lot. Vol moves; vol coming in.

T. Snapchat vol bid—why the fuck are all these scanner things false?

J. You get a Jet Ski if the fed talks—only then [see the Jet Ski chapter, below].

T. That spicy coleslaw downstairs is spicy.

Brandon. Tony?

T. Did five, then got one in the screens with rebates. Quarter commish [commission].

B. Wonder if that counts toward our tier requirements?

T. Every time I try doing it, it doesn't work.

B. We need to show Zach how it doesn't work, then we'll add it to the sprint list. He feels he's not accountable unless it's on the list. Let's hold him accountable.

To start, Tony and Jeff are having an argument about pricing Snapchat options. Tony tries to invoke quotes from the scanner, but it turns out that the quotes are out of date. This erodes his argument, and the conversation wanders to fed policy and canteen coleslaw. Toward the end of the exchange we hear Brandon talking about bringing up the scanner's problems with Zach Bauer. Zach is the head of TradeCo's off-site development team. Brandon is briefly strategizing about how he can get Zach's team's attention to fix the scanner. While we'll hear more about the "sprint list" and how Jeff and Zach's group interact momentarily, for now, it's enough to note that Brandon felt he had to conform to Zach's workflow in order to fix a problem.

ITG

ITG, at the time of my fieldwork, offered one of the largest suites of brokerage services and dark pool access in the financial world. TradeCo, in turn, bought some market access from them. However, while I was there, complaints about ITG came up repeatedly. The following exchange is indicative.

Jeff. Shadow banking out of China? Buy more stocks!

Tony. I think everything just froze.

Kyle. ITG?

T. Internet. Just ITG—call 'em. There hasn't been a day in the last three weeks where there hasn't been an issue with ITG. [*Throws glasses down*] There hasn't been a fucking day.

J. It looks like ITG is down. Tell these fuckwads to get their shit together.

T. We gotta drop 'em. This should be the last straw.

J. Some symbols I see data.

Rob. No. Everything is disconnected. Don't trust 'em.

J. It's down. I'm calling them.

T. At this point we shouldn't pay them. We've had an issue every day for the last three weeks.

J. It's dead. Should I restart? Can you tell these fuckwads to get their shit together? We'll have to just leave their service. We're restarting.

It was never clear to me what exactly ITG's problem was. But whatever was happening, Jeff's team's market access went down regularly while I was there. This particular instance illustrates how reliant Jeff and his team are for market access from third-party brokers like ITG.

Bugs across the System

As noted above, TradeCo has multiple offices across a number of global financial hubs. Accordingly, Jeff's and other's teams at TradeCo would share computer systems and Zach's team of programmers. Part of this was meant to make the organization a bit more efficient, though part of it also served a compliance purpose. Some of each trading group's activities needed to be partitioned from one another so there wouldn't be illegal collusion. Also, TradeCo wouldn't want to be in a situation in which teams were betting against each other and netting zero profit as a consequence. Given all this, a bit of what Zach and his team engineered were ways that various team activity would communicate across the firm and allow or preclude other activity. As you may have already guessed, though, these checks were a work in progress.

Jeff. Why is it half an hour instead of twenty minutes?

Kyle. We have this safety: if there are three fills in a row, there is a cool down. For some reason they need to wait for [a trader] in [another city]'s machine to send. This is all fucked up. It's a bug; a complete mismatch. Every time he pulls on SPY and Qs, I get pulled. Every time, I have to call Zach, because it's not something I can do myself. That was really frustrating.

J. That is so bad.

Here, some automated catch in the system was systematically pulling Kyle's trades. Moreover, he couldn't adjust the catch himself, he had to get Zach to manually fix it every time. Kyle, in turn, felt like he was missing good trades.

Everything

A fair amount of the time, there was no individual culprit apparent. The whole system would just seize up and no one could do anything.

Tony. I don't mind slowing down and waiting for a big down—pulling a "[specific trader's name]" as you would say.

Jeff. Anyone know the general line? I have a VIX order that's left in the market that is stale. I have a futures order that I don't know how old it is or where it came from. I can't cancel. I don't know if it's a new problem or part of the old problem. I don't know why I can't cancel. It looks broken. I wonder if I can with these futures. VIX futures are broken too. Looks like VIX futures are just broken.

T. Everything is down again. I can't cancel anything. They are just a fucking piece of shit.

As this last exchange indicates, fairly often, everything is liable to go down. If we step back for a moment, in aggregate these tech issues add up to a perplexing situation. Jeff and his team are capable of making a million dollars a day in profit (I've seen it.). Moreover, his group has out-survived sixteen other groups in their particular office and has existed for over a decade. Yet rarely does a day go by without their systems, their technology, or their connection to financial markets enraging them in one way or another. Moreover, they're unable to fix their own problems. They had to rely on Zach, about whom, until I met him, I was half convinced only existed as some group hallucination—a scapegoat on which to pin their technological tribulations. It turns out, though, he's real. Zach's situation, too, offers a way to understand why these highly skilled traders are so often at the mercy of computer problems that they don't always understand and often can't fix. In a way, Zach embodies all these tech issues and personifies Jeff's team's estrangement from their own work.

The Chauffeur Problem

Recall from the preface that there has been an exponential growth in electronic trading across all financial markets over the last few decades. This, in turn, has come at the expense of in-person and over-the-phone trading. Simply put, the vast majority of trading now happens in electronic order books located in data centers in a couple American suburbs (specifically in Secaucus, Mahwah, and Carteret, New Jersey, outside of New York City, as well as Aurora, Illinois, outside of Chicago; see MacKenzie 2021). These order books, in turn, are only accessible via computer intermediation. As such, there has been a structural shift in the professional world of traders. Increasingly trading firms are becoming technology firms. Also, Jeff and his team and groups like theirs can only speculate and set prices provided that they can sit on a sophisticated, semiautomated trading system of which they control some parameters but that is largely allowed to operate according to its own logic. Put another way, instead of primarily and exclusively making trades, Jeff and his team both make trades and supervise an automated system that makes many, many more trades than the team would ever make personally. Given this balance of activity, Jeff and his team increasingly find themselves at the mercy of these systems and their maintenance.

This sort of shift and its implications has been attested in the wider literature. Emanuel Derman (2004), a physicist and professor at Columbia University's engineering school, wrote a memoir, *My Life as a Quant*, in which he talks about being one of the first quantitative analysts at the financial services firm Goldman Sachs. He notes how at the start of his career, finance people, traders, and the like didn't quite know what to do with a trained scientist like him. As time went on it became increasingly apparent that Derman and other quantitative analysts are able to generate models of financial markets and activities that make money. Increasingly, too, large financial service companies could not operate without the sort of technological and scientific sophistication people like Derman could supply. Derman's rise, in turn, upset the functional and prestige hierarchy of finance firms.

Conventionally there has been a distinction between the people that make money (traders, bankers, and so on) and the people that cost money (IT support, building maintenance, administrative staff, and so forth). The difference was often referred to as a distinction between "front office" and "back office" (see Ho 2009) or money makers versus cost centers. Conventionally, science people and computer programmers, if there were any around, were strictly back-office people, the expendable help. However, given the sort of market environment people like Jeff and his team find themselves in, the help, folks like Zach, are increasingly indispensable. This also seems to be a pretty general predicament in times of rapid technological change.

Historian Kevin Borg (1999) describes a case that is paradigmatic of this sort of social shift in his essay, "The 'Chauffeur Problem' in the Early Auto Era:

Structuration Theory and the Users of Technology" (see also Barley 1986). The Chauffeur Problem is as follows: in the early days of the twentieth century cars were starting to emerge as a mode of transportation. At the time, they were extremely expensive, difficult to maintain, in need of constant repair, and, essentially, only accessible to the extremely wealthy.

Before the emergence of the car, the wealthy had gotten around in horse-drawn carriages. In addition, the wealthy would often have multiple horses, stables, and liveried servants to care for the horses and drive coaches. Moreover, the wealthy expected servile deference from these servants. Borg suggests that when the car began to replace the horse-drawn carriage as a mode of conveyance for the wealthy, the wealthy transferred their expectations of how their horse servants should act to how their new chauffeurs should act. Borg suggests that this is pretty typical of moments when technological changes offer new affordances to people and classes who did not have them before—people simply expect social relations to stay the same as they're more or less blind to the implications of the new technology.

The car demanded far more expertise and savvy than was required for caring for horses. Moreover, lacking people with such expertise, many wealthy car owners could simply not make use of their cars. Given this newfound leverage, Borg describes the situation:

> On a summer Sunday in 1906 a *New York Times* headline told a man-bites-dog story: "Chauffeurs Lord It Over Their Employers." Chauffeurs became a serious problem for wealthy motorists during the first decade of the twentieth century. They extorted commissions and kickbacks from garage owners, took their employer's cars out for joyrides at all hours, and exhibited a brazen disregard for social decorum. They did not behave as servants. (1999, 797)

Chauffeurs were able to exercise newfound scope for action and new privileges and powers as a result of technological change creating a niche in which they became indispensable. The parallels to Zach and Jeff's situation are obvious.

Both Jeff and Brandon started their careers as pit traders on options exchanges.[1] This means they started their career physically in the middle of markets that they and others created through the course of market hours by yelling and signaling buy and sell orders to one another. They were the market makers, the front office, the money makers. And they had support. They had runners to take their orders and clerks to register and clear their orders.

They had accountants and support staff to maintain the firm's position. But they also had a large degree of autonomy and could operate in and of markets and feel separate from their interchangeable support staff.

Now, however, Jeff and his team rely on Zach and his people, regardless of how they feel about their work. Zach, like an early twentieth-century chauffeur, is simply indispensable. He becomes increasingly more so, too: the longer he stays at the firm, the more he knows TradeCo's system, and the more customized those systems become all in response to the mechanization of the larger financial environment. The following conversation illustrates Jeff's group's relationship to Zach as well as Zach's method and process (NB: Zach failed to show up on a day he was scheduled to come to Jeff and his team's office).

Tony. He's not here because Walt [a partner and everyone's boss is] not here.

Aaron. That's the end I got to in this process. Anyone understand this? It's not me, so I asked somebody else.

T. How does stuff fail? How does tech fail? I built this scanner eight years ago, and it doesn't break. They are supposed to be professional coders. My code is sloppy and it always worked—only time it broke is when VIX changed its server. I don't understand how Zach broke something that breaks every day. What is so hard about that. I don't understand how code could break. Once you're done with it, it's math and algorithms.

A. They keep pushing updates that they don't test.

Brandon. What if inputs change?

T. Don't change inputs.

B. What if exchanges change?

T. Easy fix.

B. What if the exchange lies to you?

T. Should be an easy fix.

B. All I'm saying is that it's not impossible. I completely agree with Tony's frustration. The internet at night is working. When you wake up in the morning, and it's not, the modem is still on and plugged into the wall, like, fuck you.

A. Systems break down all the time, but it seems like ours . . . work approximately, and then don't work.

Kyle. My friends at coding firms, they present code, and they present . . . and they get questions and edge cases. They test for edge cases.

B. He doesn't adopt that model for man power. According to Zach, a lot of small firms do that. It makes me marginally less angry.

A. In that situation, you have to be marginally more receptive.

B. He doesn't understand why people are angry.

A. You can't take it personally when your shit gets criticized for not working.

B. You believe you did your best.

A. It's not working for us.

As is probably apparent, Jeff and his team had no shortage of work that they wanted Zach and his team to take care of for them. The task of technological innovation and integration seemed to be endless. Jeff and his team, too, had been preparing for Zach's visit. And he just didn't show up. Zach's absence leads Tony to reflect on how little leverage they have over Zach given that they both share the same boss. The team then talks about what in Zach's process bugs them.

It turns out that Zach and his team were practicing a form of technological production and management called Scrum or Agile. What this practically meant is that teams like Jeff's would prepare tasks that would go on "sprint lists." These sprint lists are meant to be managed by a tight group of six to ten people who work in very close conversation with each other, giving each other daily reports and holding each other accountable to daily milestones over the course of four to six weeks. This management technique is meant to foster close collaboration of a team and allow the team to produce programs quickly. It basically works. But given the size of Zach's team, and that the demands of TradeCo far outstrip his team's ability to complete everything, Zach and his team end up prioritizing some projects and abandoning others. Moreover, they rarely if ever look forward and test or look back and do maintenance. Put another way, Jeff and his team become beta testers for unproven software that often has both internal bugs and glitches as well as issues integrating with their complex patchwork of existing systems. It's worth noting, too, that this relationship to technology was in part a deliberate strategic choice—TradeCo has decided to spend less than it might on technology and more than it might on traders, making a bet that smart, motivated (and agitated) professionals will make do with a buggy, technological patchwork.

On the face of it, it's not hard to understand why Jeff and his team are angry so often and swear as much as they do to let each other know about problems with their technology. I think, too, it's worth dwelling on this anger for a moment as it helps make Jeff and his team's problems a bit more generally applicable to other times and places in which people feel alienated in the context of new technology in their work. Often when dealing with structural features of the economy, as when I characterize wage labor and technology writ large, it's easy to lose sight of how an individual navigates these large-scale features of capitalism.

In the introduction, I noted that anthropologists had observed that when people deal with economic transitions, they tend to get angry or despairing and tend to personalize general economic processes in terms of their own lives (see again Weiss 2021). In what follows, I'd like to draw on some existential anthropology to offer an interactional account of what technological alienation feels like, throwing some light on where, specifically, people's anger and rage and misapprehension is coming from.

In thinking about different emotional responses that people have to new technology, anthropologist Michael Jackson (2002; see also Piipuu 2017[2]) suggests a framework that dwells on some the basics of what humans want and need in their ongoing lives. Jackson starts from the premise

> that all human beings need to have a hand in choosing their lives, and to be recognized as having an active part to play in the shaping of their social worlds. As a corollary, I approach the meaning of what people say and do in terms of the degree to which they accomplish a balance between controlling their own fate, collective or otherwise, and accepting that which cannot be decided by human will or subjected to human designs. (333)

Given this starting point, Jackson goes on to imagine that human lives are

> lived as a network of reciprocal relationships among subjects . . . [which] implies, first that human beings everywhere tend to conceive of subjectivity not only as encompassing others but as extending into the extra-human world, with the result that objects, words, and ideas tend to become imbued with consciousness and will. (344)

So, if we go back to Jeff and his team, we can think about their situation in existential terms. In order to lead their lives, they need to strike some sort of balance between control and resignation. However, it would seem that they can control far less of their lives than they would like. As is typical in a capitalist context, their technology, their systems, and their relationship with the technologist Zach and his team all set up situations in which they have far less control than they feel they should have. They want to trade, to make bets, to compete, but their screens are constantly refreshing, and Zach isn't showing up.

It's significant, too, how they react to this lack of control over their technology and their technology people—they get angry. They swear. They yell. They vent. Jackson suggests, "when the machine does not conform to human expectations of reciprocity or fair play, we get distressed and angry, much as we would if a person behaved unfairly towards us or failed to acknowledge a gift" (2002, 336).

> First, strong emotions arise spontaneously when we are frustrated in our attempts to comprehend and control others or objects. But secondly, and most importantly, we work on and play up these emotions, making them the means whereby we "magically" recover our sense of lost power over others or objects. Nursing ill-will towards an enemy, cursing an errant computer, kicking a flat tyre, or pitying oneself for one's inability to stand up to a tyrant will not necessarily effect a change in the object or other, but may reverse one's experience of one's relationships with it. One, becomes imaginatively and retrospectively, the determining subject of the events that reduced one to the status of an object. . . .
>
> The problem is that this process involves splitting self from other—a split that may become entrenched and habitual, as in luddite views of technology, chauvinist views of asylum-seekers, and racist views of foreign bodies. (2002, 338)

What Jackson suggests is happening when we get angry at technology, or people for that matter, is that we are responding to what we see as a lack of control in our own circumstances. We get angry in order to reassert ourselves and our control over our environment in relation to that which threatened us. There is also a danger in this sort of a response, as the contempt necessary for anger may become a permanent way of figuring relationships to people and things. In this way, larger economic forces and technological phenomena become personalized in individual, local role expectations.

Given the rapid change that has happened in the technological entailments necessary to trade on markets, and given the way these technological changes have reduced the power and stature of traders and raised the fortunes of tech people, Jeff and his team's routine anger at their computers and their computer people is unsurprising. Basically, they run into obstacles to doing their job and fulfilling what they understand as their social role multiple times a day in the form of complicated computer systems that they can't fix. Tony sums it up succinctly when he says, "I don't understand how code could break. Once you're done with it, it's math and algorithms."

Part of Jeff and his group's ability to function as a profitable trading team is dealing with and triaging their technical systems daily. Moreover, given their role as traders, and the increased importance of tech people and computer systems in their lives, they are frequently not able to do their own jobs to their own satisfaction and, well, they get mad. This, though, isn't the only way to exist on markets or to deal with new technology. Borg (1999, 804) suggests that some new car owners did in fact become skilled mechanics themselves. Faced with the same technological shifts, some drivers embraced the new technology and learned it. This, then, is another way, for a few people at least, of coping with the new affordances that technological change brings. In the next chapter, then, we'll see what happens when a trading firm becomes the machine.

3

The Greatest Trader in the World

Across three multiday field trips spread over about a year's time from summer 2018 to summer 2019 and due to an interest in explainable artificial intelligence (see Borch 2022; Borch and Min 2022; and Min and Borch 2022), my colleagues Christian Borch and Bo Hee Min got to know a trading firm—we'll call them Bradford Partners—that had a far different relationship to technology than Jeff and his colleagues did at TradeCo. Bradford traded interest rate products as well as currency and commodity futures. Interest rate products are financial instruments tied to some predicted future interest rate (such as what a government or municipal bond might pay or the interest on US dollars held in an overseas account). All these products have a chain of expiration dates and an interlocking calendar of expirations, much like the options that TradeCo trades.

TradeCo's and Bradford's different attitudes to their electronic systems is particularly interesting in part because Bradford's founder, CEO, and CTO were all financial professionals working successfully in the early 2000s and saw the rise of computerization and automation just as Jeff and his team did—an incontrovertible reality of the financial universe, one that needed to be reckoned with for survival. Whereas Jeff and his team held onto their idea of themselves as traders, in control, and with a fantasy of subordinate technologists, Bradford Partners took a different route: Bradford abandoned a prioritization of human agency through trading and became their system (named LINUS).[1]

To understand what becoming the system means, though, we have to dive into the professional history of the firm's founder, the firm's CEO, and the firm's CTO and their voyage away from being a fairly typical finance firm built up around traders to a firm that subordinates traders to a central automated machine system. Recall Jackson's (2002) point that so often frustration, anger, and alienation come from a human existential failure to control aspects of their lives that people feel they ought to be able to control. What we'll see is that the founder's alienation from his own firm and his uncertainty about its future provided the opportunity for the CEO to act on his dream of a healthy organizational culture and the CTO's aspiration to give technology a central, privileged place in a trading firm (see Min and Borch 2022). In turn, we'll also see how this shift in priorities served to diminish and dismiss a number of more traditional traders, functioning as a microcosm of the larger finance industry.

One brief caveat before we begin: the account I'll offer from Bradford is largely from the point of view of management. And even when nonmanagerial voices come in, they largely come from interviews that were set up by Bradford's management. Given that, it's reasonable to presume that the story we get may be idealized, from a different class position, or at least a bit more schematic than the daily experience of working at Bradford. Also, given that we're spending so much time thinking about alienation and what labor feels like in the context of changing technology, it's worth keeping in mind that improvements in labor's productivity through automation may in fact feel great for management insofar as it diminishes or eliminates willful, specialized traders that are themselves hard to manage. Really, this is *the* dream of much capitalist automation (Chiang 2023b).

Now, to Bradford's history.

The CEO identifies Bradford's inflection point precisely. In a follow-up conversation around a previous draft of this chapter the CEO told me that at a dinner celebrating the ten-year anniversary of the firm, Bradford's CEO had no idea what to say nor any sense of what the future would hold for the firm. Bradford started with the founder and some colleagues making a number of profitable trades. In the mid-2000s they had added some rote automation around their click trading and had brought in a number of individualistic, competitive traders.[2] The founder had no idea where any of it was going. He didn't like the people they had brought on to the firm. The trading techniques seemed idiosyncratic and didn't point to any larger strategy. So, when called to speak at the anniversary, the founder had no words.

This was all the more disappointing to the founder, because he had aspirations to form a healthy organization in which people enjoyed working and did so with a shared sense of purpose as opposed to his past experience in other parts of banking.

> When I started the company, working in Japanese banking was a pretty miserable experience for me. Basically, it sucked the soul out of me, it sucked the drive, it sucked the enterprise, initiative. And I love Japanese culture, but I don't like Japanese work practices. When I started Bradford, I really wanted to make it everything Japanese banking could not be or was not. So, there were dress codes [in Japan]. [By contrast,] I wanted it so that people could come and go as they pleased. Very few rules. The only rules that we had were just what the regulators forced us to have. And that just concentrated in making it a fun, happy place. And that's all well and good when it's a small company with a few people. But when you start to grow, you can't just have that kind of way of developing. Because that's what we did, and mistakes were made, and dead ends were gone down, and so, in the same way of my trading approach.

Elsewhere in Min and Borch's interviews, people described some of these dead ends and mistakes: as the company grew, they brought in a number of traders who did not fit with this larger, fun, open culture. They instead focused, as the traders on Jeff's team do, intensely on the nitty gritty of winning their trading game. The founder eventually realized this was untenable and turned to the CEO for help imagining a better future. In a way, the CEO had been preparing his whole life for this sort of moment.

Before coming to Bradford, the CEO had started his career as a floor trader and then had run a retail bank in an OECD country (the Organisation for Economic Co-operation and Development, a group of thirty-seven capitalist democracies). All through his career, he had maintained an interest in psychology and organization studies with an eye toward creating a kind, value-driven, purposeful workplace. In his own accounting he had prioritized working with positive, honest people and had tried to pay attention to the sorts of institutions that allow those people to flourish. However, Bradford's identity crisis was the first time he was able to have the power and resources to act on an organization and shape it at the level of its day-to-day culture and processes. What's interesting about this moment, too, is the founder actually does allow the CEO the latitude and the capital to make a more pleasant firm without having much sense of what this should look like in practice. That said, neither the CEO nor the founder had imagined a firm built around an automated, adaptive machine-learning system that would both design strategy and execute trades.[3] For this vision of the future to crystallize, the CEO would have to meet the CTO.

The CTO also had a long career in finance. Before the 2007/2008 financial crisis, he had worked in a large American financial firm in which performative aggression was the way people asserted their wants and, in his words, where "it's entirely okay and expected to be a c——." Beyond enduring this manner of aggression, the CTO had become accustomed to technology being low in the bank's estimation of its own priorities (cf. Pardo-Guerra 2019). He noted, "a lot of firms view technology as a cost center within the financial world. Basically, it's like maximize the payout to the . . . traders, minimize the cost to any cost center." Put another way, if money needs to be cut from a budget, "cost centers" like technology came first. So when the CTO came to work at Bradford, he was tired of working in places where people were mean to each other in a default way and he had come to see the marginalization of the technologist in finance firms as being deeply misguided, particularly given the rise of automation on markets.

Once they started working with each other, the CEO and the CTO began collaborating around their common overlapping aspirations in shaping their own workplace. With their values in mind, they set about imagining what sort of a firm could both be pleasant to work in and actually keep up with the accelerating technological demands of trading and not rely on any given trader holding any number of proprietary strategies. Naturally, this would require automation of some sort. But it would have to be of a different kind from the automation that operated at Bradford before the founder's identity crisis. The CEO noted the limitations of the old Bradford's ability to innovate its technology in a reflection he made on the way trading firms tend to operate:

> Many, if not most, prop groups are really just a collection of trades. . . . They're just a collection of trades that have a functional organizational wrapper around it. They're not a business, per se. They're a trade. They masquerade as a business that does trading, but I think therein lies a very interesting distinction. If you're just a collection of trades that has a functional wrapper around it, the technology is a servant to that. It's a cost center, because the real value in the business, where the value is extracted from the business, is really extracted from the trade itself. And so you often see trades degrade.

In the CEO's eyes, as long as you focus on individual trades and individual traders, and setting aside the ego and aggression they may bring, technology will necessarily be subordinate to those all-important traders. Technology is always an enabler and a cost center.

To get around this built-in problem in financial service firms, the CEO and CTO decided to create an adaptive machine-learning system. Rather than create a system that automated strategies that traders themselves came up with, they would create a system that would trade, and then based on the results of those trades change the system's strategies. In the language of machine learning this would be a sort of ever-evolving "neural network,"[4] meaning that the system would take inputs in the form of market and trade data, constantly readjust the weighting that would go with various inputs, and then produce outputs in the form of new trades and new strategies. In a follow-up interview that I conducted with Christian, the CEO and the CTO explained the point of developing a system like this via an elaborate and somewhat macabre metaphor: they asked me to imagine a golden-egg-laying goose that eats its own eggs. And then makes more golden eggs. And then eats those. And then makes more eggs. Ad infinitum.

Aphoristically, the goose that lays the golden egg is a turn of phrase that is meant to convey the fact that it's not just some reward or wealth that's important (e.g., an egg made of gold) but the mechanism to continually create more and more wealth (the goose that lays said eggs). In the land of allegory, we're meant to be careful so that we don't kill a goose that lays golden eggs—we always want to protect our wealth creator, and not, say, eat it short-sightedly. So, conventionally, in a trading firm there would be an assumption that traders make strategies. In turn, making strategies would be the equivalent of laying golden eggs. So, one wants to cherish, and coddle, and remunerate one's traders. However, the CEO and CTO basically don't accept that equation anymore.

To the CEO and CTO's mind, individual traders create toxic cultures around strategies that inevitably degrade due to intense market speedup and competition. What the CEO and CTO wanted to do was to create a computer system that eats its own eggs to learn from its trading outcomes: a goose that eats its own golden eggs, and then because of this act of filial cannibalism, makes even shinier, more valuable eggs in an endless sequence.[5] This, then, is the business model the CEO, the CTO, and the founder would pursue—an adaptive machine-learning system, and then a firm built around that system. To do this, though, Bradford would have to do away with the culture of the individual trader and instead develop a technology firm that focused on collaboratively tending to and managing their automated-trading system.

In contrast to a trader-focused firm, the founder here offers a post hoc, reflective, high-level gloss on how the machine learning and the organizational structure and practices of the firm have come to hang together:

[A company] that is safe, that is, where people are entrained. Where we are like a flock of birds that are flying together. There isn't one bird that is leading the flock in the direction it goes, but when there is a subtle change in one of the birds, all of the other birds change direction and flow and that way we can hit that kind of mythical state of flow where we're all the same kind of people: we feel safe; we feel self-supported; we're working toward a common goal; we have a common sense of ethics, morals, and standards. So, I'm very interested in the social biology of what it means to be an individual; what It means to interact with other people; what it means to interact in a company and out in the world.

Then, also, there is the philosophical idea of machine learning. I'm very taken by the evolutionary structure of the brain: you've got the emotional brain, the intellectual brain, the lizard brained; you've got the left hemisphere, the right hemisphere, and all the different things that they do. And, I'm particularly interested in left-brain thinking. Left-brain thinking being the closed system that creates a model of how the world should be, and your decision-making runs through that process. Whereas the right brain is the open brain, that is open to what could be, but is not yet modeled.

It kind of struck me as quite an important thing that we're actually doing when we're creating a machine-learning system: it takes a certain amount of historical data, we have the methodology, and we give it a goal to solve, but what we're actually doing is creating a left-brain system. It is a pure left-brain system. And animals don't work that way; humans don't work that way. We have evolved over hundreds of thousands of years as humans and millions of years as animals, and the process by which evolution is endowed with the survival mechanism is to have a left brain to deal with the world in a certain way and a right brain to deal with the world in a different way. There is a huge danger in machine learning that we just create all of these left brains that have no ability to sense that the world is changing, or black swan events could happen and things like that.

The design of what we're trying to do with the company as a whole is to try and build that right brain around the left brain. So, we're not there just creating this child, pushing it out into the market and leaving it to fend for itself. We are giving it support; we are giving it an environment; we are utilizing what humans can do, how humans have the ability to train their right brain and to be aware of dangers that may not be apparent from six-month's-worth of microsecond by microsecond validated data. We're a long way from a machine having any sentience or anything approaching the right brain's openness to the worlds it finds. And so, my idea is: can we build this kind of lovely, gooey company, friendly, happy together kind of company that will take our child and nurture it and give it what it can't do?

Later in the interview the CEO clarified somewhat more pragmatically:

We decided, actually let's build this system to create a system. LINUS became not just the heart of the business, but LINUS became the purest manifestation of every man and woman in this company.

This is remarkable. The founder understands the firm that the CTO and the CEO built as a nurturing symbiotic environment for LINUS, a learning, computerized trading system. Moreover, the CEO clarifies, they see LINUS as the personified embodiment of everyone who works at Bradford. Again, this is a proprietary-trading firm like TradeCo. Though Jeff's group and Bradford trade different things—interest rate products versus options and volatility products—they are both traders having to reckon with electronic markets and calendar spreads. Bradford's management, though, has decided to go all in on a computerized system, a personified, named machine-learning trader that will represent all of them, a system that is analogized to a child making its way in the world. This is a far, far cry from Tony's lamentation of their system *just* being "math and algorithms"; and is distinct from Jeff and his team's anger and rage at and alienation from their tech team.

LINUS represents an alternative and perhaps an opposite way of imagining and then dealing with the changes that have come to financial markets, changes that so regularly enrage and hamstring Jeff, Tony, Aaron, and the rest at TradeCo. However, the LINUS route, as is the case with any technology that increases productive abilities, isn't open to the same number of traders it displaces because of the increased capacity for action that LINUS can undertake. What is more, LINUS also and arguably increases managerial control over trading. Given this, dwelling a bit more on where LINUS came from and how the people at Bradford work with LINUS will help to understand a bit more of the fate that faces people when computerized and automated systems confront and constrain them. In what follows, I'll show the shift in role that traders, the CTO and CEO, and the founder all had to imagine to allow the possibility of a LINUS. Then I'll show how LINUS operates in the firm—specifically, how the people at Bradford personify LINUS and then design appropriate managerial processes for this personified, learning computer system.

Slouches Towards . . .

Again, if we take human existence as basically relational—that is, we can understand how people feel about and lead their lives from the point of view of the relationships they make and, in turn, the control they feel they are able to have over the course of their lives in forming and acting in these relationships—technological change can be extremely alienating. People form relationships with the inanimate or insensate all the time and expect the universe to respond largely along human norms. Put another way, technology and nonhumans more generally are supposed to reciprocate and oblige humanity's wishes and desires. When they don't, people become alienated and occasionally angry. In the context of capitalist wage labor, in which increased productivity due to technological change accumulates as a matter of course, this sort of estrangement is basically inevitable.

The Chauffeur Problem highlights how this existential predicament can compound. It's often not just a fractured relationship with a thing. That fractured relationship with a thing also can come with rebalanced relationships with people. For TradeCo this has meant both anger at technology and a historically unprecedented role for Zach, TradeCo's chief information officer. At the core of this anguish, though, is TradeCo's insistence on staying traders, on being the ones who gamble in defiance of the ever-looming specter of automation. Bradford's management saw this same dilemma over the past few decades but chose to stop building their business around traders.

In another interview, the CTO explains:

[That trader] used to have a trading book, doing some other specific trading. And he was so bought into it. And the thing that was interesting about [the trader] is, he's the first person that I've seen to, as a trader, give up the, "I'm going to sit and make my own PnL, and my personal sense of self-worth that is going to be attached to that." He said, "Actually, [LINUS] is the future, and I'm going to make the long-dated bet that this is the right way."

Most basically, in whatever firm, the rise of automated, high-speed trading technology has offered novel affordances for acting on markets that have threatened the traditional autonomous role of the trader. No longer can someone relatively independently make their own way and tend to their own profit and loss statements (see also Souleles 2020b). Faced with this, Bradford's surviving traders gave up their primary personal investment in their role. Other Bradford traders who couldn't or wouldn't support the rise of LINUS left the firm.

LINUS Understands

For Bradford's managers, the first step toward LINUS was shedding a sense of themselves as individualistic traders who made money according to their wits and as reflected in their own PnL ledger. The second step was imagining how they would work with LINUS. Again, this is where Jackson's existentialism is of use. Jackson suggests that we should pay attention to the sorts of relationships people form with the other things in their lives. Moreover, he notes that people tend to personify nonhuman objects and imbue them with the expectations of human relationships that are governed by reciprocity and mutual obligation. Given that, the metaphors relating to personifying that a senior software engineer uses to talk about LINUS are telling:[6]

> We have LINUS. It has its own competence and character, and we try to understand its skillset and scope. As we go to make changes to it, then, if we see okay here's a new candidate [for] LINUS that's been proposed by one of our research teams who's done some experiments. So okay, we think LINUS understands better this particular skill, as evidenced by this result from the research. Should we, what should we do with that? Should we take it to the market? Should we ask more questions?

The software engineer suggests that the linchpin of working with LINUS is whether or not LINUS *understands* the changes that Bradford's employees are making. It's not so much a matter of functioning or doing particular tasks but a question of understanding. This would suggest that LINUS can, at a meta level, fathom what is being demanded of it and act accordingly. Put another way, understanding suggests that LINUS is capable of grasping human intention.

In addition to understanding, LINUS is able to learn. Bradford's chief technology officer explains how this dynamic unfolds:

> The more [a trader] understands technical matters and details of LINUS, the better he can contribute inside of it. That, in particular, is a theme. So, getting to know LINUS, we had a series of "Bradford Teaches" [events] that were called "getting to know LINUS." And the idea is, to influence LINUS, you have to know him. So, we would specifically have a mission, say, "your participation will be proportional to your understanding. Let's try intentionally to get people to get together and do that."

Bradford still has traders, and traders that are distinct from programmers and engineers. But as we've come to expect, their independence is diminished. They generally don't trade on their own anymore and serve as a sort of check on the actions of LINUS. Here the CTO is explaining, again, that "understanding is necessary." The more a trader understands why LINUS is doing something, the more likely they will be to contribute to LINUS's growth. It's worth noting, too, that as the CTO shifts to talking about "knowing" LINUS, LINUS shifts from an "it" to a "him."

This metaphor work wasn't just fleeting. In another interview the CEO introduced the idea of developmental stages that the founder referenced above as he slipped between talking about Bradford culture and LINUS.

> Are you able to genuinely engage me and understand me, so we can have [a] deep and profound relationship? This is important to our culture, but it becomes spectacularly important in terms of our strategy because we don't write rules for [LINUS], we have a relationship with it and try to coach it. And as it gets wiser, through each passing day . . . as he gets wiser, it's like a child. Our ability to influence it will start to degrade. I have two daughters; they are wonderful. My wife and I, we have a wonderful healthy gorgeous relationship with them. But we raised them to be, just like [the Founder] has for his two daughters, we raised them to [be] emancipated. And then, one day they become emancipated.
>
> You're like, wow, how did you end up with an opinion of your own? And like you encouraged that. LINUS is like that right now, it's young and so it's like my daughters being six, seven years old. Mom and dad still matter profoundly. We didn't negotiate with our girls, we set parameters, we encourage, we call that empowerment or parameters with empowerment. But as they

evolve more and more of their cues and more and more of their development derive from those cues, are social cues, and you would know that as sociologists.[7] And so, too, it is with LINUS. The more it trades in the market, the more that it's exposed to the market, the more it really understands that its objective function is, actually, it's prosecuting its objective function pretty faithfully and you want [to] talk to me about changing what I do? I don't think so. So now, all of a sudden, we have to see the world through its eyes. We need to have a deep, profound relationship with it. We need to change our operations so we could have that . . . like a child, it gets away from you, it just stops listening to you and it doesn't stop listening to you because it doesn't like you, it just actually thinks that it's not well served by listening to you.

LINUS has eyes and sees the world. LINUS understands and grows. LINUS is like a child that gets away from its parents. LINUS acquires wisdom. LINUS is simultaneously part of Bradford's office culture, the avatar of Bradford's values, and the embodiment of all who work at Bradford. LINUS is the best that Bradford has to offer. In the words of the CTO,

> So [Bradford] is on a mission now, to get to make the best trader in the world. We're going to do that by increasing his scale, increas[ing] the scope of what he does by going to new markets and exchanges, and increasing his skills.

The LINUS Production System

First Bradford abandoned the idea of what a trader is, an idea that TradeCo still holds onto in Jeff's group. Then Bradford personified the computer system in such a way that they bent the firm's operation toward catering to LINUS's traits. LINUS is like a child who grows, learns, and develops and finds some sort of autonomy. Given that, LINUS needs an open, supportive, and attentive human environment to flourish and become the best trader in the world. The final step in illustrating how LINUS and Bradford's humans coexist is to show a bit of the process of maintaining and updating LINUS. Here, then, is a senior software engineer explaining how running LINUS is like running a manufacturing process.

> Just making LINUS better and making it a better trader, extending its reach to more markets, increasing its skills so it's better able to cope with what it's trying to trade today. So that starts to feel more repeatable, it's not ad hoc

anymore. Every time we take LINUS out of the market, dust it off a bit, polish it up, send it back out, every time we go to a new market, it's gonna be eighty, ninety percent the same. So, that starts to be much more repeatable. That starts to feel much more like manufacturing.

The software engineer is suggesting that there is a rhythm to working with LINUS. He goes into the market every day. And at the end of every day he comes out of the market. His new rules are analyzed to the extent that humans can parse his changed logic, and perhaps up to 10 to 20 percent of his objectives, tools, and sensibilities are shifted. This regular process is where the manufacturing logic comes in.

Yes. So, there's a whole body of work around what we call "lean manufacturing." So, it really comes from the Toyota production system, which is all great. You might be expecting me to launch into a discussion on how we then apply that to us, but I will talk of some of that, but we try to put our own twist on it—we've called it, "regenerative manufacturing." So, we're trying to pioneer that space, which goes in a slightly different perspective. . . .

So, what on Earth has this got to do with Bradford Partners and trading? Why on Earth am I talking about it? You know, there's no trucks outside our door with all different materials. So, for machine learning we can really think of two primary resources that we consider. One, and the biggest one, is actually me and us, all of the people. Because it's our skills, our energy, our passion that is getting put into the creation of our products, of LINUS. And the other is data. You'll often hear it said that data is the food for a machine-learning strategy. Without that data to learn from, it can't learn how to trade a particular market. So, you've got the data and the energy of the people, that's our biggest inputs . . .

With machine learning, you have the data and you have the strategy and it will learn the rules. So, every day, every night, we'll take it out of the market, it will learn some more rules, put it back again. Does that completely solve our resources problem? Can we say that we are now free from resource constraints? Because we don't have that traditional half-life problem, have we just switched it for a different problem? So, we still need the data and we still need energy. So, as we build a model that will, LINUS can now trade this particular market, and we ship it out the door of our factory, and we move on to the next market. It's not like something we just ship to our consumer. It's in the market, we still have to support it, we still have to make sure that it's the proper conduct, we need to monitor each day, we need to combat the degradation [of] returns over time. So, it doesn't go away. There is an operating cost associated with that, and also if you want to keep improving it, then we're manufacturing it, we're taking it back. So, there's very much this cycle of going into the market, calling it back, being improved, going back in. And so, we continue to add products to our baskets, to trade on different markets.

This process that the software engineer gestures toward is precisely what TradeCo was lacking. The software engineer is gesturing toward a regular and efficient process of testing and analysis and development and surveillance (see also Pardo-Guerra 2019, 226–37). Moreover, all of this happens in house, in the same place as where the supervisory traders work, in the same place where the quantitative analysts develop strategy, all swaddled in the same supportive, nurturing, learning office culture.

Toward a Synthesis

Bradford's shift to LINUS has not removed the need for skilled market generalists of the sort that work on Jeff's team. There are just fewer of them and they work in a different capacity. Bradford's head of market risk explained:

I've been involved with the LINUS products and sort of helping out there when and where I can, with the quantitative nature. So, on one side you have a lot of very technical information, higher skilled expertise, very narrow, and on the other side, it's me and that's basically a guy with broad market experience, over numerous years and just picked up tricks along the way. So, basically, what we're trying to do is aggregate those two experiences into one and try and help out the machine-learning suite in a five-dollar saying, you probably say, cover off the blind spots. As you know, sometimes they're not as quick as they possibly should [be]. So, you bring experience to assist them with that.

The head of market risk is helping LINUS with what LINUS doesn't know to pay attention to, helping with the blind spots.[8] As an aside, it's interesting, too, that LINUS fairly quickly becomes "products" and "the machine-learning suite" in the trader's telling. LINUS also doesn't receive a gender from the trader. LINUS's blind spots, too, could be pretty fundamental.

So effectively, when I came back, I noticed that there was one of our particular, one of the more dominant contributions toward the firm's PnL was misbehaving. I just couldn't understand why it wasn't exhibiting the characteristics you want to see in that certain portfolio. And that portfolio was very used to trading stable curves. Curves that are relatively flat and just basically flex slightly like that, so you trade the noise back and forth. And that's good while it lasts, but when curves start to move because the plumbing underneath the market changes, or the direction of capital underneath, basically the sentiment in the market, changes for whatever reason—usually for technical reasons these days, because of the federal reserve or the central bank likes to play games. So, the technical reasons behind it will not be picked up in data prior to that, if it's actually a new modality of injecting or subtracting liquidity, that's not in the data ever. It hasn't been, we started in two thousand eight, it's changed, it's morphed as we've gone along. We've seen different central banks take different controls of different parts of the curve, all around the world. That was never in the data. That's where human trading experience can say, we got a problem here.

The scenario the head of market risk walks through illustrates well the role a human can play with LINUS. In a given interest rate product with different calendar expirations, like treasury bonds, the interest rate of each instrument can be plotted on a curve into the future. The curve is meant to reflect the fact that as you get farther away in time, money should be more expensive, and the curve should have an upward slope. The price of different interest rate instruments compared to the shape of the curve tells a trader a lot about how markets are behaving, which prices are reasonable and which are not, and how things may shift in the near future (see Zaloom 2009).

The head of market risk says that the shape of the yield curve is a basic assumption that quants would have standing behind their inputs to a system like LINUS. In turn the presumed shape of the curve would stand behind a number of LINUS's actions and form a specific view on what LINUS could reasonably expect from a market. Put another way, their curve would stand as an axiomatic assumption from which a number of other sensible actions could follow. However, LINUS doesn't (or didn't at the time) have a mechanism to get back to these sorts of assumptions and revise them. The head of market risk suggests that there are all sorts of large influences on the shape of a given market's yield curve that would affect the features of the market that LINUS wasn't noticing. This is where a human with a lot of experience, who can toggle between different levels of analysis, could diagnose LINUS's problem and work with quants and developers to fix the system.

———

For Tony, his computer systems were just math and algorithms. For Aaron they just didn't work. For the whole TradeCo team, no small amount of their invective came from their technology behaving in ways they did not like. Their technology reflected back to them, often in the guise of the ever-elusive Zach, the steadily diminishing and fragmenting role and status of the human trader as a laborer in the world of finance. Technological advancement and the development of automated-trading capacity force traders into a more circumscribed, less independent role. What this looks like in day-to-day life is that traders are forced to relate to complicated nonhuman systems. Jeff's team of traders often relates through anger and frustration, creating a sort of irritated agency that allows them to reinvent themselves imaginatively as actors who have more control than they actually do. For all this, Jeff and his team preserve much more space for action than a comparable trader at Bradford. This, too, is key to TradeCo's business model's ongoing profitability. In their words, they're comfortable making bets on themselves. It's possible that this frustration and friction is simply the price of taking those sorts of risks given how markets currently work.

By contrast, Bradford Partners has taken a different route through technological change. Many of them have abandoned the idea of an independent trader or even a team of traders and have instead rebuilt a cohesive company around an automated system, LINUS, and that system's daily maintenance and analysis. Bradford personifies LINUS in order to relate to LINUS. With this personification, Bradford Partners is able to imagine developmental stages, milestones, and forms of willful agency that LINUS displays. In this way personification makes LINUS intelligible, and, probably, staves off much of the anger and resentment that pops up at TradeCo. Central to Bradford's technological priorities, too, is a gamble on the relative importance of a risk-taking independent trader in the context of contemporary, highly automated financial markets. At least at the time of writing, it's not clear whether Bradford or Jeff and his team have the correct balance, whether one will survive the other, or whether a messy coexistence is the way of things to come. Still, it's worth noting that to stave off alienation, resentment, and stagnation, Bradford Partners has abandoned willful, unruly traders and has become the machine.

4

On Markets: Rallies and Flows

[The government's response to the coronavirus] makes me realize that if America was attacked by aliens, our first response would be to lower interest rates.
Michael Nguyen, tweeting @nicepantsdude, March 17, 2020

There is fear in this market. Jeff is displaying fear.
Aaron Meyers, junior team member at TradeCo

In the minds of Tony, Zach, and everyone else at TradeCo, as well as in the minds of LINUS's enablers at Bradford, computer systems exist as a way for traders to access various financial markets. As interesting as Scrum or Agile software development is, or as wild and brilliant a metaphor for capitalist alienation as it is to create a totemic machine-learning system to replace all of your traders and personify the collective soul of the people in your firm, in the minds of just about everyone I've talked about so far, computer systems exist as a means to access various financial markets and find profitable trading opportunities. What's more, traders conceptually and verbally collapse all these financial markets, all these trading venues, and will often just talk about "the market" as their arena for professional activity and as an entity that has knowable traits, moods, patterns of behavior, and eccentric dispositions. The last block quote in chapter 3 illustrated this tendency.

Bradford's head of market risk talks about the "plumbing" underneath a market that gives it a shape and a pattern. He also talks about "market sentiment," or a mood and affect that can influence the universe of financial activity and trading opportunities. Aaron's quote in the epigraph at the start of this chapter is another example of this global metaphoric use of the word *market*. Here *market* stands for the trader's arena of professional activity and a place where aggregate trader emotions are manifest, in turn affecting market behavior and trading opportunities. This chapter, then, will show what the traders at TradeCo mean when they say *market*, illustrate how their idea of a market stands in for the limits, constraints, and opportunities of their professional activity, and specifically what they thought of "the market" and "markets" at the time I was watching them.[1] In this way the market for a trader is the possible universe of moneymaking opportunities, the environment in which one can act. As you might expect, Jeff and co. were frustrated with how their market was behaving.

Unicorns Grazing on the IPO Cycle

One thing that came up again and again is that Jeff and co. felt that people were overvaluing stocks, and that stocks were trading at prices that were not justified by their underlying businesses' economic activity. While I'll hold off for a moment on explaining the mechanism by which they thought stocks were overpriced, the phenomenon of stock price inflation was particularly clear as they talked about Uber's IPO on the day that it happened (NB: an IPO is an "initial public offering" and is the first time a company's stock is publicly traded on a financial market. Put another way it's the first occasion that noninsiders can invest in a company and buy its stock).

Uber is (or, perhaps by the time you read this, *was*) one of the first app-based ride-sharing companies. The basic business model was to develop a cell phone–based program (an "app") that would allow you to "hail" a driver, a worker in their own car, to pick you up and take you to your destination. The app would coordinate the ride, direct the driver to you, process your payment, and give drivers and passengers a way to rate each other. Another part of Uber's business model was to expand aggressively, disregarding local labor laws and laws governing taxis, to capture an ever-increasing market share. Also, Uber, as far as I was aware at the time of my work at TradeCo, had never been profitable (Schleifer 2019). From a market share point of view, Uber's goal was to outlast its competition and establish something of a monopoly in ride-sharing, similar to Amazon's role in online retail or Google's role in digital advertising.

Uber set its initial stock price at US$45 per share, which implied that the company should be worth US$82.4 billion (de la Merced and Conger 2019). On the day of the IPO, it became apparent that Uber wouldn't maintain that price level, and the stock fell into the thirties. In the year or so between its IPO in May of 2019 and my writing in March of 2020, Uber has largely traded in the 20s and 30s, periodically and briefly cresting into the 40s. At the start of the COVID-19 pandemic, Uber plummeted to around US$14 per share. At the time of the IPO, Jeff and his team felt that Uber was overvaluing itself since it had never made money. Moreover, they hoped markets would recognize this and punish Uber by driving its stock price down. They also felt this and wished this for most other stocks they traded. That day, their wishes were partially fulfilled.

Jeff. [*Singing*] Goodnight Irene, goodnight Irene, I'll see you in my Ambien-fueled dreams. [*Talking*] This IPO cycle, this unicorn cycle—people have been talking about it for a decade.[2]

Aaron. It's going to certainly change tech valuations.

J. Forty-two [Uber's current share price on IPO day]. They fucked all these people. For the banks, that is a no-no. That is a no-no. They got owned. They just can't find bids. The banks are going to have to backstop this. Lyft [another ride-sharing app, already publicly listed] is shitting itself. We got this right. We talked about this. We even got this right. Very very nice. Big whoosh, ten handles.

A few things to note—first, Jeff is happy with how things are going—he's singing. Given his conviction that Uber was overvalued (as were stocks more generally), his team anticipated some downward movement with the IPO. Moreover, he's crowing about the banks that screwed their investors by overvaluing the stock initially. Mechanically, for an IPO to happen, one or several banks give Uber money for shares ("underwriting"), which the banks then sell to investors who can then sell those shares on open markets once the stock is traded publicly. From a pre-IPO investor point of view, if they are able to buy the stock for less than people on the market will pay on IPO day, they have made money (say, if Uber traded above US$45). In this case, from Jeff's point of view, the banks fucked all those people, and the markets are appropriately punishing people who bought overpriced stocks. This schadenfreude does not last.

One of the market leitmotifs in the background of the time I spent with the traders was US president Trump's trade war with China. Trump's economic policy was largely incoherent and based on imagined injuries sustained from perceived slights cast by other countries on the United States. This "policy," such as it was, manifested in the application of tariffs or taxes on imported goods. One such target of these tariffs was China. Trump felt that China had built manufacturing capacity at the expense of the United States (in addition to other grievances) and applied a series of tariffs on imported Chinese goods. Given that the Chinese and American economies are so intertwined, this led to concern among the traders about American companies' supply chains. This also led to a steady drip of news from the president's administration meant to encourage markets that a resolution to the trade war with China was just around the corner and would be resolved in America's favor. One such announcement came in the course of Uber's IPO day which, from the point of view of Jeff and his team, irrationally sent the markets up.

Tony. Uber is just flying now.

Jeff. Everything is flying. The whole market is flying. Everything is flying except for PCG—that can't go.

T. Fuck us. And banks [can't go].

J. There has to be some sort of news.

T. It's Mnuchin [US treasury secretary]. Fuck him. Ten minutes ago.

J. No, no. We just went up ten handles in the last minute.

T. Dumb people are just catching it now. Fuck. Fucking ITG.

J. We must be massively synthetically long with VIX. That's what it's looking like.

T. Uber is flying.

Rob. Front futures are down fifteen cents.

J. It is. It dropped, dropped forty-four handles and the future is down for the day. You live in the alternative universe now, because the problem that causes the market to go down is the same one [that causes it to go up]. Now, I refit everything to lose another hundred grand [US$100,000] in VIX. We must be so long because of the downside stuff. We are hemorrhaging money on the VIX. We're not making it elsewhere, either. We own so many fourteen puts: ten thousand seventeen and sixteens, and another ten thousand fourteens and fourteen and a half. Weird, when I did the risk yesterday it just didn't show up as that. Now the sodomites are going to fuck us in the ass on every position.

Aaron. Get that down; it's very important: the sodomites.

Daniel. Who are the sodomites?

T. People we hate.

J. People who cook books to market-make a position. Effectively, whatever they
have on, they aggressively bid or offer to make things favorable.

T. The big guys do [it].

J. It's just stupid. VIX vol just came in fifteen points—an exact carbon copy of
yesterday. [We] finished the day with no fucking [trade] deal.

Despite a promising start, Uber's IPO day ended up in disappointment for
Jeff and his team. Things begin well—Uber is overvalued, as they suspected,
and the market bids down its stock. This gives Jeff and the team the opportunity to explain a bit about what they think is going on in markets currently—
stocks are overvalued, particularly those of tech IPOs. Moreover, they see
this cyclically, pointing to a ten-year "unicorn" cycle in which venture capital
money has been loose and easy to come by. This could have been a happy day
for TradeCo, as they stood to see their idea of how the market should operate
valorized in Uber's pummeling. However, it was not to be.

At some point, the US secretary of the treasury made an announcement
about progress on the US-China trade deal. No concrete deal mind you,
just some comments about hypothetical progress. This turns the market's
attention from Uber to SPY, an ETF based on the S&P 500 stock index. SPY
and its related stocks started to "fly" up. However, futures related to SPY
did not. This created a doubly confusing situation for TradeCo. First, as
near as they could tell, stocks were going up because of the intervention of
a member of the United States government's executive branch announcing
nonnews about economic policy. Second, futures didn't seem to be following stocks and were still depressed. For this reason, other market participants, under the guise of a homophobic slur for biblical sexual deviants,
were going to metaphorically anally rape the TradeCo team. The day was
ending poorly.

Jeff, Aaron, and Tony's characterization of the "sodomites" is noteworthy
too. They're identifying a class of actor who manipulate the market's ability
to accurately price stocks according to their own gain. In this case it's some
amorphous combination of agents of the US federal government and the
banks that structured Uber's IPO. At other times they would refer to "flow
whores," momentum traders who chased trends blindly and stupidly. In the
trading room, whores and sodomites, as indexes of morally repugnant de-
viance, stand in opposition to heteronormative, manly restraint and proper
and economically fundamental market action. The market and its villains,

though, could expand and contract depending on circumstances turning in a way that aggravated Jeff and the team.

Secretary Mnuchin on the news. Tariffs may or may not be removed depending on negotiations.

Jeff. How is this positive? He's just trying to goose fucking stocks.

Tony. Play along!

J. No!

T. You have to!

J. I'm not a fucking lemming.

T. Lemmings are the only ones who make money.

J. Lemmings get slaughtered eventually. [*Mocking*] We have a great relationship [with China]. We've been talking for two years and we have no deal. There won't be a deal and everyone fucking knows it. VIX is about to go through its fifth strike today.[3] Twenty-eights are now in play. [I/they] want to buy the twenty-eights back for a penny.

T. At least we did the Twitters. Ten thousand. Whoosh up. Apple, high of the day. That's a fill, a really good fill.

J. A lot of fucking morons on Wall Street. Seventy handles now.

This sort of sequence should look pretty familiar at this point. Vague news from the US federal government leads to some sort of market rally—some index has gone up 70 handles (and counting) at this point. Moreover, Jeff and Tony think this is both nonsense and are unable to do anything about it. They think Mnuchin, the US treasury secretary, is manipulating markets to go up. They also think their colleagues on Wall Street are a bunch of lemmings who are marching in lockstep out of all sense of financial reality. All this, too, is how they describe markets—markets have whooshes and have participants (sodomites and whores). Markets get manipulated. And markets set the context for TradeCo's actions.

What exactly, do they mean by markets?

I'm Done with This Day

The saga of Uber's IPO, Secretary Mnuchin's intervention on markets, and the resulting calamity engulfing TradeCo's positions is meant to be an example of how Jeff and his team think about markets. The best way to understand what the traders at TradeCo mean when they talk about markets or the market is to understand that they are both referring to the actual stock exchanges and venues on which they trade as well as the larger metaphorical totality that is the arena in which they compete with other traders and try to make money. Moreover, Jeff and his team explicitly mention markets infrequently. Rather, markets are often the antecedent noun in an observation, the implied context for a "whoosh" or for a "rally." These disembodied, impersonal, contextually vital phenomena all happen on markets or on *the* market. Knowing about this second expansive sense of the market and markets is necessary to understand the constraints under which Jeff and his traders feel they operate.

In a moment, I'll walk through the basic qualities that markets have—how markets and their conditions have a temporal duration and have attributes that affect everything occurring in their financial universe. Moreover, I'll explain a bit about how apperception of current market conditions provides the grounding for sober analysis, provides a sense of constrained possibility, and, most basically, consistently makes Jeff and his team unhappy, despondent, or enraged. Before I do that, it'll be helpful to explain a bit of my thinking around how I understand markets for TradeCo traders as a sort of metaphorical, conceptual ground in which they imagine their activity and through which they understand what they can and can't do. It may seem vaporous, so some clarification might help.

The sort of cultural anthropology I'm a practitioner of takes seriously the notion that humans understand their lives in terms of their relation to other people and in the context of large imagined social realities such as, say, a national community such as "the Danes" in Denmark, a global community or the "Umma" of the Muslim world, or the movement of "the class struggle" cutting across all of history (e.g., Graeber 2001; see similarly Anderson 1983). Many of these are as-if propositions that are generally unvoiced grounding conditions that allow people to build on and (try to) lead lives of meaning and of value. These sorts of propositions create context. One example of this that is close to the idea of the all-encompassing market that I'm identifying at TradeCo is Hannah Appel's (2017) explanation of the "national economy." Appel notes that in many national and international governing contexts, say at the level of national economic planning or at the level of international lending to specific countries, the "national economy," as measured in aggregate economic statistics such as Gross Domestic or Gross National Product (GDP or GNP), is taken as the most important attribute for analyzing a nation and understanding how well or poorly it is doing (for a history of these measures, see Coyle 2015; for these numbers' limitations, see Kennedy 1968).

Appel notes that seeing a country in terms of its national economy is fundamentally an "as-if" exercise, an act of imagination by which "objects like national economies come to exercise much of their power, while remaining contingent and contestable" (2017, 296). Over the course of the twentieth century and on into the present, this as-if way of thinking about a country has had tangible effects on specific nation's access to international credit and the terms on which it was offered. The national economy understood in terms of GDP or GNP became a grounding condition for the flows of wealth between nations.

We hear local reverberations of this idea of a national economy every time a politician talks about how great or poorly "*the* economy" is doing or every time a newscaster talks about what's going on with *the* economy or every time a member of a central bank meets bad news with an interest rate cut in order to help *the* economy. In each case individuals are using the metaphor of the national economy to understand a large group of people they need to relate to in their world. Moreover, their metaphor of choice, "the economy," makes it easier to pay attention to certain things in a society (things that are countable, such as employment statistics or bank balances) and ignore things that are not amenable to quantification (such as happiness, joy, or job satisfaction) or do not fit in economic theorization to begin with (solidarity, love, or an appreciation for beauty). The economy becomes the metaphoric precursor for understanding a country and imagining what one can and cannot do in terms of governing. The market, in turn, operates similarly for Jeff and his team and becomes the agent of their alienation.

Most basically, market attributes are rooted in a unit of durational time. That is to say that over some period of time markets have more or less stable predictable characteristics. The most basic characteristic was the ability to make money in a given window of time. Among the traders, some unit of market time was "over" or "done" when nothing more would happen and there would be no more opportunity to make money. After a flurry of activity, one of the guys would say that "today is over," or, "I'm done with this day." It'd often be offered as an ironic commentary on how boring conditions were and how they'd have to pay attention to the market regardless. The irony could expand too. On my first day in the office, a Monday morning in February, I heard Brandon say to no one in particular, "This week is over. This year is over." A few months earlier, shortly before that new year, the VIX had spiked up to around 30. By the time I arrived in February of 2019 the VIX had descended into the teens and was an index of calm, boring markets without much going on. For Brandon the week (much less the day) as well as the year was a vast expanse of expired possibility (cf. Guyer 2007).

Within a given temporal moment, markets could also have directional movements: things can whoosh up or whoosh down collectively. Things can also be "fucking choppy" or move quickly and be "high fucking octane." This can also lead to basic evaluations of market conditions. Conditions on the market can be "fucking stupid" or "fucking crazy." Moreover, traders can arrive too early or too late. One day, Jeff speculated that it might be too early in the day for a real rally, and Tony confessed, "I'm so terrified to fade [to ignore] this rally, though." For traders, in a basic way, when they think about the market, specific units of time meet up with varying qualities and set out, hopefully, knowable possibilities for making money (compare to private equity investors' ideas of investment time in Souleles [2019b, 129–53] or Bakhtin's idea of the chronotope [1981, 84ff.]). In this way, the market and its current characteristics allows the conceptual grounding for Jeff and his team to do their work.

The Spooz Will Fucking Rip

Most basically, thinking about a unit of time meeting up with qualitative possibility allows Jeff and his team to imagine different possible futures for markets and the sort of trading opportunities those futures might bring (see Beckert 2016).

Walt. I had this thought this morning after the conversation last night. Regarding the possible outcomes for the trade war, the real risk is probably on the upside—upside Spooz [S&P 500 future]. If there is a deal, both sides will claim victory as loud as they can. No one will really know who caved on what, but the Spooz will fucking rip.

Tony. At least one hundred handles.

Jeff. I though the consensus was sixty to eighty.

Here, Walt is talking about the likely outcome of Trump's trade war with China and speculating that, if it ends, it'll end in a muddle of mutual recriminations of victory. A clear analysis of the consequences of the trade war won't be apparent to market participants, and people will blindly bid things up. Moreover, this bidding up will take the form of bidding up S&P 500 futures contracts (Spooz). Also, when S&P 500 futures go up, their underlying equities tend to follow, leading to a cascade effect where the whole market goes up all at once. Walt suggests, too, in this market environment the real danger would be being inadequately long and thereby not being able to take advantage of that sudden rush up in the market.

Jeff, Tony, and the rest of the team would periodically have these sorts of sober, high-level strategic conversations with Walt. Walt was the partner managing their group, and he would walk through from time to time asking how everything was going and offer his opinion on things going on in markets. More often, though, commentary and analysis on the market was sharper and suggested very basically that the market was wrong (and often inscrutable).

At one point the market seemed to be going up for no particular reason, and the team was trying to figure out what was going on.

Jeff. New highs. What the fuck is going on? VIX is down twenty-five points now. New highs—this is just unbelievable. What the fuck has changed in the last two hours?

Rob. How far are we since we started?

J. Two-ninety-three.

R. From Monday we already are there.

J. This Monday, after the Friday close, we almost fully reverted about thirty away. Yesterday, up forty-four then dropped twenty—over halfway back about thirty more to go. The crazy thing is, vol is down so absolutely, being outrageously crushed again. We're in an alternate universe. Before Trump came out today, they were already hitting this. They made sixty-five on the vox side, scalping another sixty in the equities. One twenty—not even coming close. Not even in the ball park.

They don't have a clue what they're doing. They're just piling on momentum. It could be a market maker. It could be a market maker with a high-powered system instead of something volatility heavy. They market-make against themselves to try to flip out a third of a penny. They keep squeezing in and squeezing in. They market-make against themselves for a third of a penny. It's silly market-making activity. They push things—rates, vols, skews. Their theory sometimes creates an opportunity for it. Their theory makes you suffer short term losses. It's nauseating. It's a trade and fade sort of thing. They deflect and buy ten for fifty—offer at fifty to buy 'em and sell 'em at a period of time. They get two rebates; it's a half a penny move. [We're] not fast enough to do that. [They] spend hundreds of millions. Ninety percent of their orders are sellers. If the market wasn't rigged, and actually went down the other side . . . All they want to do is churn at a level.

Tony. That's all they want to do. The want to make their rebates.

J. It's so fucking outrageous the type of shit you see right now. Epic levels of rigging—that this could happen in 2019.

T. Is it?

J. Astonishing. I thought it was astonishing when Yellen and Bernanke were complicit in rigging the stock market every single day. It is beyond reproach. It's the most shocking thing I've seen in my entire career. They're just making shit up. Oh, we may do this in six months on autos. China is our friend and we want a deal. People are trading on this stuff every day. It makes doing our job virtually impossible.

T. We really do have an impossible job.

Daniel. I don't know how you guys make money.

Kyle. [*Laughs*]

R. We make money.

J. Sometimes.

T. Whoosh up, banks.

This exchange puts us, again, on familiar ground. The markets are going up, and Jeff can't figure out why. What's different about this exchange, though, is Jeff and Tony bounce off of each other and riff on how they see markets (see Beunza and Stark 2012 on "resonance" and "dissonance" in trader deliberations). Basically, Jeff identifies two things that lead markets to behave in ways that he thinks they should not: "news" or announcements from important people who should know better (in central banks or in governments), and the behavior of high-frequency, highly computerized market makers. These two activities feed on each other and put the market in a place that Tony and Jeff think is wrong.

First, the announcements and the news: Jeff and his team felt that one reason stocks were overvalued, that Uber's valuation could be as high as it could be, was a steady trickle of vague "news" from authoritative sources to which markets responded by going up in a coordinated way. These are the lemmings of an earlier reflection. Second, high-frequency market makers: Jeff says that there are fast, sophisticated market makers that make manipulative trades against themselves to collect rebates on exchanges. What this means is that a lot of opportunity to trade on markets is basically "phantom liquidity," bids and offers that you couldn't collect if you wanted to—they simply disappear ahead of your own order. This has the effect of freezing markets in a particular price band and then churning around that price band. It also has the effect of excluding slower actors like TradeCo from making money. Taken together, this set of circumstances enrages Jeff and Tony:

Tony. I hope Yellen dies. Hopefully Yellen dies, then we can have a down day.
Jeff. She'll go down as one of the greatest villains in history.
T. Really, those that came before: Bernanke and Greenspan, those are the real villains.
J. If they just keep rigging it until everyone dies, then no one will know.
T. My kids and my grandkids. Nah, fuck my grandkids.
J. I'm like a parrot, new highs [*squawk voice:*] new highs, new highs.
T. When I leave, I want to leave something. Maybe, I'll make a bobble head that says, "new highs, whoosh up."
Aaron. I would absolutely shoot myself.

Over and over again, this conversation repeated itself—the market went in a direction the team did not feel was warranted, the team couldn't do anything about it, and they would loudly declaim the people they felt were manipulating markets and trading stupidly. They would indicate a time over which they were analyzing markets, characterize what one might do on those markets (not much, usually), and then impugn the people they thought were doing the manipulation. And so, their assessment of markets generally made the traders at TradeCo unhappy.

———

Before any trade can occur, traders need computer systems to access markets. Once they have those computer systems, they need to understand the market on which they're trading. They need to make sense of what attributes the market has and how long those attributes will last. This market analysis becomes the grounding condition of the sort of financial activities that Jeff and his team do. Moreover, these analyses largely point to the perceived perfidy of market manipulators and serve to make Jeff and his team variously unhappy, aggrieved, and enraged. How might we understand the source of this anger?

In her ethnography of futures traders in Chicago, Caitlin Zaloom noted that, "During its hundred-and-fifty-year history, the [traders in the trading] pit had garnered a singular place among trading technologies, too. The CBOT

[Chicago Board of Trade] defined the market in futures every day. Chicago traders were proud of their part in modern market history" (2006, 56). I think there may be something general about this sentiment. Like many of the pit traders Zaloom observed, Jeff and his team *make* markets and see their contribution to the financial universe as being sort of intermediaries that allow markets to function and liquidity to be ever present in a capitalist mode of production. They identify with markets; they feel in a basic way they create markets, and they are proud to be traders and offer a service.

However, Jeff and his team often feel they can't do their job because of ambient market conditions—the limitations of their technological reach on the one hand, and the malfeasance of powerful political or technologically sophisticated actors on the other. In TradeCo's estimation, agents of the US federal government seem to take it as their responsibility to encourage people to recklessly bid up stock markets at the expense of a given capital market's auction mechanism finding some sort of accurate (or at least a fundamentally informed) price for a company or a financial instrument. In addition, more sophisticated computerized traders churn at narrowly set price levels, shutting out people like Jeff and his team. Just as technological breakdown led to anger, irrational market conditions lead to rage.

Writ large, Jeff and his team feel estranged from the markets that they themselves make. An examination of another form of market making, that of the people who work on and create exchanges, will bring some perspective to Jeff, Aaron, and Tony's rage at the faceless lemmings and political grifters wrecking their markets.

5

Eternal Optimizers

Despite being "market makers," Jeff and his team felt estranged from the markets they traded on. In a basic way, they weren't in control of how things traded, who participated, or how markets in aggregate responded to news. Moreover, this sort of alienation was reflected in their language—markets were generally the unvoiced, metaphoric totality of the arenas they traded on and were often manipulated by powerful political actors or heavily computerized competitors. Here and there, they comment on rebates or tick sizes or fee structures or enforcement mechanisms. Moreover, they're able to discuss the vagaries of this sort of market design fluently. But generally and practically, markets are left in the abstract. The team at TradeCo doesn't talk much about markets as places that people deliberately design.

This lack of dynamic reflection, perhaps unsurprisingly, is in stark contrast to the people who work at the actual exchanges (the NASDAQs, NYSEs, and CBOEs of the world), the specific markets on which Jeff and his team trade, at which Zach sets up collocated servers, or to which ITG provides market access. Put another way, everything having to do with the trading arena that Jeff and his team often voicelessly elide has been deliberately designed by people working at specific exchanges, under specific regulatory supervision, and with their own ideas of what a market is and what it should be. More to the point, the ideas of people designing and working at exchanges only partially overlap with those of Jeff and his team. As the sociologist Juan Pablo Pardo-Guerra notes of the technicians who built the London Stock Exchange, "market engineers held clearly moralized views of markets that they sought to bring into being. Through technology and purposeful design, trading could be made better—perhaps even more socially virtuous" (2019, 133).

Over the course of the larger AlgoFinance project, a number of us spent time interviewing and visiting people who worked at exchanges. At the time of writing, we (mostly my colleague Bo Hee Min, given her interest in the regulation of financial markets) had talked to twenty-four people working at exchanges in the United States and Europe. Their specific details are enumerated in the larger informant chart contained in appendix C (anyone who has "exchange" in their employer description). But, to give some sense of their occupational diversity here, our interviews included executives, software developers, economists, data product creators, testing managers, and market surveillance people. What emerges across all of these interviews is a much more nuanced sense of both what a market is and, crucially, how one might design, change, engineer, and, perhaps, if you're lucky, optimize a market for given ends.

To put some precision to this more nuanced sense of what a market is and could be, I did a close analysis of the way that the word *market* was used across 553 instances in a subsample of six interviews (in our coding convention [see app. C], these were interviews b010, b012, b023, b024, d034 and d035, and BN002—one chief technology officer of regulation, one senior VP economist, one senior testing manager, one chief operating officer, two software developers, and one head of core market equities and market analysis. The people also worked at five different exchanges). I picked this particular subsample for its occupational, interviewer, and exchange diversity—sort of a maximal informant diversity within the cultural domain approach. Now, to many, six interviews may seem like too small a sample size. Granted, this would be the case for many ends. But there are a few things to keep in mind that I think make this sample work for my purposes.

First, when accounting for cultural, meaning, or relational data (such as the shared meaning and use of a specific important term),[1] there is research (Weller et al. 2018) that suggests that within a given cultural domain, the elicitation of list items in an interview (say, examples of types of a larger category—for instance, all the types of fruit you can think of, or an inventory of all the ways people use the word *market*) may reach saturation fairly quickly. Saturation is simply the notional point in interpretive work at which the researcher can find no new data (see Guest, Bunce, and Johnson 2006).

Saturation can occur quickly if the researcher samples a population that is cohesive in terms of its shared cultural understanding and given that researchers probe extensively in the course of their interviews, eliciting a broad range of responses (Weller et al. 2018). For my sample, then, we may take the universe of professionals that design and operate exchanges as being extremely cohesive, given that this professional milieu involves highly specialized technical work in which people with similar backgrounds in finance, mathematics, the sciences, or economics circulate in a fairly limited universe of trading firms, financial service firms, and exchanges over the course of their working lives. As to the amount of elicitation in our interviews, we conducted semistructured interviews that ranged from around thirty minutes to over two hours on the long end and that probed informant's careers and the work they did.

Beyond a cohesive population and interview probing, it's worth noting, too, that my larger experience over the past few years doing fieldwork on automated stock trading and my familiarity with our team's larger corpus of data give me a degree of background knowledge on markets generally and exchanges specifically that allow me to interpret this interview data. Plus I'm only interested in the highest level of classification related to the word *market*. So, for the limited purposes of illustrating with a bit of precision how exchange people differ from the traders at TradeCo, we might take my sample as adequate.

Across this subsample of six interviews, again, there were 553 uses of the word *market*, which I condensed into ninety different propositional statements. In turn, I sorted these propositional statements into five distinct definitions/uses of *market*. An example will offer a lead-in to the general categories I identified.

At one point, b012, a senior VP chief economist at a public, American financial exchange, offered the following hypothetical situation about routing a specific order to one market exchange or another given latency or timing considerations: "I'm willing to put a thousand shares at risk, a thousand euros at risk in the **market**. I'll put eight hundred euros on the primary exchange two hundred euros somewhere else. Okay. That's arbitrary; and it works because, as you know from these guys, adding time to the decision-making process of their trading computers is a bad thing."

At the level of analysis I'm concerned with, this statement is interesting because of the way b012 is using the word *market*. Here, he is characterizing a market as a place or location in which someone can place risk. In turn, I can condense this into the following propositional statement: "Market as a place where you put risk." And then, I can categorize this as an instance of the affective or metaphorical descriptions of markets (along with six other propositional statements), combine this with thirteen related "practical descriptions" of markets, and we have an umbrella category of "MISC Market as a qualitatively described place." The larger schema I came up with for the ninety propositional statements follows (see app. C on the use of the word *market* for all the propositional statements):

- Markets as manipulable spaces (the things that exchanges see as mechanisms to shape markets, 34 total)
  - Umbrella concepts to understand markets (concepts through which practitioners understand manipulation, 14 total)
  - Orders and speed (the mechanics of buying, selling, and accessing, 16 total)
  - Data and information (the information that buying and selling generate and the way it is distributed [sold mostly], 4 total)
- Markets as made up of participants (the various people who are on markets, 17 total)
- Markets as exchanges that are competing and interacting entities and businesses (15 total)
- Markets as a thing that people do naughty stuff to (10 total)
- MISC market as a qualitatively described place (20 total)
  - Practical descriptions (13 total)
  - Affective descriptions (7 total)

What's interesting for our purposes about this schema is that it fairly quickly illustrates the difference between how exchange people and Jeff and his team think and talk about markets.

To be fair, there is some overlap, particularly at the descriptive level. For exchange workers and their practical descriptions of markets, markets are places with prices. Markets also have volatility and relative levels of liquidity. More generally, markets are places of variable size, places with good and bad information, and places with multiple venues. In terms of affective or more metaphorical work, markets are things to which you have obligations. Markets are things with nuances to be understood. Markets can be a place where you have no idea what is going on. Finally, and pleasing to the categorical structuralists among us, markets are places that can be dirty or clean (as in Douglas 1966). These descriptions are all categorical and basically static attributes that markets (and exchanges) have at one time or another. In addition, this is basically the way that Jeff and his team describe markets. They go up and down; they have volatility and opportunity; there is or isn't liquidity; there are multiple venues; they respond to news, and so forth.

Where TradeCo and the exchange professionals depart, though, is across most of the other categories. Exchange professionals see markets most basically as places to design and change, *not* as preexisting givens (see, again, Pardo-Guerra 2019, 133). The most frequently occurring category across the subsample of interviews with exchange people was markets as something that can be manipulated or deliberately designed. Along these lines, exchange workers observed that markets had macro- and microstructure (echoing disciplinary economics' partition of the world into the "macro" and the "micro"); markets, following legal regulatory imperatives, should be "fair and orderly"; markets can be transparent, opaque, and modeled; markets have the option of being electronic; markets evolve; and markets can, in the spirit of economic reasoning, be optimized.[2]

Whatever angst Jeff and his team have, day in and day out, this angst from the point of view of exchange workers is, at least partially, optional. The primary arenas of manipulation that exchange workers see, too, is the way traders interact with exchanges, that is to say the orders they send and receive, as well as the information that traders have access to in a given amount of time. Moreover, the manipulable dimensions of markets set the conditions by which people can or cannot commit financial crimes on markets (the naughty stuff in my schema, or perhaps the rigging that Jeff and his team were concerned with) as well as the means by which exchanges compete with one another for order flow as businesses *as well as* public utilities.

Hold 'em, Fold 'em, Walk Away, or Run?

The stakes of market-design work are extremely high. Financial markets, the place that Jeff and his team collectively reference and trade on, are one of the largest ways that societies allocate wealth (Hart and Ortiz 2014; Ortiz 2020). Via the auctions and order books, churns and whirls, rises and falls of markets, market participants are valuing companies and derivative financial instruments and allocating wealth according to those valuations. Market participants are deciding how much money Uber or Lyft are worth. And market participants are deciding the value of United States sovereign debt or the exchange rates of numerous national currencies. The decisions market designers and operators make about the specific mechanisms of those markets affect who gets money and who does not and how that process can and should happen. The decisions exchanges make affect how angry, frustrated, resigned, or elated Jeff and his team will be.

Specific exchanges are institutions with often extremely complex sets of rules and procedures for the operation of their markets. All exchanges, though, at their core have a relatively simple mechanism, a "matching engine" sitting on a server somewhere (usually in a suburb) that takes incoming bids to buy and offers to sell and pairs them according to some set of auction rules by which buyers and sellers are matched (Pardo-Guerra 2019; MacKenzie 2021). This auction mechanic can take the form of time priority, as in first in, first out, or FIFO, in which orders are paired as they come in. Orders can also be joined according to a pro rata logic in which anyone with a posted bid or offer will get some portion of a match that comes into the exchange and through the matching engine. Even at this simple stage, you might be able to see the way FIFO matching would benefit relatively quick-moving traders, traders who put bids or offers at the front of a given price-level queue, whereas pro rata matching gives everyone a chance to get an order filled but has the hazard of people potentially putting larger orders than they could actually consummate in order to get a larger prorate share. These sorts of design decisions, particularly as they pile on and compound each other, become rapidly and interrelatedly complex.

Moving one step beyond the matching servers at the heart of financial exchanges, designers also need to think about the way that trading firms communicate with matching engines, that is to say the form that orders can take on an exchange. Orders are basically of two types—limit or market. Limit orders have particular price parameters attached to them: say, I want 1,000 shares of Uber provided that the price is not above US$20 per share. Market orders, by contrast, are only for a fixed quantity of stock at whatever the best price is at the moment of the order. Say I want 1,000 shares of Uber at whatever the market price is currently. If the market price happens to be US$15, I pay it; if it happens to be US$150, I pay that too. A limit order could make sense if you were trying to carefully calibrate an investment. A market order could make sense if you need cash or stock for some functional reason now.

So far, so simple. But by adding constraints on time and transparency and contingencies related to other prices as well as by adding multiple steps that orders should take to be executed, things can become exponentially complicated. An example from NYSE Arca, the exchange that Jeff and his team had trouble accessing at the start of my fieldwork, will illustrate this. Don't worry if the following list is bewildering or only partially makes sense—the complex accumulation of contingencies is the point.

On NYSE Arca there are three primary order types (market, limit, and inside limit orders), each of which has three potential temporal modifiers (day, limit IOC, and limit routable IOC orders). Then there are four auction-only orders for the occasions when normal matching shifts to a different auction format (limit-on-open, market-on-open, limit-on-close, and market-on-close orders). Then there are four types of orders that are conditional and are partially or wholly undisplayed to other market participants (reserve, limit nondisplayed, midpoint liquidity, and tracking orders). Then there are two types of orders that are contingent on or pegged to other market activity (market pegged and primary pegged orders). Then there are four orders that are designed not to route to other exchanges, a possibility the National Market System is meant to ensure (ARCA only, ALO, IOC ISO, and day ISO orders). Then there are three orders that contain specific routing instructions for sending on to other exchanges (primary only, primary until 9:45, and primary after 3:55). There is one type of cross order (limit IOC cross), one specific type of market maker order (a Q order), and, finally, seven miscellaneous order modifiers (proactive if locked/crossed, self-trade prevention, STP cancel newest, STP cancel oldest, STP decrement and cancel, STP cancel both, and nondisplay remove modifiers) (all from Intercontinental Exchange 2020). It's worth noting, too, that every other exchange (twenty-three official exchanges and thirty-three alternative trading venues) has its own suite of orders offering subtly or dramatically different mechanics for those who trade with them.

Beyond the brute complexity of the list of order types on Arca, there are a few repeated dimensions along which the exchange is allowing traders to control their order behavior. We might summarize these dimensions as having to do with (1) access; (2) transparency; (3) information sharing; and (4) contingency. Depending on the way traders manipulate these dimensions, traders are able to behave and present themselves in different ways on markets, allowing themselves various advantages and disadvantages. That said, it can be hard to imagine the significance of all this complexity, particularly given that most of us don't work in a firm like TradeCo. And even if we did, we'd probably only have partial access to the universe of order mechanics.

Given that, a game-night analogy, followed by a few specific historic examples of market design on actual exchanges, will help us appreciate what manipulating these dimensions does for market participation and, ultimately, the allocation and distribution of wealth in society via capital markets.[3] This, in turn, will open the floor for some ethnographic reflection on the people who do market design at exchanges and make for a profitable comparison between how they see markets and how Jeff and his team see markets. First, though, to poker night.

Let's say it's Tuesday night at 8 p.m. and you're sitting around a table playing poker with your friends. Take a moment and put that image in your mind with some specific people.

Poker is a game in which some portion of a deck of playing cards is distributed to some number of players such that everyone has a "hand" of cards. Each player holds and evaluates their hand; and, crucially, they don't show it to the other people they're playing with. Different versions of poker deal with the construction and ranking of hands differently, but the gist of all versions of the game is that you're taking turns betting on your hand being the best without showing it to the other people you're playing with. In turn the people you're playing with decide to either meet your bets ("check"), "raise" your bet with a new, higher bet of their own, or "fold" their hand (leave the game and never show their hand) all depending on whether they think their hand will be able to beat your hand if and when all hands are revealed at the end of the game. The money coming from these rounds of bets go into a common "pot" in the middle of the table, waiting for the eventual winner.

There is an element of skill and odds counting involved in poker—some awareness of how likely it is to get a particular combination of cards helps evaluate your hand's likely success. But there is also an element of confidence, reading your opponent's faces, and competitive gambling as well. You win either if you have the best hand at the end of the round or if you've got everyone else to fold and you're still holding any hand at all (if you win this way, you never have to show your hand). Much like in a financial market, there is potential to win on merit or on confidence (see also Bjerg 2011). Also like in financial markets, there is an element of competitive pricing as well as an element of presumed secrecy. You only partially know what your opponents can have in their hand or how they value it. Similarly, you only can see displayed bids and offers on the order book. You don't know the rest of the person or firm's portfolio, their risk tolerance, their margin, or their other trades or even how fast they can move. You most certainly don't know their exact strategy. How, then, can a game unfold in the midst of all this ignorance (see also Souleles 2019a)?

At our hypothetical poker night, before each round begins, everyone "antes" or puts a bit of money in the pot to buy the right to participate in the next round of poker. If the ante amount is a couple dollars, most people with jobs and not too much debt will be able to play and will probably pay for each round mechanically just to stay in the game. If the ante moves up to US$50 or US$100, those same people may hesitate. If the ante moves up to US$10,000 or US$100,000 just to see some cards, we can imagine that most people simply won't be able to play poker at this game night. The amount of money you have to pay to access the game is an element of the game's design. Similarly, on financial markets there is a technological and data infrastructure that people need to buy into to participate on markets as well as a margin requirement, a sort of insurance they need to post with exchanges in case their portfolio unwinds. In a rough way, too, the more firms spend, the better they'll be able to participate. Conversely, the less you spend on speed and data and margins, the more limited your market participation will be. This is how relative access can shape market participation and behavior.

Stick with the same poker night. Let's say we've solved the ante problem so everyone in attendance can afford it and everyone is playing. Let's say that once the game is underway, the group has decided that if you put an extra US$10 dollars in the pot at any point in the game you can look at one card, chosen at random from someone else's hand. Even if you've never played poker and are first encountering it in any specificity here, you can probably gather that being able to see cards in this way would allow you to have more information than anyone else you're playing with and would probably shift whether you would hold 'em, fold 'em, walk away, or run.[4] This ability to gather information about other people's hands would represent a change in design to the game that would tilt things in favor of people who paid extra money for a bit more information. One analogous situation on financial markets has to do with buying access to data feeds that are faster than the national market feed such that certain market actors know about price movements faster than other participants and can, in turn, make inferences about future price movements. Another analogous situation on financial markets is the ability to place hidden orders on exchanges that only get activated in certain contingencies. Very basically, if other traders can't see these hidden, resting, contingent orders, they can't be sure what orders are waiting for them on the market. Access to information radically shifts how the game works for them.

One last example from poker night. Let's say we've solved the ante problem, and we've gotten rid of the ten-dollar peekaboo. Now, however, we've decided that people can play multiple hands at the same time. You, as an individual, can play as many hands as you'd like in a given game, provided you've anted up for each of them. Normally when you play poker, everyone has one hand with the same number of cards, everyone can only see one hand, and everyone bets, checks, or folds on only their one hand. Imagine, though, that there are seven hands at the table, and three are controlled by the same person (if you go back to your mind's eye and your own imaginary poker night, you probably have a pretty good idea who *that* person would be, sitting smugly across your table).

That one person with multiple hands would have a massive information advantage over the other players; that one person would know where almost half the held cards are. Moreover, they could coordinate each of their individual hands' betting, checking, or folding to bamboozle the other people at the table. In this way, different levels of participation offer the possibility of different levels of contingency, manipulation, and coordination. As we'll see shortly, many exchanges are designed to specifically mitigate this sort of coordinated, contingent behavior (which is often categorized as forbidden behavior or even a crime—all manner of manipulation, such as order stacking, layering, or spoofing).

What our imaginary poker game should illustrate is the way the competitive balance in even a simple game like poker, or a simple set of market and limit orders, shift as the conditions of the game shift. We can see this, too, if we examine a few examples of the priorities placed in actual exchanges.

Arranging the Trading Crowd

Ellen Hertz's (1998) book *The Trading Crowd: An Ethnography of the Shanghai Stock Market* is, as far as I am aware, the only anthropological study of the creation of a financial exchange (for a sociological history of automation on stock exchanges, see Pardo-Guerra 2019). What's more, it takes very seriously the role of market design in affecting investor behavior and larger societal distributional outcomes. Hertz notes the significance of the Shanghai stock market (also known as the Shanghai Stock Exchange or SSE), explaining that she did her fieldwork in 1992 at "a particular moment in the history of China's experiments with economic reforms, the moment when this symbolically charged 'capitalist mechanism' was first officially promoted on a large scale in one of China's most important cities" (Hertz 1998, 1; for an update on Chinese financial development, see Petry 2020). Put another way, the Shanghai stock market comes at an interesting moment in China's economic life and offers a sort of departure from strictly centrally planned or controlled business life. A capital market could take power away from the government and grant it to the holders of wealth and allow them to finance firms according to market mechanisms instead of state priorities.

After all, it's worth recalling that one of the things that most aggravates Jeff and his team is the possibility that agents of the US federal government might be manipulating financial markets. For Jeff and his team, for these markets to operate correctly or efficiently they need to be "free" of interference from governmental planning. This, then, is the conundrum of the Shanghai stock market—How do you raise foreign capital for Chinese firms? How do you use this capitalist market mechanism without ceding control of your companies? This, then, is where market design can come in. Just as markets can be legally required and then designed to be fair, open, and orderly in the United States, so can Chinese markets be designed to accumulate foreign capital while preserving some form of state control.

The first element of market design for the Shanghai stock market came at the level of shares offered for trade.[5] Hertz explains:

> The single most important aspect of China's stock market design which insulated it from international finance capitalism was the creation of two distinct markets for company shares, one for domestic investors ("A" shares) and another for foreigners. This second market, called the "B share market," was authorized in late 1991 as a means of attracting indirect foreign investment. (1998, 12)

These B shares, which were available to foreigners, pay dividends but do not allow for control of a company (nor are they issued in enough quantity to allow that to happen in any event). Later in the book, Hertz produces a chart summarizing ownership shares in fifty Shanghai joint stock companies (56–57). In only thirteen companies do foreigners own any shares, and in no companies do foreigners own a majority of shares. Moreover, the Chinese state, as opposed to Chinese individuals, owned an outright majority of twenty-six companies. So, at the level of market access in the form of what can be traded and what cannot, the Chinese government is able to maintain ownership of companies and collect foreign indirect investment.

A second set of features of the Shanghai stock market exist to prevent the possibility of fraud and to allow for market supervision. Moreover, at the time of their adoption, these mechanisms were ahead of their time in many American and European markets.

> The market's operating procedures depended on four main attributes, all of which were as modern as contemporary financial technology would allow. The first was a fully automated computer matching system, which paired buy and sell orders by price/time priority. The second was centralized clearing and settlement by the SSE, a feature which distinguished it from all other stock markets in the world where, by contrast, trading, clearing and settlement of shares are generally handled by the Exchanges, stock brokerages, and clearance companies respectively [as far as I know, this is still the case]. Thirdly, the market was entirely scriptless (*wuzhichua*); a few companies had printed stock certificates in the early phases of the share-holding reforms, but these paper certificates now had no economic value except as souvenirs and no paper certificates of share ownership circulated on the Shanghai market. Rather, and this brought us to the fourth feature of the Exchange, all transfer of stock ownership was centralized in the SSE computer. Individuals had a record of ownership in the booklet they were issued when they opened their registered "stock account" (*gupiao zhanghu*) though an authorized brokerage. This feature, our guide [on a tour of the exchange] informed us, was obviously related to the "Situation in the mainland": with automated stock transfer centralized at the Exchange, it has become impossible to carry out black market transactions. "Without a single arrest, the black market was entirely eliminated, and accounts registered with the Exchange have risen from 20,000 to 700,000," she said, smiling. (Hertz 1998, 34–35)

Taken together, these features of the market do a number of things. First, they function to telegraph modern efficiency—everything is electronic and internalized. Second, these features allow for supervision of trades and preclude the opportunity for black market and fraudulent transactions by internalizing all trading, transfer, and clearing. Moreover, this consolidation and internalization allows for a level of market surveillance unheard of in other stock exchanges.[6] Seemingly simple decisions such as the form that shares should take, where clearing should happen, the amount of electronic trading, and the form of records one would keep all structure the sort of trading that people can do on exchanges.

Closer to home, Michael Lewis (2015) in his book *Flash Boys* explains how the implementation of the National Market System in the United States led to a situation in which relatively "high-speed" traders would have an undue advantage over other market actors. The idea with the National Market System and the SEC's Reg NMS was that stock trading in the United States should be subject to competition and no longer dominated by the New York Stock Exchange, NASDAQ, and their affiliated brokers. Instead, there should be a national market of exchanges on which trades would get routed to the best bid or the best offer nationally. To facilitate this, there would be an aggregate market feed, the SIP, which would alert market participants to the best bid and offer on the market and where to find it. This arrangement, though, was subject to predation.

Newly competitive exchanges needed to make money as they stood to lose market share and fees for trading because of newly national competition, so they devised pay-for-play and pay-for-data schemes. Firms could pay extra money to locate a server at an exchange to have a speed advantage in reaching an order book. Trading firms could also pay for a direct data feed from a given exchange that would show market changes faster than the SIP. The combination of colocation and faster data feeds would allow trading firms with this speed advantage to arrive at any exchange faster than anyone else, given some change in a market.

Lewis's book *Flash Boys* is the saga of this market situation and the story of an insurgent exchange IEX whose designers sought to create a trading venue that would neutralize these high-speed advantages to trading. Lewis explains the cost of these speed advantages in the mid-2010s:

> The effect of the existing system on these savings is not trivial. In early 2015, one of America's largest fund managers sought to quantify the benefits of trading on IEX. They detected a very clear pattern: On IEX they tended to trade at the "arrival price"—that is, the price at which the stock was quoted when their order arrived in the market. If they wanted to buy 20,000 shares of Microsoft, and Microsoft was offered at $40 a share, they bought at $40 a share. When they sent the same orders to other markets, the price of Microsoft moved against them. This so-called slippage amounted to nearly a third of 1 percent. In 2014, this giant money manager bought and sold roughly $80 billion in U.S. stocks. The teachers and firefighters and other middle-class investors whose pensions they managed were collectively paying a tax of roughly $240 million a year for the benefit of interacting with high-frequency traders in unfair markets.

Anyone who still doubts the existence of the Invisible Scalp might avail himself of the excellent research of the market data company Nanex and its founder, Eric Hunsader. In a paper published in July 2014, Hunsader was able to show what exactly happens when an ordinary professional investor submits an order to buy an ordinary common stock—in this case, 20,000 shares of Ford Motor Company. Hunsader has the advantage of access to microsecond-level data on everything that happens in the U.S. stock market—what amounts to a movie of the action. All the investor saw was that he bought just a fraction of the stock on offer, before its price rose. Hunsader was able to show that high-frequency traders pulled their offer of some shares, and jumped in front of the investor to buy others and thus causing the share prices to rise. (2015, 279–80)

The basic problem that Lewis identifies in the US in the mid-2010s is that traders can't trust prices that are listed on exchanges. When people try to trade or get large orders across a matching engine, all the prices, all the liquidity that was there evaporates, and prices go up, generally at a persistent cost to all non-high-speed market participants.[7]

The workers at IEX, though, decided that these issues of market design could be solved by even cleverer market design. Lewis explains:

> Creating fairness was remarkably simple. They would not sell to any one trader or investor the right to put his computers next to the exchange, or special access to data from the exchange. They would pay no kickbacks to brokers or banks that sent orders [what others call "rebates"]; instead, they'd charge both sides of any trade the same amount: nine one-hundredths of a cent per share (known as 9 "mils"). They'd allow just three order types: market, limit, and Mid-Point-Peg, which meant that the investor's order rested in between the current bid and offer of any stock. If shares of Proctor & Gamble were quoted in the wider market at 80–80.02 (you can buy at $80.02 or sell at $80), a Mid-Point Peg order would trade only at $80.01. "It's kind of like the fair price," said [someone at the exchange]. (2015, 178)

IEX, through a combination of order design, pricing structure, and physical infrastructure choices, created an exchange that would mitigate the ability of traders with faster technology or more information to take advantage of the other traders that make up the majority of the market.

Hertz and Lewis both illustrate the way that simple changes to market design can radically affect the scope and scale of play possible for market participants (see Pardo-Guerra 2019). In one case the form of the share or the visibility of trading restrict access to capital markets and foreclose a whole category of fraudulent activity. In the other, order types, fee structures, and the rearrangement of technical infrastructure can neutralize one form of high-frequency actor profiting at the expense of other market participants. This sort of discussion, too, puts Jeff and his team's frustration in a new light.

Though the traders at TradeCo often talked about the features of markets as though they were a fact of nature, attention to those who design exchanges illustrates that much of what characterizes a market is not a given. Rather, markets are designed, often to the benefit of some and the detriment of others. Hertz illustrates a case in which the state, Chinese nationals, and non-Chinese foreigners are integrated differently into a financial market. Lewis illustrates the way the majority of the US financial system could be bent to benefit relatively few traders at the expense of others and how somewhat simple design in other exchanges could neutralize that advantage. Given all this, the rigging and the manipulation that Jeff, Tony, and Aaron all decry are not necessary features of their market lives. Perhaps it's that fact, coupled with the fact that there really isn't anything for them to do about their circumstances, that makes them so unhappy.[8]

6

A Nice Chianti for Our Trading Partner, the Target Bomber

Right around May 8, 2019, some calendar expirations for derivatives based on the Chicago Board Options Exchange Volatility Index, or the VIX, had come due, and some weird, frenzied trading was happening. Recall that the VIX is a heuristic, numerical index representing how much volatility, how much movement there is on financial markets. A higher VIX implies more volatility and more price uncertainty in financial markets. VIX derivatives are contracts that make a bet about how high or low the VIX is going to be and place buyers and sellers of that contract on either side of those bets (MacKenzie 2018c). Standard interpretation of the VIX would have it that the higher the VIX is, the more panicked short selling there is in equities, the more fear there is on markets (see Wigglesworth 2018). For a number of years, leading up to the market crash around the COVID-19 pandemic (at which point the VIX went into the 80s), VIX was historically mostly extremely low (in the teens), with periodic spikes and then a return to lows (admittedly, this history only goes back to the VIX's inception after the 1987 stock market crash).

On this day in May there was an unusual amount of selling at a loss, of expirations that were set to come in. Moreover, the selling was both in large, regularly sized quantities or "lots" as well as in small, one off "odd lots." This suggested to Jeff and his team that someone sophisticated, maybe a hedge fund investor, maybe a European (maybe a Frenchmen?), were puking—liquidating their position and selling everything they could at a loss so as to salvage at least some cash out of some investment mistake. Still, TradeCo didn't, and probably wouldn't ever know exactly the identity of the person they were trading with or what their strategy was. Market design had it that the trades came through a broker in the pit or over the electronic order book with no explanation in both instances. However, Jeff and the team did have some analogies:

Daniel. Is this the same thing as the Target[1] guy? [Previously they'd told me about a get-rich-quick trader who worked at Target and traded VIX.]

Brandon. The guy bought puts [options to sell] on Target and built a bot net to blow up the local Target.

[Longer conversation in which it came up that there were multiple Target-affiliated VIX traders. Brandon and I were talking about different ones.]

Jeff. It's similar at its core. This guy is trading tens of millions. The Jason Miller guy was just selling futures. The guy yesterday was selling a fuck ton of calls [options, as opposed to futures]—closer to five hundred thousand; three hundred sixty thousand; close to one hundred million.

D. Will you ever figure out who that guy was?

J. Maybe there will be an article written about him. Love to take that guy for a beer.

D. Least you could do.

J. Take him for a nice chianti.

Tony. I'm sure that guy made some money for his clients.

J. When that guy's clients get down to Q 2, they're not going to be happy.

Aaron. The Target bomber is a registered sex offender.

B. I did not make that up.

A. Sixteen thousand dollars on puts, expected to make 131,000 to four hundred thousand dollars by blowing up a ton of Targets. He offered ten thousand dollars to a guy to place ten of these bombs. That's a lot of his money.

T. [*Laughs*]

Here, I'm asking Jeff about this person who was making these trades that ended up being pretty lucrative for TradeCo. I'm just trying to figure out what they know about the people they're trading against. As I've suggested elsewhere (Souleles 2019a), Jeff and his team don't, and actually can't, figure out who is behind these trades—again, market design prevents that and ensures a baseline level of ignorance of the other people trading against them in the markets they're on. But they do have speculation about the identity and strategy of the person they're trading against, and that speculation partially structures their own trading activity. Most basically, in this instance, because they see someone puking, they assume that they're either not sophisticated, like the Target guy, or they're sophisticated and they've made a crucial mistake. Either way, the people Jeff and his team are trading against are out of their depth in managing a VIX position, and those poor marks end up puking, thereby creating profit opportunities for TradeCo.[2]

To be more specific about this particular instance, they have some analogous situations in mind about people affiliated with the American big-box store Target to help make sense of the sort of person they're currently trading against. A bit more on these Target traders that Brandon was confusing will introduce us to the larger dilemma Jeff and his team face matching trades to potential trading partners and subsuming both of those in a coherent strategy.

A Tale of Two Targets

In trying to understand how I should think about the potential puking Frenchman, I was asking Jeff whether this situation was like that of the "Target guy." A bit earlier, I was similarly asking about the VIX and who is trading it and why it behaves the way it does. In response to this Jeff and his team told me about a guy I later learned was named Seth M. Golden (Thomas 2017). (Jason Miller, the person Jeff mentioned, incidentally, was yet another VIX day trader from Florida jumbled up in the team's collective recall; Loder and Banerji 2017.) So, what were the Target guys doing, and how did TradeCo respond?

Tony. We just need things to trade in general for us to make in any product. I feel like volumes have been zero. In trading off of Kudlow's [director of the US Economic Council] coked-out press conference, we dropped seven handles in one clip based on China news from ten years earlier. We're trading against machines. That's it. It's pointless.

Rob. Target manager, Jason Miller, pound those VIX.

T. Yeah, Jason Miller, that's right.

Jeff. Jason Miller, Target manager, has been pertinent to our business for a number of years. Shorting the VIX—hot retail. He does a future roll into the front month. All the retail guys point down to eleven, two, settle at ten, and make a quick ten percent profit. The guy appeared in a *Wall Street Journal* article about how much money he was making compared to working at Target. Everyone was shorting the VIX. We need people in our markets.

Here, then, is a breakdown of a few different traders and how those traders in turn affect the TradeCo strategy. Since they're market makers, Jeff and the team need some baseline volume of trade for their business to operate. Moreover, these trades have to be real, or organic, and not just with machines, automated market makers who just churn to no end. Trading with them is pointless. By contrast the Target traders are "retail" traders, or "dumb" money, and give the necessary random churn to markets on which Jeff and Tony profitably market-make.

So, the VIX trade that Jeff is describing Jason Miller doing is, for Jason Miller, premised on the VIX never going up and staying mostly flat. What this means is that as a product of a long stretch of tranquility in the markets, people who know relatively little about the VIX are able to short far-out expirations on VIX futures contracts, then, as expiration approaches and the VIX doesn't go up in value because volatility is not going up, collect a profit and roll that profit into future expiration dates. This works so long as the VIX never goes up. This is basically a bet that (1) as derivatives contracts approach their expiration date, they will become less valuable because the VIX is unlikely to move wildly and there is less future risk, and (2) the VIX won't change, and in fact in the long term it will trend down, so there is no danger in being wildly out of the money with these derivative contracts. This is another version of profiting by selling portfolio insurance at a premium, similar to one plank of TradeCo's business logic that Jeff explained at the start of the book. Once the VIX goes up, this trade falls apart, and the trader who was shorting VIX contracts would be liable to pay out however much the VIX went up.

Seth Golden became the poster boy for this trade. Landon Thomas (2017) of the *New York Times* describes Golden's day as follows. "Each morning, at the market's open, Seth M. Golden, a former logistics manager at a Target store, fires up the computer in his home office in northern Florida and does what he has done for years: Puts on bets that Wall Street's index of volatility, the VIX, will keep falling." Landen goes on:

Mr. Golden also believes that in the decades since the VIX was introduced in 1993, its long-term trend has been to push consistently downward. Yes, there will be spikes as during major cataclysms (9/11, the 2008 financial crisis) and other less tumultuous events (a devaluation in China, a North Korea crisis or even a presidential tweet). But after every spike of fear must follow a longer period of calm, Mr. Golden contends, which he argues, is a perfect scenario if your bias is to always bet against fear. "The nature of volatility is that it desensitizes over time," he said. "Which is why the index has been tracking down for so long."

What's particularly interesting here is that whereas Jeff and his team see market tranquility, ever-increasing stock prices, and low volatility as the product of deliberate manipulation of financial markets in the form of political intervention and policy action, Golden sees the VIX's behavior as a natural fact. Also, at the time of the *New York Times* profile, Golden had done quite well for himself: "Mr. Golden, who is 40, lives in a suburb of Ocala, [Florida]. Since he has been shorting VIX, he says his net worth has gone to $12 million from $500,000 in about five years." Though a crash later knocked him down to US$3,000,000—a 75 percent drop in his portfolio (Langlois 2018). This, then, is our first Target-affiliated resident of Ocala, Florida, involved in market speculation.

The second Target-affiliated market participant from Ocala, Florida, had a slightly different scheme, though it also involved future prices (Aaron says above that he was buying options to magnify his potential gains) and the assumption that stock prices always and eventually go up. The United States Department of Justice, US Attorney's Office, Middle District of Florida (2017) describes Mark Charles Barnett's (48 and also from Ocala) plan as follows:

> According to the affidavit supporting the criminal complaint, Barnett offered a confidential source (CS) $10,000 to place improvised explosive bombs in Target retail stores along the east coast of the United States. Barnett created at least 10 of the explosive devices, disguised in food-item packaging, which Barnett delivered to the CS on February 9, 2017. Barnett then asked the CS to place the explosive devices on store shelves from New York to Florida. He also provided the CS with a bag of gloves, a mask, and a license plate cover to disguise the CS's identity from law enforcement.

Barnett theorized that the company's stock value would plunge after the explosions, allowing him to cheaply acquire shares of stock before an eventual rebound in prices.

In the language of the street, Barnett was planning on "buying the dip" in the stock price in anticipation of a future rise. What distinguishes Barnett from most traders (though not from activist-investor hedge fund managers) is that Barnett sought to manufacture his own dip.

Two Target plans from Ocala, Florida (and a third VIX day trader from Boca Raton), are all jumbling around the team's mind. These stories serve a role too. They allow the team to personify some of the people they're trading against. One genre of people they imagine out there are people who are not terribly skilled or sophisticated with managing a VIX portfolio, people who are hammering down VIX prices with the assumption that the VIX naturally always goes down. In a way, too, they're all interchangeable. The puking Frenchman could just as well be one of those guys from Ocala, Florida, trying to blow up Targets to goose the stock price. For all it matters, these are some of the sorts of people, the rubes and inexperienced day traders and criminals, who are shaping the markets they are on.

What the Target traders illustrate, too, is a smaller instance of the team making sense of other market participants and adjusting their behavior accordingly. Again, by design, traders can't know many of the people they're trading against, but it doesn't stop them from knowing some, speculating about the others, and then acting accordingly. What follows will offer an overview of who they think is out there and what they're up to.

And the Devil Walks In

Most trades that TradeCo makes are automated and pass without specific notice, save, perhaps, in the constant aggregate monitoring of the group's position. However, numerous trades come through other than automated channels and are the subjects of constant negotiation, analysis, and debate. They could be simple trades of one or another type of security or derivative, or complex multiple "legged" trades with various balanced components and calendar dates of derivative contracts with evocative names (strangles, butterflies, condors, etc.) reflecting what they might look like plotted on a graph of their likely return over time. (For a textbook overview of these sorts of trades, see Hull 2018, 251ff., or Sinclair 2010.) The latter, multilegged trades often had to happen personally as they could be so specialized, esoteric, or low volume that there wasn't an automated way to fill such orders. This is another niche that TradeCo could fill. As an aside, periodically these complicated trades come to the VIX pit, and people pause to enter them into a spreadsheet to come up with an aggregate price.

Trades could come over ICE chat—the electronic chat platform that the traders sit in with their various brokers and traders from other firms. Trades can also come over the phone in the form of a broker asking someone at TradeCo to make a market and offer a price to buy or sell something. Trades can also come in various trading pits. Occasionally these trades were mutually beneficial and noted as such.

Tony. We're not day short Apple. We should be day long Apple.
Brandon. I bought lots of puts. I thought the vol was too fucking cheap.
Jeff. What do you think you pay on this? Pay up to forty? I'm trying to talk, too much—fuck him. Wait. No, no. We want him to be buying back. I'd pay up to forty-two, I think.
B. He is good at this. If you type to him and he talks to him, it works.
J. But, this is the order we've been waiting for all day. I don't want to miss this.

Here, a mutually beneficial trade shows up in the ICE chat and allows Jeff to fix what they see as an error in their day's position. One minor interesting note about this—Jeff's first inclination was to imprecate their potential savior ("fuck him"). Only later does he realize that this is actually a good trade for TradeCo and pursue it. Jeff's initial impulse to be contemptuous was far more typical of how they commented on the people seeking to trade with them, as in the following:

Jeff. Alright, here we go.
Tony. Big uptick in Apple vol.
J. May 18, twenty-two call spread. What, you give 'em thirty-eight? Fuck this guy.

Why, then, the contempt?

Well, because of all this market-design imposed ignorance, the TradeCo guys are never quite sure whether they're being taken advantage of or whether the person seeking to trade with them knows something that they don't that will shortly lead to a bad outcome for TradeCo. Given this, hostility and contempt seem fairly reasonable responses:

Jeff. [*On the phone*] Hello. What? Sixteen-ten. What's your offer? How can you be a nickel away on VIX nowadays? Um, you guys are like a nickel away, maybe a penny away. Not just you—forty bid is my absolute best, and even that I don't like. [*Hangs up*]. He's a nickel away? Give me a fucking break.

———

Tony. How hard is it to get SPY options? To be able to trade them?

Brandon. Buy call spreads and sell puts. I told that guy to fuck off. He calls us, we do all the work and then we don't get a commission. Fuck him. He's wasting your and my time.

———

Jeff. We just went up twenty-five now from the lows. Twenty-five million, pending the three [inaudible] flexes. We're flying.

Tony. What is flying?

Brandon. Spooz.

J. Snort some Adderall [*joking, jumping up and down*].

[*Rob slams the phone and knocks it off its receiver*]

Walt. The fuck happened?

B. Got fucked by a broker.

Rob. I said cancel, then he said you're already filled.

———

Tony. Chron is 40 cents lower. That guy fucking knows it. It's trading with the devil.

Brokers misprice things. Or have you to do all the work. Or, most basically, they fuck you. Sometimes, you're even trading with the prince of darkness himself. Over and over, when orders came in or requests for prices came across their desks and those orders or requests rise to the level of verbal acknowledgment, there is contempt mingled with the apprehension that people are going to take advantage of the folks at TradeCo.

This contempt, too, could congeal around existing relationships and shape the ways that folks at TradeCo repeatedly interacted with people in their networks or firms with which they did business. One of my favorite instances of this was with a broker, Chuck Mark, whom they referred to as Cheatin' Chuck. With Chuck the invective would often seem to come out of nowhere, although it was probably prompted by a fleeting offer on an ICE chat. Still, it made for funny listening:

Brandon. None of these chips are moving.
Tony. Apple is down five percent. Go fuck yourself Mark.

————

Rob. Calls in the VIX offers, I guess that's it.
Jeff. Chuck, this guy just doesn't fucking stop. He's selling a calendar, buying them all—it doesn't fucking stop. Fourteen-fifteen, what's your bid? Nah.

————

[On their radio news services: "A Chinese delegation is still coming to America for trade negotiations, but will be smaller than planned."]
Jeff. It's a small delegation, buy some stocks.
Tony. DHOOOOKAY, buy stocks.
J. Buy futures. Come on Powell [chair of the US Federal Reserve], click the button faster, only got an hour left. He's gotta be freaking out.
Rob. Never mess with Jeff.
T. Fuck you, Chuck Mark.

————

Daniel. [Referring to the CNBC financial news playing in the office] They were just interviewing a psychic.
Jeff. It's another arm of the government propaganda to buy stocks.
Aaron. Oz Perlman is in on it.
Tony. We're flat bank deltas. The effect of the trade war has been perfectly priced in.
J. All the Robinhood customers [a phone-based retail trading app] had to get flushed. There's only one down market day to get retail out.
T. Fuck yourself Chuck Mark.
D. Is that the same as Cheatin' Chuck?
Rob. That is the same dude.

Trading with Chuck is so bad that he gets his own sobriquet, and every time, near as I could tell, he rose to the level of verbal communication, the trader's profaned his name. Put another way, if you worked at TradeCo and this broker came up, you could assume he was pushing some shit and you ought to avoid it. I have a record of three other specifically imprecated brokers as well as a trove of broker offers that never rose to the level of explicit naming but that did warrant complaining profanity.

Also notable is Jeff's aspersion of "Robinhood" customers. Robinhood is (or perhaps *was*, by the time you read this) a smartphone-based platform and app that allows users to link to their bank accounts and trade financial instruments free, that is to say, with no trading commission. Robinhood was founded in 2013 by Vlad Tenev and Baiju Bhatt, who met as undergrads at Stanford while majoring in math and physics respectively. In the estimation of *New Yorker* staff writer Sheelah Kolhatkar, "Robinhood has become successful . . . by following a trajectory similar to that of other tech companies: behaving aggressively in pursuit of fast growth" with 13 million users and a claim of US$35 billion in user trade profits as of 2020 (2021, 33–34).

In January and February of 2021 Robinhood and its users made a name for themselves via the concerted pursuit of "meme stocks," that is to say stocks and trading strategies that were hyped in online message forums such as Reddit and Discord (most prominently, the subreddit r/wallstreetbets). One stock in particular became indicative of Robinhood traders' swarm potential—over a few days, through mass action, traders managed to bid the price of stock in the mall video game retailer GameStop up around 1,800 percent to highs of around US$350 per share.

What makes GameStop particularly interesting is the way traders were not just buying and selling stock but strategically using options to drive up prices. Various strategists on r/wallstreetbets had noted that hedge funds were enthusiastically shorting GameStop stock, meaning they were betting that its price would go down.[3] When people short stocks they run into trouble when the price of those stocks actually goes up because they have to buy stock at the newly increased prices. The higher the stock price goes, the more of a loss there is for the short sellers. Also, because of the nature of shorting stock, at some specific point short sellers are forced to buy stock at whatever price they come to. The r/wallstreetbets traders had realized that they could increase the price of GameStop stock not only by buying shares outright and refusing to sell them despite short seller demand but also because they could also buy options contracts that would force market makers like Jeff and his team to buy (and therefore bid up) lots of stock to hedge and insure TradeCo's growing option position, leading financial times journalist Robin Wigglesworth to observe that options trading had become "weaponised"

(Wigglesworth 2021).[4] This is part of the peril of being a market maker: if people want to buy options, you've got to sell them, and they can force you to create large, absurd positions in order to hedge your options activity.

The reason that Jeff is complaining about Robinhood is in part because he thinks their reasons for trading are, if not stupid, at least ill conceived and ill informed. GameStop, again, is illustrative. The business case for GameStop is weak—it is/was a mall-based retailer who buys and sells physical copies of used video games. Online retail threatens malls, and downloadable video games threaten the market for physical copies of games. It's unclear that on business fundamentals that GameStop valuation should have gone up by 1,800 percent. Rather, trading seems to be motivated by nostalgia for what GameStop means in individual traders' lives and a collective desire to stick it to merciless short-selling hedge fund traders. Put mildly, these are trading motivations to which Jeff has trouble relating.

In addition, the traders didn't restrict their hostile, suspicious contempt to individually named brokers or swarms of retail traders. There was one options brokerage firm in particular, Ebbtide, that seemed to bring and offer them nothing but bad trades. As such, the mere mention of their name would lead to lamentations.

Brandon. Is intel coming in?

Tony. No, it's coming in in thirty minutes.

B. I'm trading with Ebbtide; someone fucking kill me. One thousand.

T. Alright.

B. Right here [*slaps chest*]: Uh, uh, uh, uh, staying alive.

[*Plays the song,* "Flip That Flow"]

Aaron. RIP this guy. This song is so absurd.[5]

———

[Here, Jeff is both talking to the normal team as well as a pit trader in another location about some trades, some of which are with Ebbtide.]

Jeff. What was our total on that one, eighteen or seventeen-fifty? OK, that's blottered. Thirty-nine-oh-five. The total is forty-four-oh-five. OK, should be clean on everything. 4,405 total. I bought thirty futures against it. We could probably do something else. Blottered 4,500 as a place holder in Op Mon just to see how it affects our group. I agree, I'll do that. That is fucking good. Yeah, talking about that guy coming in and puking it. Did they send us our first one, seven hundred? This call spread is new—1,500?

Tony. Apple vol is right back up.

J. VIX vol is on the highs. Did you lead at both legs? I'll track and make sure the position looks right.

Brandon. It's in. I did it. I'll do it to my crash. I can do this.

J. Fuck Ebbtide.

T. Lee, lets coordinate this. He's going to have thirty thousand more to do. How many are you going to do? We have the bullets, theta-wise to do it, I think. We would end up short about five thousand for next week. We can always trade the regular May against it. [*On the phone*] Hello? I'll do one thousand one-oh-five if you go it. Cut me to five. I did the last print fine. [*Off the phone*] Trying to cross the whole thing. Don't let him do it. Fucking jackwad. I tried for thousand to let you know. I said I may or may not get it, but twenty-one futures.

Ebbtide was a universal object of derision while I was in the office. The mere prospect of trading with them made Brandon revolt and led Jeff to extra aspersions. Looking at the brokers that made up their most frequent manual and announced trades, we can see the way some of those trading partners get habitually typified as incompetent or predatory and are then treated with suspicion.

One final note about this sort of reflexive contempt—it wasn't just reserved for random day traders and the brokers who came and went as part of the daily round. Traders at TradeCo also could evaluate their own groups this way, particularly since some trades that they and others would do could restrict other trades within the TradeCo organization for compliance reasons. One instance of their complaining about a group who did not seem long for this world follows:

Tony. I don't know how I lose twenty-five grand in Lyft today. Do you know? We don't have a position. We're paying three grand a day in theta. It's up six percent. I give up. I literally give up.

Jeff. [On the phone] Hello? Fucking stop. I'm not doing these thirty dollars [*off the phone*]. twelve-forty risk reversal in May [*mocking nerd voice*] go fuck yourself.

Kyle. What part of, "they lose money every single day," did you not understand? Every single day.

J. I don't know how it is possible to lose money every day just throwing darts at a ticker. Actually, I think on Friday they made nine grand then lost twenty grand. No fucking idea in my wildest imagination if this is possible, in this burgeoning new office [in another city]. These are new guys we hired out there to do some skew strategies.

Aaron. They work out of a basement.

J. We cannot stop buying options. There were pennies and two pennies. It's just crazy. The options selling down banks is something to behold. This baba is up to forty.

K. Raised it back up.

J. More than fifteen people picked up, you need a security guard. We don't need it, just wait a few days.

T. Part of me says we should just buy one thousand puts in random names and risk three hundred grand for a fuck load of money.

J. Definitely think we sell out all of our long deltas.

Theta refers to the time risk of holding a security or derivative and can be expressed in terms of the Black Scholes Merton equation used to price options. The traders use *theta* metaphorically to refer to the cost of holding their positions. In this case Tony starts off, wondering how it's possible that they're paying theta given that they haven't taken a position one way or another on Lyft and are presumably just doing normal market-making work. This leads to a larger discussion of a new group at TradeCo, one who is doing "skew" strategies, or is placing bets on derivatives that have different prices but the same underlying asset.

It's a trade that assumes that these differences are capable of being arbitraged and one can build trades on the expectation that there will be some form of convergence in price on into the future. At least that's the idea. Jeff and his team don't think this new group is particularly good at it. Rather, they seem to be steadily losing money and are doing no better than throwing darts at a stock ticker. In turn, Tony thinks that maybe the darts-at-a-stock-ticker strategy might prove more productive than their own.

Only One Losing Day

Across the trading partners that bear mentioning, the traders at TradeCo had a certain amount of suspicion and contempt. I suggest this has to do with the nature of market design on the exchanges on which they operate. They don't get to see the totality of other people's positions, much less their ideas or strategies, much less know them personally. As a consequence, they are left to fill out imaginatively the identities of the trading partners they encounter and then change their strategies accordingly.

One sort of trader they encounter are the big movers who are out of their depth. These can be retail traders as in the gentlemen from Ocala, Florida, or the swarm on Robinhood. These traders can also be European sophisticates who don't know how to run their VIX portfolio or need to cash in their VIX for its insurance value. Either way Jeff and his team know these people are out there, periodically see them blow up, and are more than happy to provide a market for them to liquidate their positions in a discounted rush.

Another sort of trader that Jeff and his team encounter is much more professional. These are the brokers and brokerage firms that populate their ICE chat and call their phones. These traders know what they're doing, and in the imagination of Jeff and his team, they generally have an angle that involves taking advantage of TradeCo if they can. As a consequence of this, Jeff and his team have developed a reflexive contempt toward most of this class of trader. Chuck Mark becomes Cheatin' Chuck, and Ebbtide makes everyone want to wretch. This sort of professional discourtesy is even extended to other flailing groups within TradeCo, as the commentary on their new group illustrated.

These traders—retail, human brokers, and internal—do not exhaust the universe of people Jeff and his team imagine as being on markets. We've already heard about political actors and central bank actors. There are also regular institutional traders—pensions, sovereign wealth funds, and the like that move relatively slowly and buy and sell over long, somewhat predictable time horizons. These probably make up much of basic market movements, and they send their orders through large, automated institutional brokerages and make up much market background noise. Finally, we've also heard about mechanical or automated actors, the LINUSes and the Citadels of the world. To close the chapter, it's worth spending a bit more time on how TradeCo figures these traders.

Whereas retail investors, crooked brokers, and dysfunctional traders all offered a way to react and a way to trade, mechanical, automated traders often lead to resigned defeat—the end of the game and alienation crystallized. A number of times above, the traders have noted that they're just trading with machines, or that they've been flashboyed and that there just isn't anything to do.

Tony. You could respond, let's say eighty-six cents. Ask for six cents of edge. That's my bid.

Brandon. 2,500?

T. Sure. What did I buy here?

B. Fuck. Ugh.

Jeff. Losing streaks just get longer and longer. Winning streaks can get longer too.

T. Such a Debby Downer.

J. You didn't listen to me with what I said.

B. [My friend said that he had] one losing day in a seven-year career at Virtu.

J. With no regulation, that's either fucked up or they're cheating.

Aaron. Lots of small winners.

B. Half the days, I lose money. The other half, I hope I win more. [Virtu] offered to move [my friend] to [a sunny city] and he hesitated.

A. I would personally not want to move to [that sunny city].

T. It's not sad enough for you.

J. [You like it here with] terrible weather and depressed people.

Here, Brandon is pondering a losing streak. And he's doing so by comparing his ability to make money and win to that of a friend of his who works at the high-speed, automated, market-making firm Virtu. Brandon notes that this guy said that they had but one down day in a seven-year run. By contrast, Brandon hopes to do slightly better than breaking even.

One other day I asked Brandon and the team about exactly this: How could they stay in business when people like Virtu were in the market never losing? While they didn't directly answer my question, they did offer some insight into the issues of market design they were dealing with and why, again, their future work as traders was by no means guaranteed. Here's Brandon:

> VIXB options used to be listed in quarters, then eighths, then nickels. Around 2007 a thing called the penny pilot happened, and [the tick size of these] options went to penny widths. Quarters to 12.5 to nickels to pennies for a lot of options. That brings in the high-frequency surge rush. We think that we maybe make a half a penny on a trade if we make a great trade. [With penny tick sizes], most trades now make a tenth of a penny.

Brandon is suggesting that the tick size of stocks—the minimum increment a stock can move up and an element of market design—affects the profitability of market makers. Firms like TradeCo need things to be wider than a penny to make money given how much they make on each stock. Firms like Virtu and Citadel don't because they're completely automated and trade at huge volume and scale. Brandon continued:

When they said pennies, there were two thousand stocks listed in pennies and it broke people's models and broke people's machines. It broke execution platforms and people had to invent all these auction mechanisms. There were market structure issues. The faster guys and the bigger guys fragmented liquidity even more.

Setting the minimum tick size would seem to improve the efficiency of markets as stocks and derivatives could move at ever more granular increments. What Brandon is suggesting, though, is that an adverse effect of this move is to diminish the number of market makers in a given trading environment. There are only so many traders who can profitably market-make with penny spreads. Jeff comments as follows in the same conversation:

> I think the exchanges, they want one or two giants for liquidity, and all the little guys [e.g., the Robinhood traders] who generate big commissions. Pennies work for the biggest guys, and they work for the little guys. It's somewhat inadvertent, but the more market makers you have, the more efficient the market is going to be. The bigger risk you already start to see is that there are only two or three market markers. Then, the little guy gets fucked, hard. The little guy is going to get screwed and then retail execution quality will decline.

Here, Jeff is making an argument about the trajectory that markets are on that has some similarities to Michael Lewis's diagnosis of the problems with the rise of the National Market System. What Jeff is suggesting is that exchanges prefer a situation in which they have one or two market makers and the tick size is as small as possible. (Why they might prefer this has to do with ideas about what an efficient market should be as well as business considerations of the sort of data and access fees that can be extracted from big market-making firms.) What Jeff says happens under these circumstances is that liquidity and competition actually goes out of a market. Michael Lewis suggested that a lot of the orders posted on markets in the mid-2010s were phantom because high-frequency traders would pull away from real buyers and reprice faster than those buyers could adjust. Jeff says the same thing happens when one or two market makers crowd out everyone else. Execution quality goes down, as does available liquidity.

Jeff and his team bear witness to these sorts of markets every time they get stuck trading with machines and chasing phantom liquidity. The prospect of these mechanical markets leads the traders to despairing speculation reminiscent of a reflection that sociologist Jenna Burrell made about the role of automated computer algorithms in society:

> In addition to the polarization of a public discourse about algorithms, much of what is new in this domain is the more pervasive technologies and techniques of data collection, the more vast archives of personal data including purchasing activities, link clicks, and geospatial movement, an outcome of more universally adopted mobile devices, services, and applications and the reality (in some parts of the world) of constant connectivity. But this does not necessarily have much to do with the algorithms that operate on the data. Often it is about what composes the data and new concerns about privacy and the possibility (or troublingly, the impossibility) of opting-out. (2016, 2)

Here Burrell makes the point that it's not so much what automated computer algorithms do in any given circumstance and with whatever source of data that leads to concern about them in a given society but rather the fact that these new algorithms seem inescapable. This echoes the Marxist observation about the inevitably and inexorability of estrangement in the context of wage labor and limitless, uncoordinated accumulation both of wealth and of productive capacities. The traders at TradeCo know what to do with French hedge fund sophisticates and Target terrorists as well as predatory brokers. They're all people that they can match wits with and strategize around. By contrast, when they get flashboyed, there's nothing to do and nowhere to go but sit back and lose money. Huge, automated market makers change the basic reality of being a trader on a market. Maybe they should just throw darts at a board and trade based on that?

7

They Don't Tell You That There's No Price

Of course, those automated-trading computer algorithms that get Jeff and the team down at TradeCo, those monopolistic and inescapably predatory algorithms from Citadel or Virtu that seem to be harbingers of a future for human traders that is vast, dull, and money-losing, well, those algorithms have to come from somewhere and from someone. We met one such group in Bradford Partners and their avatar LINUS. One thing that made LINUS and Bradford intelligible for our purposes is that they started as traders and adapted to new market conditions along a timeline that is roughly concurrent with that of Jeff's group at TradeCo. By contrast, many firms as well as much computer talent and many techniques for computerized trading actually come from beyond finance altogether (e.g., Pardo-Guerra 2019). As such these people and processes bring ideas about markets to trading that are foreign to those of financial professionals. Moreover, they structure their algorithms and market participation accordingly. One such example of this is Brad Olin (d033), who runs a hedge fund trading firm. His origin story and a description of his learning curve in working on markets will illustrate what Jeff and co. are up against.

In the course of my interview with Brad, he told me a bit about his background. Brad is both a tech person and an entrepreneur, and had worked at and founded a number of companies that made use of surveillance and tracking algorithms to do things like monitor and help with people's health. Brad explained the business model to me:

Brad. I worked at . . . a wearable body, a modern company [that] made a wearable [piece of technology] that measured what kind of activities you did, how well you slept. It was kind of a precursor to things like the Fitbit [a bracelet that tracks individual fitness and health data].

Daniel. You were ahead of the curve on that one.

B. Mhmm. We were way out of the curve, way too early if I'm honest. If we started that company five years later, we would have done much better.

D. What was the idea of starting that?

B. With that one? It started [with] guys who were designers and/or wearable experts and were on a couple other wearable projects. They just thought, "Hey we can get a lot of information by using machine learning and data." Data synthesis [and] fusion was a big topic back then, and we could basically make much better predictions than the others out there.

D. Sure, sure. Did it work?

B. Yeah. It actually worked very well. We had the most accurate wearable body monitor for measuring you know the number of calories you burn and we got bought by [a big company] in [the early 2010s]. After I left, they killed it.

So, this is where Brad is coming from. He doesn't start as a finance guy, rather he's an itinerant tech guy. At this particular company, they had the idea of using machine-learning algorithms, that is, bits of computer programming that iteratively change their own program based on some set of data they receive, all in order to serve some sort of personal health monitoring and advice function. In Brad's estimation the technology was good and ahead of its time. This, in turn, is why the company got bought.

There are a couple things in this narrative that are worth noting. First, machine-learning algorithms are a thing to be dropped into this particular business. The algorithms and the computer people don't need to have any sort of necessary connection to health or health care for this to be appropriate. Rather, in Brad's estimation, these programs are things that can just be added in to a larger business model or plan. Brad's specific attitudes echo a pervasive belief among technologists and tech entrepreneurs that technology is always the solution to any societal problem, an attitude that journalism professor Meredith Broussard has called "technochauvinism" (2018, 7–8; see also Boyd and Crawford 2011; for a similar phenomenon in finance, see Ho 2009 and Souleles 2019b; and in consulting, see Stein 2017 and Chong 2018). From this perspective, local knowledge about, say, finance and financial markets is more or less irrelevant.

The second thing to note is that Brad is itinerant. He's working at a place for a while and moves on to something else. Life is a long hustle; a string of ideas, largely concerning applying computer programming techniques to various businesses and industries. This sensibility led him to trading. Rather, this itinerant sensibility as well as a specific fantasy led him to trading.

After the wearable health technology company, Brad eventually started his hedge fund. Here, Brad made use of the same logic with the wearable company—apply machine learning to some industry and make money from the ensuing alchemy:

> We were pretty unconstrained about what we asked the system to do, so when we started we thought, you know, machine learning is pretty powerful. We'll just apply machine learning and it will come up with a great [trading] algorithm and we can all be on the beach, right?

The fantasy here is a money machine, an autonomous computer algorithm that teaches itself how to make profitable trades. A computer algorithm that works so well that Brad and his colleagues could lounge on a beach and watch the money roll in.

The fantasy didn't quite work out. Recall that Brad didn't actually start in finance, and at the time he didn't know anything about finance. He has since learned a lot, but as part of this interview, I spent quite a bit of time asking him to explain what he didn't know and what he'd learned. A brief enumeration of some of the things he came to know about markets will illustrate how little he knew about finance and the potential of algorithmic cockiness to overcome market ignorance.

Brad. It's sort of funny. We started back in [the mid-2000s]. We had seen the confluence of big data computing and computer science algorithms getting better, and we realized there's so much data coming out of companies that there was going to be a time when computers could find strategies faster than the humans could. That was going to happen at some point. It would be a John Henry–like moment and we said, "let's be a part of that, because this is going to happen again." I think we were a little early. Some of the changes that happened over ten years were the world catching up to this idea. And some of them were us actually building the infrastructure that we needed in order for this to happen. So, it was also, us, honestly, learning about the markets. There was a tremendous amount that until you actually dive into it, no one tells you.

Daniel. [*Laughs*]What are some things?

B. Well, they call them brokers, because that's what they do. They make you broke-er. The data is not clean. Like it's this huge mess of data. We're actually transferring from one data vendor to another one right now for our primary data sets, and the differences are utterly amazing.

D. Like what?

B. Like when a company splits up, which company in the past gets to keep the ticker [the stock ticker symbol that identifies it on markets]. Right? Cause it totally changes the history of all of the market if you do it differently, right, eh? and some of these break-ups are massive and mergers are massively complicated. Mergers are the ones that when you're looking back at it there's two tickers going into it and only one coming out.

D. Jesus.

B. The company chooses that one, right? But when you're looking back at it in the past you have to assign that common ticker to one of those two companies.

D. Yeah.

B. So, which one gets the history? You make this assumption that you can know what the price of a security is. It's a myth. There's no price for a security. There's a market.

D. No, it's spreads on tons of different markets.

B. That's right. Yeah. And the movement of Bitcoin and crypto currency in general is a great example.

D. Oh god, it is so not standardized.

B. Yeah, yeah. I was trying, I bought a little tiny bit of Bitcoin.

D. How long ago?

B. I bought about a year ago, so I'm very happy, yeah.

D. Good for you.

[Bitcoin chat interlude]

B. Anyway, there's other data things like, so people revise your data. That's a problem for machine learning because when you have fresh data for today, they'll be like what should I trade today? You don't have it revisioned yet, right? And so, data vendors who revise their data without telling you, they're the worst. We had one that for dividends would report that the company had "none" dividends and a null number if they had never given a dividend ever. But as soon as they give a dividend, they will retroactively go back and replace all those "nones" with "zeros." So, machine-learning algorithms, they just bias the companies that [show] "zero" dividends instead of [the companies that show] "nones" [and] will make money because they both exist long enough to give a dividend and eventually get dividends. It's cheating.

D. Jesus. So, do you know how to deal with this? Do you, like, have to find a data vendor that like—

B. You have to find good data vendors, yeah. You have to unclean your data right, to give the system the noisy data, and you have to work really hard to give the system the noisy data, and you have to work really hard to have point-in-time data so you know when events changed [relating to] something in the past.

D. Got it. OK. So, what are all the things they don't tell you?

B. They don't tell you about a lot of things. They don't tell you about how much leverage costs [the cost of borrowing money], right? Academics almost never worry about leverage. They don't tell you.

A lot of the basic nature of trading is you need to have liquidity. Liquidity is really the thing that matters. And there are various assets that look like they don't have much liquidity but really do and vice versa. So, the other issue with liquidity is it's very much subject to behavior of the market. So, you can get a flash crash, right? Even in superliquid assets, if all market makers run away, then your three sellers can just crush the market.

D. So, there's all this like real market stuff that you just don't know about going into it.

B. Right. Oh, you think there's one price. There's not one price. There's n different exchanges all trading at different prices, [at] different instances between each other, right?

D. [*Laughs*] But, I have this precise machine-learning algorithm, but there is no price.

B. Right. No, no. There is no price.

[Interlude on price and broker algorithms]

D. Got it. What other things they don't tell you?

B. Raising money. It seems like you should just be able to go out and be like, "hey, we're really smart. We've got great algorithms. We've been trading for a year. Give us your money," right? No, it's not how this works.

Brad's forthcoming interview is a great illustration of what nonfinanciers don't know about markets. To start with, Brad notes that he didn't really understand the roles of brokers—that is, people who take your orders to market. He didn't understand that one part of trading cost has to do with paying brokers to execute your trade. He also didn't understand the heterogeneity of trading data—that different vendors and different exchanges have different conventions and formats for their data. He illustrates this by explaining the conundrum about thinking about the price history of a company that has merged or split—how should one think about this when feeding it to a machine-learning algorithm?

Then he explains that he didn't know about leverage or margins—the credit accounts that people have with exchanges that allow them to trade at higher amounts than the cash they have. This sort of leverage has a cost that impinges your ability to trade. Then there is raising money for his hedge fund—people don't just give him money because he's good at computers. This surprises him. He was used to the opposite. And, finally, he laments twice that there is no price. Recall that contemporary financial markets are essentially constant auctions, electronic order books made up of posted bids to buy and offers to sell with a spread between the two. There is no price, there's just constant bidding, auctioning, and crossing the spread. In retrospect there can be an average across dimensions like time or volume or both. But basically, there is no one, current price.

What's telling in all of this is how little Brad knew about financial markets despite being convinced at the outset of founding his hedge fund that he could conquer those markets. And, in a way, he's been vindicated. He runs a profitable hedge fund. He didn't know how trading worked; brokers, leverage, margins, and pricing were all foreign. He didn't know the networks through which he could access investment capital. He didn't even know how to analyze and think about the data he was going to get. Yet he got into markets anyway. And he did so, in his words, because he had great algorithms. What I suggest here and over the rest of the chapter is that understanding what he and other computer people who get into finance ("quants," if you will) think about their algorithms shows the outlook and explains the actions of the people who are flashboying Jeff and his team and creating markets and exchanges from which Jeff and his team feel increasingly estranged.

Into the Algo-verse

Algorithms are tricky to define. Most basically, we can understand them as automated bits of computer programming that do tasks according to the logic of their code. Some algorithms can learn from their own actions, as in machine learning. Some algorithms work semiautonomously. Other algorithms require lots of attention and input from humans or other algorithms. So far, so simple. What makes algorithms tricky, though, is that it's difficult to understand when exactly they stop and start—what counts as part of the algorithm (Coombs 2016). Moreover, it's difficult to account for the fact that different groups of people treat algorithms differently, much less understand why Brad's algorithms are so lucrative.

Sociologist Robert Seyfert (2016) makes this point in an article that among other things, suggests that to regulate algorithms you can't limit yourself to their computer code:

> A demand to reveal the inner workings of algorithmic codes is formulated from a very particular perspective that assumes that operations are in fact operating from inside the [black algorithmic] box. For trading firms, algorithms are relational entities and can only be understood in context and in relation to other algorithms. . . . Thus, attempts to understand the complexity of [High Frequency Trading] cannot consist in revealing as much code as possible. Rather, it must consist in looking at the way code operates and interacts in "real" life. Most importantly, it needs to understand how this operation and interaction is perceived by different actors. Because different participants perceive the "same" information differently and act on it differently it is important to do comparative-cultural analysis. (273)

Seyfert is highlighting two things that are particularly important for our purposes. First, the context of an algorithm, its development, and its deployment matter for understanding it. And second, algorithms and humans work together to do things. These insights are important grounding for understanding what exactly Brad is getting at in suggesting that investors should throw money at him because he has good algorithms. Anthropologist Nick Seaver (2017) clarifies, in terms of methods, what a study of algorithms that takes into account this sort of complexity should do. He notes that the definition and deployment of algorithms, and whether, to informants, those things have any sort of concurrence are empirical questions (2), and advocates a variety of creative ethnographic methods to tease out the various ways that algorithms both sit inside of as well as make up social life.

Mindful of the capacious nature of algorithms and hesitant to reduce them to their root code, I chose to approach what an algorithm is and thereby what an algorithmic trader is, how they act, and how they spoil Tony's day by inventorying the ways that the quant traders we in the AlgoFinance project talked to understood algorithms. Across our interviews, Kristian Bondo Hansen (2021, 609) suggests that we talked to seventy-three people who specialized in algorithmic or quantitative finance and trading (people with quant or programming or machine or computer in their job descriptions). From that sample, I created a subsample of seventeen informant interview transcripts and collected 235 instances of the word stem *algo-*, which I then condensed into 121 discrete, declarative statements about algorithms. All told, this is the same maneuver I explained and did in the chapter on markets.

One tiny distinction: I needed to use more informants here for algorithms than I did for markets because the definition of algorithm is a bit more diffuse and the actual instance of the word *algorithm* is less frequent in conversations than *market* was. The informants I selected were meant to be different from one another across career stage, researcher informant network, and geographic location. The informants as well as the 121 discrete algo statements are enumerated in the appendix on the use of the word stem *algo-* (app. E).

This algo exercise generated the following schema:

- Generalizations about algorithms (30 total)
  - Algorithms have behaviors (19 subtotal)
  - Algorithms have limitations (6 subtotal)
  - Algorithms do good and important things (5 subtotal)
- Algorithms conjure both specific people and specific arrangements of people (17 total)
- On building algorithms (23 total)
  - Algorithm building has an aspirational, imprecise, often metaphoric component (11 subtotal)
  - Algorithm building has a precise, technically specific component (12 subtotal)
- Algorithms have trading abilities and limitations (45 total)
  - Algorithms have specific trading abilities and features (36 subtotal)
  - Algorithms create specific results and conditions in markets (9 subtotal)
- Algorithmic miscellany (6 total)

While I'll use specific examples of the above elements of this algorithm schema throughout the rest of this chapter, what's of immediate use to us are the generalizations quants offer about algorithms. The generalizations are particularly interesting because they're not specific to finance and do not portray algorithms as directly analogous to the human traders they are displacing but point to what quants think algorithms can do in the wider world, often regardless of context.

Most basically, quants say, algorithms solve problems. They fix inefficiencies in complex, leaky, component-filled projects. They create a fast society and allow you to teach the machine to be a scientist. Algorithms are far away from the path and pattern recognition of pigeon-brained humans. What comes out across these good things that algorithms can do is a sense of speed, science, and surpassing humans. That said, algorithms have to do all these good things via behavior that is idiosyncratic to algorithms and often tacitly juxtaposed to human behavior.

In this vein, algorithms produce things that are unexpected, behave in ways other than how they are supposed to, and have their own world. Within this unexpected, proprietary world, algorithms can have a complex relationship with one another: algorithms can analyze other algorithms; algorithms can know and follow each other; algorithms can also ingest data and become automated. Algorithms can have distinct behaviors. Algorithms can look for statistical patterns, can be tested against one another, and can detect attacks. Algorithms can be implemented, can be knowable by people, and can be supervised by humans. Put another way, algorithms need to be supervised to make sure they do what they say they're doing.

What starts to emerge across the general typification of algorithms is that in many important ways they can supersede human abilities—human abilities to process, to sort, to analyze, and to act. Moreover, algorithms do this by means of distinct, often autonomous behavior in their own algorithmic realm. In this algo realm, algorithms interact, observe, follow, and attack one another. Perhaps, because of all this autonomy, humans need to supervise algorithms. Moreover, algorithms have a number of distinct limitations.

Because algorithms are reliant on the data that one puts into them, they can be overfit to that data. This means that they can operate admirably with their training data but in the real world fail because they have been solely accustomed to a too-predictable environment. Algorithms can also have biases either due to the lack of vision of their programmers, the nature of the data they are fed, or the environment in which they operate. Algorithms can be difficult to understand. Algorithms can follow rules for knowing and categorization that make no sense to humans. Despite this lack of intelligibility, algorithms can predict things about people's daily lives, unsettling human's sense of themselves. Cutting across these limitations is the upsetting danger algorithms can pose.

Altogether, these features of algorithms, attested to by the quant traders we interviewed, start to illustrate why Brad thought folks should throw money at him for being an expert algo wrangler. Algorithms, after all, have the ability to do better than humans in all sorts of realms of endeavor. For this, they're complicated, sneaky, duplicitous, and dangerous. Surely, you'd want a professional taming your algorithms? Truth be told, Brad's bargain gets better and better the more you know about what algorithms can do on markets and the sort of people that come with them.

Algo, Smash (Volatility)!

Given the nature of our research on the AlgoFinance project, it's probably not surprising that the single largest category of commentary on algorithms had to do with what algorithms are able to do on markets and how those abilities affect markets writ large.

Starting functionally, quants feel that algorithms can trade; put another way, they can buy or sell. Algorithms allow you to apply the scientific method to trading, and make you or your firm distinct from a human stock picker. Algorithms can also trade futures and options. Crucial for the guys at TradeCo, however, is that trading options is more complicated than trading futures or trading the stock or other underliers for an option. Taken together, algorithms are able to perform basic market functions. This functionality in turn allows for algorithms to take on specific market roles.

Algorithms can replace human brokers and route orders. Algorithms can follow specific strategies and can be trend following or mean reverting. Algorithms can also be used to automatically hedge a portfolio position against risk. Algorithms can determine the optimal place to put an order. Algorithms can also simply market-make. Almost any genre of market participation can be assumed by an automated computer program. This is largely to do with some of the more specific abilities that market algorithms have.

Algorithms can make trading strategies. One might even distinguish between simple optimizing execution algorithms and strategy-generating algorithms. Algorithms can figure out correlations between different financial instruments and assess related movements that one might expect. One can use algorithms to determine the bottom in a given market. Algorithms can

even take on board financial economic theories of market micro- and macrostructure to make their calculations. These abilities, though, come with
constraints. Just as, from a general point of view, quants see limitations attending the exciting abilities of algorithms, so, too, do quants see market
algorithms having specific potential and constraints.

Algorithms can deliver investment results by allowing a trader to build
and scale edge (advantage in trading), to hold positions for longer periods
of time, and to avoid adverse selection. That said, algorithms can be inappropriate for some markets. Algorithms and their strategies also have a life
cycle, which generally ends in the algorithm and its strategy's irrelevance
due to outcompetition from other algorithms. Algorithms can have difficulty
assessing the permanence of price change (as in LINUS being unable to understand a shift in the yield curve), can reduce trading inventory, and, most
basically, can lose shitloads of money.

What begins to emerge from the quant account of algorithms on markets is, again, an appreciation of the various human roles that algorithms
are able to fill, often in a capacity that exceeds their human counterparts.
Despite that, algorithms have constraints—they have life cycles and don't
always seem to understand the context in which they operate. Extending
these abilities and limitations, quants see distinct effects on the larger market environment because of the emergence of algorithmic trading.

Algorithms support a trading environment that is zero-sum. Algorithms
can be market makers but grab as much value as possible from the order
book. Algorithms follow each other when they trade, thereby smashing volatility and smoothing markets. Algorithms make it hard for your orders to
get filled—it's often difficult to understand why this is the case. Broker algorithms might take your trade and then sell back to you at a higher price. On
the plus side, algorithms and their application in trading have the potential
to drive better pricing in the lower echelons of stocks and futures by making
spreads smaller. Algorithms can be a force magnifier and allow traders to
do thousands of orders a day, twenty-four hours a day, while only having to
touch things by hand no more than a handful of times. In another quant's
estimation, it's unclear whether all the resources used for algos in financial
markets is good or bad for society.

What starts to come from the quant explanation of how algorithms affect
markets are many of the things that Jeff and his team specifically lament.
The quants note that algos can reduce volatility and lead to unpredictable
price swings (see also Borch 2016). A lack of volatility makes it difficult for

all but the fastest market makers to operate. Moreover, the quants observe that algorithmic market makers can suck all the value out of an order book and churn trades, selling your own positions back to you at a loss. Moreover, these quick actors act to narrow spreads, again making it less profitable for other market makers to function and leading to a winner takes all scenario for this sort of speculative trading.

One further entailment of the rise of algorithms are the people like Brad that the algos conjure. One thing the quants observed is that algorithms had a knack for arranging and rearranging people. Most basically, algorithms require high-level ideas people. Because algorithms can be wickedly smart, they can support wickedly smart traders. Moreover, an algorithm can contain the whole investment committee. These sorts of requirements and condensations lead algorithms to drive hiring practices. More specifically, algorithms require people who are in high demand to run them. Perhaps put another way, algorithms are employed by scientists and specialized researchers. Moreover, algorithms in trading are so new that the people who do them by definition cannot have gotten their jobs because of family ties. Put more sharply, algorithms are used by people who are not the big swinging-dick banker bros. More generally, algorithms presuppose an algo trader way of doing things that is more academic and cerebral than a pit trader way of doing things. Algorithms allow you to not care about who is in the market save for whether they are informed or not.

These algorithmic personnel self-assessments illustrate the distinctions that quant traders draw between themselves and what they see as older or more typical finance people and traders, and they illustrate, granularly, how structural changes in an economy can happen because of the increased scope and productivity of algorithmic systems and, in turn, how these structural changes are understood in the local language of a specific group of people. To quants, algo people are scientists in high demand; they are precise and succeed by their own merits. Employing algo people allows you to have disdain for more conventional trading and who is in the market. This sentiment is echoed, in fact, by Jim Simons, the founder of one of the most successful quantitative hedge funds, Renaissance Technologies. In his book about Simons and Simons's fund, Renaissance Technologies, *Wall Street Journal* reporter Gregory Zuckerman writes,

> Until then, Simons and his colleagues hadn't spent too much time wondering *why* their growing collection of algorithms predicted prices so presciently.

They were scientists and mathematicians, not analysts or economists. If certain signals produced results that were statistically significant, that was enough to include them in the trading model.

"I don't know why planets orbit the sun," Simons told a colleague, suggesting that one needn't spend too much time figuring out why the market's patterns existed. "That doesn't mean I can't predict them." (2019, 150–51)

Algorithms come from science, are precise, and are created by scientists (see also Lowrie 2017). Markets are just another arena with phenomena and are interchangeable with any other field or arena that scientists should look at. It doesn't really matter what other traders are doing. TradeCo can parse the various Target bombers all they want. For the algo traders and quants, all that human noise is just abstractable to mathematical formalism, raw data, and a series of theories and predictions. It doesn't really matter from this point of view why a market moves—be it due to government intervention, manipulative electronic trading, ill-informed retail investors, poorly designed market environments, fundamental changes in corporate or business performance, war, a global pandemic, or something else. All that matters is the modeling and the results. Specific people are nowhere present.

A Day in the Algo Life

On another day in another financial center, I had the opportunity to sit down with Horace Banning (d029) and his team of quant traders and do another generic interview about their background and their work. Horace and his team are market makers in currencies and futures and can often make up 20 percent of a given market they trade on. Moreover, they claim above average returns and to be in the top 25 percent or so of their space. Now that we've met Brad, a quintessential tech outsider to finance, and heard generically how the quants we spoke to think about algorithms, the interview I did with Horace and his team will afford the opportunity to put the analysis in this chapter together with a string of interview excerpts. Altogether, this data will show the difference between how Horace and his team and how Jeff and co. understand working on markets.

The first distinction has to do with that of being a trader versus being a quant. I noted that a few members of Jeff's team started as pit traders. I also noted that Jeff and his team still think of themselves as traders, risk takers, and gamblers, or at least oddsmakers, of a sort. This outlook on trading sees it as a sort of individual competition of matching wits. By contrast, Horace and his crew see a break in the sort of old-school pit trading mentality and the more scientific work that they currently do. This came out in how one trader on Horace's team narrated his own background.

Trader number 2. I was on the floor trading.

Daniel. You were in the pit? You're tall.

Trader number 1. He's a big guy. It helps.

T2. There were a lot of former athletes down there. I remember, one of the guys at the back where I was down there, was in his eighties or so. And he hired a former football player because he could lift him so he could signal. Like, he physically, like there's a physical aspect in that that's appreciated.

D. So is what you do now different or similar?

T2. Fantastically different. So much of what happens down there is relationship based. It's in theory supposed to be the first person that if a phone call comes in from Goldman, they want to know the market in a certain [way], and the first person that quotes isn't necessarily the first person that gets to trading with Goldman through the broker. It's basically the person that's been there the longest. Everyone quotes the same a reasonable amount of the time, so there's like a seniority priority, basically, which is illegal.

[Conversation about the networks in the pits]

T2. I just felt like [I was] working in a museum.

T1. You were the exhibit.

T2. Yeah, I mean there were literally people walking by watching us. So, you could kind of see the writing on the wall. It was a lot of people in there, forty-year-old guys that were making a living out of there. [They] could probably retire, but they were working with their friends and getting paid. However, it wasn't a good place to start really.

D. What year did you get out?

T2. I got out of the pit in 2012.

D. Wow.

T2. And I got in in June 2010, and out early 2012.

[Conversation about closing the pits]

T2. I think the most exemplary thing of how old it is, when I got my actual badge and we, like paper traded with the hand signals and everything you were supposed to learn to do it with—we're trading options for Deutsch marks. [They] don't exist anymore. And [the fake options] expired the month I was born.

Elsewhere, Trader 2 made the point, "no one cares how big or how old you are when you trade on the screen."

What comes across in Trader 2's transmigration is an amalgamation of the various distinctions the AlgoFinance quants drew between pit traders and quant traders. Pit traders rely on networks and do each other favors. Pit traders rely on their own personality and physical advantages. Pit traders use an archaic, inefficient, and potentially corrupt mode of market making. By contrast, no one cares whether you're a dog when you trade behind a screen. Screen trading ushers in a more efficient, more fair mode of a market.

Another distinction the AlgoFinance quants made between their mode of trading and what came before and what other humans do is that their approach was transparent, logical, and scientific. Earlier in the interview, I asked Horace about how his team puts their approach to trading into practice. Here is how he answered:

Horace. So, the market's no different. I can build models for specific scales and specific horizons and specific levels of error, but I have to understand what those are for each of those levels.

Daniel. And is that formally or practically built into your guys' processes here? What does that look like?

H. I wrote a paper on it [*laughs*]. I've kind of expressed that view publicly. I'd be happy to give you a copy of the paper.

D. Sounds great. So, maybe it'd be helpful then to sort of describe—I'll read the paper later, but what is the process of development of an algorithmic strategy look like here?

H. See, I'm a scientist. So, it's applying the scientific model to the trading strategies. That's really it. I gave a keynote at a conference a year or two ago, and I saw a bunch of people from my competitors sitting in the audience, and so I had to change my introduction [to] just flat out say, look, I'm going to stand up here for the next half an hour and I'm going to talk about applying the scientific method to trading. That's what this talk is about [*laughs*].

D. How was it received?

H. It was received very well, but there's no secret there. It's just making sure you understand your hypotheses, that your hypotheses are testable. If it's not testable, it's not a good hypothesis. You know, did I fit inside my constraints and objectives? And, how you can get all that done and again as [another trader] said earlier, that's really about just putting all the pieces together. There's no secrets in any of the individual pieces, but the process is only valuable because it puts all the pieces together in a way that makes sense.

Being on the market is simply a matter of applying the scientific method, applying hypotheses, and being open and transparent in your methods (to a point). To put a fine point on it, this is not how the traders at TradeCo see their work. Again, Jeff and his team are taking risks, matching wits, imagining opponents, and automating much of that logic to operate at volume. Horace and his team aren't really doing that. One final interview extract will illustrate this contrast.

One thing that preoccupies traders of whatever sort is a fear of getting taken advantage of by hitting a trade that ends up being bad because of information of which you are unaware. Recall that this motivated a huge amount of the skepticism Jeff and his team had toward Cheatin' Chuck and the rest of their brokers. There are a variety of ways to describe this getting taken advantage of—one more technical way would be to call it "adverse selection." Here is how Horace and the crew felt about mitigating adverse selection:

Trader 3. We try to minimize adverse selection. That's what [Horace] means by trying to get out of the way, right?

Daniel. Got it. So, tell me, how do you minimize adverse selection?

Horace. Well, you have some idea of a fair price. And, as your idea of the fair price, you know, changes, right? You're going to adjust your bids and offers. And, so, adverse selection in this case typically comes from the price starting to move. You know, getting some price momentum in one direction. And, if you don't cancel and back up quickly enough, then you get a bad fill, that's fundamentally adverse selection.

T3. But it's really us trying to figure out if we think adverse selection is coming. It's kind of like a lot of different tiers. We could go from, you know, a simple kind of probability model all the way up to something more like machine learning.

H. Yeah, so start from, you know, basic conditional probability. Stop at the inside market. You go into the various macrostructure models about action in the [order] book, about the dynamics of the order book, and you know, then beyond that you can, as T3 said, get to more sophisticated models that are looking at trying to predict prices. Not just looking at probabilities of a price change, but you know, actually trying to do predictions.

D. And how present are these different ways of analyzing markets in the various algorithmic strategies that you have? Is there like an element of each of those types of analytics in all of them? Could you walk me through an example of what that might look like?

H. Yeah, so I think you can start from thinking about a probability of a take up or take down, right? So, conditional probability mode, so you can build that model using any number of statistical models, you know, from basic stats one-oh-one type stuff, all the way up to the most sophisticated Bayesian classifier.

Avoiding adverse selection is simply a matter of selecting the right sophisticated Bayesian classifier. What's so difficult to understand or execute about that?

———

A chapter ago I suggested that Jeff and his team can never really know who they're trading with because of the nature of the market design of the exchanges they're on. But the TradeCo team does have a number of imaginative shorthands that shift how they behave and how they take risks and make trades. That said, one form of imaginary opponent stopped them in their tracks—the times when they felt they were just trading with machines. Here, we've seen a bit more about the people who trade with machines and have come to appreciate some of the grounding assumptions of the algo-verse. Algorithms are powerful, universal tools for aiding or superseding human beings in all sorts of settings, including markets. Moreover, these algorithms are built by scientists according to a logic that is imported into financial markets and often reflects a disregard for local knowledge manifesting in a sort of technochauvinism. This mode of reasoning doesn't really care about who is on the market or why they're behaving the way they are. It's all just data to model. In paraphrasing Jim Simons's words, who cares why the planets go around the sun so long as we can make money on 'em?

8

Why Would You Buy an Electric Car on Jet Ski Friday?

This book started with a fairly basic question—How is it that Jeff and his team made money, particularly given that there were so many things on and off markets standing in the way of their performing the simple task of being market makers? My suggestion across this book was that if we paid attention to the things that agitated them, the things they saw fit to swear about, we would gain a feel for what it's like to work in an atomized market environment increasingly dominated by automation and computers and with less and less control over the specific circumstances of your own labor. Moreover, this could be taken as a specific example of a sort of alienation and estrangement that comes with wage labor and the development of technology that increases productive capacity and decreases the need for human labor.

We've seen specifically how the traders deal with technology, think about markets, and imagine the people they trade against. We've also seen, for each illustration, contrasting cases: one from a firm that likes their computer systems so much that their managers and tech people, at least, imagine themselves becoming it; one from the tinkerers who design and optimize the market environments that traders often take for granted; and one from the land of scientific algorithmic trading, which would like to make human trading a distant memory.

In each case, we've taken a step beyond the perspective of Jeff and his team to see a bit of what their world looks like from the point of view of the people they're interacting with via the mediation of their market environment. This has allowed me to follow the insight that your particular social location on markets partially determines how you think about and then how you act on markets (an insight which follows scholars such as Abolafia 1996; Zaloom 2006; and Beunza 2019). In a way, too, we can imagine this as the larger social and cultural grounding necessary to understand how Jeff and his team actually make money. Given all that then, here, in this penultimate chapter, I'll pursue a different narrative track and bring together this book's various threads and show how Jeff and his team made one investment decision and probably made around US$500,000 in profit on that decision, thereby heeding Hart and Ortiz's (2014) call to follow the money. To do that, though, Jeff's team had to answer the question, "Why would you buy an electric car on Jet Ski Friday?"

What Should We Buy This Friday?

As odd as this question sounds, I think it's worth dwelling on as a question of practical political economy, that is, a holistic answer to the question of how wealth is generated, distributed, and used in a given society and how financiers collect and redistribute wealth globally (Ortiz 2020). You see, I heard some version of whether it was a good idea to buy an electric car on Jet Ski Friday asked and shouted, yelled and proclaimed over and over and over again when I spent my time with TradeCo. The electric car in question is a Tesla, which exists at several models and price points and is in turn made by the US-based, publicly listed Tesla Inc., a company led by celebrity-CEO Elon Musk and dedicated to, in its own words, "accelerat[ing] the world's transition to sustainable energy."[1]

Whether or not someone would be willing to buy Tesla stock in turn affects that stock's price, which affects the ability of Tesla Inc. to raise money to finance its operations, invest in manufacturing capacity, pay workers, or keep the Elon Musk show going. This is the essential function of stock/equity/capital markets: in exchange for a piece of the company and a claim on some portion of profits, an investor gives the company capital.

So, for options traders, buying an electric car would mean their evaluation of the stock's price and making some sort of judgment about how investors will trade it and what demand for options that trading will generate. In turn this allows options traders to price the stock options they will buy and sell as market makers. They're not investing per se but pricing spreads of options and making money from being on both sides, long and short, of that liquidity-providing enterprise. So far, so good. But what about the Jet Skis?

The problem with stock, or options, or futures trading—really any sort of financial transaction—is that markets are incredibly complicated. There are lots of different types of traders acting over varied time horizons (in fact, we've met many of them), all with any number of strategies motivating why they are buying and selling, all in a government-regulated environment that spans numerous trading venues and exchanges. Moreover, market participants are mostly anonymous from and to each other.

Someone may make a long-term Tesla play because they think that its battery company will be increasingly indispensable to a global fleet of electric vehicles and decentralized power grids over the next decade. Someone might be short selling the stock because they think Elon Musk is an erratic megalomaniac who will drive his company into the ground because of a fight with America's financial regulators or because he's too distracted by tending to any number of his other companies (to name just a few, the social media platform Twitter [now part of X Corp], the rocket company SpaceX, or the satellite internet company Starlink—really, take your pick). Others might idealize Musk as an aspirational avatar of techno-optimism and disruptive capitalism and invest in stock as a meme stock in the same way that fans might buy a band's merch. Still another trader might simply be a market-making algorithm deployed by a massive hedge fund, buying and selling at the same time, perhaps ensuring liquidity, or at least churn, on a market. Beyond these strategies and perspectives are larger geopolitical realities. If China carries on subsidizing the domestic development of high-capacity batteries, one might persuasively argue that Tesla is in trouble. However, if California or Norway continue to offer a tax break for purchasers of electric vehicles, perhaps we can forgive Mr. Musk some of his perceived sins.

Even beyond the gyrations of an individual stock, certain politicians seek to act on financial markets in aggregate as the performance of American equity markets has become synonymous with the economic health of the nation and the success of particular presidential administrations. Given that, often indications of ill health across financial markets—say, drops perceived as too rapid, prices behaving with too much volatility, or even a lack of activity altogether—may kick national industrial or financial policy into action. A president may rashly declare a trade war or tweet about intending to lift tariffs. Or an agent of the central bank may seek to calm markets by fiddling with interest rates, buying up bad investments from banks, as in quantitative easing or QE, or even simply using public persuasion.

The goal of all of this is to indirectly protect the nation's economic health via shifting the baseline inputs and assumptions investors and traders take with them to market. If the Federal Reserve raises the interbank lending rate, money becomes more costly and, in turn, investment becomes more expensive as capital becomes more scarce. Investors, in turn, seem to respond to rate cuts or hikes, or even *the possibility* of rate cuts or hikes, in tangible, aggregate market moves. The traders I was sitting with had noticed this sort of government action as one more feature of the markets they were trying to figure out, often operating according to a different scalar logic than the behavior of any particular business's movements and stock price.

What made this high-level political action particularly salient for Jeff and the team was the fact that markets seemed to be digesting politics as well as news in a fundamentally different way than in decades past[2] largely because of cascade effects that they only partially understood. It seemed that any time a politician spoke on the economy, about markets, about interest rates, or regarding a trade war, there would be a near instantaneous market response, starting in the S&P 500 index futures, which would then lead to a rally or a fall in their underlying stock. Within an hour or two of announcements or news (or announcements of future *potential* news), a market swing accounting for ups of 2 percent could have happened. Moreover, there seemed to be a cumulative upward bias[3] to these swings, sending equities and all related instruments ever higher[4] with surprisingly little volatility.

The exact agents kicking off this cascade, as well as the mechanism by which futures and indexes lead equities as quickly as they do was poorly understood. Purchasers could be anyone from hedge funds with "event-driven" trading strategies to central banks[5] to automated-trading agents trained to instantly respond to the news. Cascades of one instrument's rise or fall in price affecting another's could come from any variety of imagined automated algorithmic agents trained to respond to the news or make correlational trades, or even from individual human speculators. Either way, markets seemed to respond drastically, quickly, and in lockstep with politics and news with some manner of a long-term, upward bias. Moreover, the traders felt that these aggregate swings had little to do with the fundamental economic reality of the specific equities and options and the specific companies they traded.

All this big-picture market weirdness showed up in a sort of joking fatalism in the trading group. Large macroeconomic policy interventions around things like interest rates or trade wars seemed decoupled from all this fundamental market action and, as often as not, due to the whims of fickle or feckless political actors. They came to joke that if markets were down, you could expect to see someone from the US's central bank (the Federal Reserve, or the Fed) or the Treasury Department, usually on a Friday, show up on the news, offering the sort of vaguely positive assurance that would lead to a cascade and a 1 or 2 percent rally, sending markets back up. These Fridays they came to call "Jet Ski Fridays," Fridays when markets would irrationally go up and ensure that every American could exercise their God-given, inalienable right to buy something as useless and expensive as a Jet Ski with profits from their privatized, stock-based retirement account.

Linking market fortunes to retirement accounts had a further, nuanced significance to Tesla and many other publicly traded stocks. Often these stocks make up the largest appreciating assets (outside of perhaps a home) that individuals carry with them into retirement, whether via formal, workplace-based pension funds or self-managed investment accounts. As of November 11, 2019, CNN Business reported that institutional investors (meaning retirement account managers like Vanguard and BlackRock among others) owned 51.49 percent of Tesla's stock. Moreover, specific pensions, like the California Public Employees Retirement System and the New Jersey Division of Investment, both recently and modestly increased their holdings. All this, too, puts these institutional investors in curious company, as the largest shareholder of Tesla by percent is Elon Musk, owning about 20 percent. In a funny way, then, individual retirements rise and fall according to the same fortunes that harry Tesla and Musk.

All these overlapping interests and mysterious market-moving phenomenon resulted in, of all things, some office swag: the traders made up a set of gray cotton T-shirts with green "Jet Ski Friday est. 2009" and a silhouette of a Jet Ski rider tearing through a wave on them; and, they would, well, wear them on Fridays.[6] The joke was that market weirdness and America's promise were both born out in a placid, steadily rising stock market; that promise, in turn, was cashed in at your local Kawasaki dealership.[7]

The question of this aspect of political economy, capital allocation via financial markets, and who that capital should benefit, then, is boiled down to the questions, Why on earth would you buy Tesla stock or stock options, given that markets behave irrationally or weirdly? How could your analysis of Tesla, particularly if you think it is doing poorly, stand a chance when a fed governor or an errant presidential tweet could goose the whole market? Or when some unknown cascade could link perhaps unrelated parts of the market to one another? Or when a swarm of retail Elon Musk fans could bid the whole thing up? Put another more general way, given the complexity of market environments, how does any company, let alone one as unusual as Tesla, gather capital? Considering financial markets, and put as simply as I can manage: who gets money and why?

Should Tesla Get Money?

As we've probably observed, at TradeCo topics of conversation don't tend to be discrete. People ping pong from subject to subject, often picking up threads after having dropped them seconds, minutes, and hours before. Folks feel comfortable expressing themselves, and it all blends into a long conversation. It was in this sort of mix that an argument about Tesla came up. Jeff was bothered by how Tesla's stock wasn't doing what he thought it should, and he wanted some validation, some argument, or just something from the rest of the team. A fair portion of the work that folks at TradeCo did was pricing in unusual events during their market-making activity. Put another way, they were trying to understand abnormal risk, price it, and market-make accordingly.[8] The conversation all starts with Walt, the supervising partner of this particular office of the firm asking Jeff how the day was going:

Jeff. I'm going down to the floor for a minute.[9] There isn't much grind up here. There is some bad news on Apple, but it doesn't matter. Their China sales are a big, big miss.

Walt. What about Tesla? When does that convertible bond come due?[10]

J. March first.

W. What do the vols look like?

Tony. They're in the mid to upper fifties.

J. I thought it was lower than that, low forties.

W. What about one year out, are they in the same place?

T. The put skews are very high compared to other symbols we follow.

J. The twenty-strike-put expires in twelve months. The ten put is fifty cents, which doesn't get much better. Hundreds are twelve fifty—your payoff on that is terrible twelve months off.

W. I'm thinking of buying 280s.

J and T. They're much better.

J. Well, I'm ready to pack it in. We've been carrying twelve hundred vegas,[11] nothing big. Some unknown firm upgraded Tesla and they're up like eight dollars. Tesla just doesn't trade like a real symbol. There is so much flow controlled by only a handful of people. It just doesn't—it isn't affected by news. Tesla can miss bond payments and it just doesn't matter. Someday it will.

Walt, Jeff, and Tony are talking about Tesla puts being high—that is, a lot of people are buying put options. The assumption here is that a lot of people think that Tesla's stock will go down. If the stock goes down, having the ability to sell the stock at a higher price would make an investor a lot of money. In a more limited way, an options market maker would have the ability to price and then sell lots of puts at a premium. While I was in Hub City, Tesla was trading in the ballpark of US$300 per share. If the stock went all the way to zero, owning a lot of US$280 put options would make you a lot of money. Tesla was actually down for much of the middle of 2019 following my two visits, and TradeCo's short bets presumably made a lot of money over that time. However, as Jeff points out, evaluating whether Tesla is going to zero at any given time is a tricky business.

Jeff's thesis and frustration is pretty simple: Tesla doesn't trade like a normal stock. Bad news comes out and it doesn't matter. It can miss payments or shipping targets, have terrible news about the company or the CEO, and the price doesn't change. He suggests that the order flow of the company's stock is controlled by only a few people. Also, this should remind us of the way Robinhood traders with GameStop could make use of options to raise the price of a stock.

None of it makes sense to Jeff. The thing, too, is that he's right about basically everything. Operationally, Tesla has had chronic issues meeting its own production and distribution targets and has recently announced that it would be closing all of its brick-and-mortar stores (Harwell 2019b). Managerially, Tesla's CEO, Elon Musk, is in an ongoing legal dispute with America's stock regulator, the Security and Exchange Commission, because the SEC maintains that Musk was improperly influencing the price of the stock by tweeting information about the company's production figures and potential future buyout by an investment fund. As of this writing, there was a chance that Musk may actually be held in contempt of court (Harwell 2019a). Again, this should remind us of the way an internet personality like Musk can hype a stock, make it a meme, stoke trading, and detach it from more mundane economic reality. Musk himself chimed in on GameStop and has sent the value of various cryptocurrencies up and down via his tweets and public activity (Molla 2021). Jeff and Walt both mentioned a big debt payment that was coming due. While I was doing fieldwork, Jeff speculated that Tesla wouldn't be able to make that payment.[12] And for all this, at the time at least, Tesla stock seemed to just go up.

They continued talking.

Walt. Yeah, that's my thinking too. Someday—well, it can't levitate indefinitely. That name[13] will explode. I just don't know when.

Jeff. How about that *Wall Street Journal* article about the service problems they're having?

Tony. They cut half their delivery guys.

W. Their staff to deliver cars, they cut them in half?

J. This article is about service. If you nick your bumper it takes four months to get fixed. They have no repair apparatus or spare parts. Granular short players[14] have been talking about this for a while. When a company like BMW gives you a car and three years of service, they put that on their balance sheet. Tesla isn't doing that. They're counting the parts and the repair as CAP X.

W. CAP X?

J. That's the allegation of the short players: Tesla's accounting guys are really fucking around with service plan liabilities. But it seems like none of it matters. Someday it will. Anyway, not a lot of news today.

W. See you at lunch time.

Beyond the general issues with Tesla that we heard about above, Jeff is zeroing in on a few specifics of Tesla's practices. First, he's noting that they have some large functional issues: namely a huge backlog of repairs and a lack of parts to make fixes. Beyond this, whereas most car firms book this sort of maintenance in a straightforward way, Tesla is listing this kind of maintenance as CAP X, or capital expenditure. Capital expenditures typically refer to investments in facilities or capacities in a business, not ongoing maintenance of a consumer product. So, the "shorts" are suggesting that something weird is going on with Tesla's books.

In any event, after this back and forth, with Walt suggesting that the group buy some puts and go short, I started laughing. Tesla had come up a lot, and that seemed particularly to vex Jeff. In response to my laughter, the conversation in the group went in this direction:

Jeff. I think it's very ironic that we want to short the day I'm throwing in the towel.

Brandon. We don't care. We do whatever you say. We're not out there picking options on vols. The stock is worth one hundred bucks. Tony and I put five hundred grand[15] on it.

J. We were going to buy puts.

B. If you're going to pay seven thousand dollars on a put spread, Tony and I don't care.

J. Look, this isn't just me, this is a conversation.

B. Sure. But you feel the most strongly about Tesla.

Tony. Yeah, after the earnings came out last time, I could care less. Before that, I could have carried a short position.

B. All this seems reasonable, particularly if we want to put three, four, five hundred grand on the line. I just stopped looking at thirty grand tomorrow. I'm way more angry about losing money with other positions. We know at the end of the year if Tesla trades at four hundred, we lose six hundred thousand dollars. If Jeff feels that strongly . . .

J. I don't want this to be shifted to me. If anything, you've been quoting vega.

B. We just don't care. Are you going to bitch about it when the stock goes to two hundred, and we make no money?

J. This should be a conversation among everyone. I don't want in seven months . . .

B. I don't understand why you're exhausted; this stock has been irrational for three years now.

J. It doesn't move; it doesn't react.

T. Well, it hasn't for a while.

J. In December it got rational.

T. It also dropped to 250 after fraud was exposed by the SEC.

B. I fundamentally believe the stock is worth hundred bucks. Really, just don't look at it. You feel the most strongly of all of us.

J. This has always been a conversation; it's not just my trade, not just my position. We made four hundred grand on it in the first week of January. We should all talk about it.

B. I just never seem to care.

J. Do you want to be long, short, or flat? You don't care? He doesn't care?

B. You obviously care.

J. I'm totally exhausted by the name and by him.[16] I stopped following him and all those guys on Twitter. It's just, I don't want it to be a distraction from the stuff we're doing.

B. I think that's up to you. You're the most distracted.

J. I'm not following it.

B. I don't understand what changed now. The stock hasn't reacted rationally to the news since four twenty day.[17]

J. I think it has. The reaction to the SEC fraud, that day, was not normal. Do you understand my point? Even if I ever had full accountability for this before, we should have a vote now.

T. I'm indifferent.

J. If we've got three "indifferents" . . .

T. Should we be trading it?

J. It's been sitting. Rotting.[18]

T. Does anyone want to trade it?

J. It seems like it's on BATS,[19] with the scanner.[20] We can see what happens.

[At this point my field notes simply say, "Long discussion about whether they should be trading Tesla."]

Jeff just couldn't catch a break in this chat; everyone was resigned. I want to highlight, though, what bothered him, and those things are myriad. First, he has an overwhelming sense that the market is treating information irrationally. He doesn't really know who is on the other end of trades or the logic by which they're operating. We know, too, that this sort of ignorance is endemic to electrified, automated, and speedy financial markets (Lange 2016; Souleles 2019a).

Jeff is also bothered by the firm's accounting practices. Since Tesla is a publicly traded company, it publishes financial reports at regular intervals. Specifically, he's skeptical of the way they're accounting for their ongoing maintenance. He's worried that by burying the cost in CAP X, they're not accurately accounting for how expensive maintenance is. Moreover, there are specific supply chain problems with replacement parts. These sorts of questions get at how one might fundamentally analyze a company like Tesla.

We know, too, that a tremendous number of assumptions are built into the valuation analysis of companies (e.g., Souleles 2019b) and that often fundamental analysts fail to beat chance stock picks (Leins 2018). Yet these sorts of company analyses "become successful through the formulation of . . . forecasts as persuasive stories" (Leins 2018, 10). Jeff is engaged in an act of deliberation and persuasion—he's telling a story based on accounting about a company that, incidentally, other short players are also telling about the future value of Tesla. It just so happens that this story is proven wrong again and again by the general, irrepressible rise in the stock market generally and Elon Musk's ongoing defiance of business gravity.[21] It's worth noting, too, that long after this episode with Tesla's debt payment, Tesla's stock rose to US$400 per share in mid-2020s, was trading in the 800s around January 2021, and as of July 2021 was trading in the 600s. Later, after a three-way stock split, as well as Elon Musk selling off billions of dollars in shares to purchase Twitter and Musk's subsequent very public distraction by running Twitter, Tesla's market cap plummeted from its 2021 peak of US$900 billion, to a December 2022 valuation of around US$355 billion (Waters 2022; see additionally Hughes and Flood 2022; for reporting on the stock split, see Kolodny 2022). It is unclear to me, and many others apparently, what Tesla should actually be worth.

Jeff also is keenly aware of the actions of the SEC, a government policy-making and regulatory agency that, among other things, polices the quarterly financial filings of all publicly traded companies and the ongoing operations of all American stock markets. Specifically, the SEC is investigating Elon Musk for manipulating Tesla's stock price via his erroneous reporting of potential buyouts and its valuation; and this conflict, in turn, is playing out in public via statements and the federal courts. Douglas Holmes (2014; see also Riles 2018) has pointed out that other government actors and central bankers have increasingly used public address as part of their efforts to affect people's behavior. Moreover, again, the traders at TradeCo saw the heavy hand of government actors on and in financial markets as leading to possible cascade effects across various market financial instruments. It's easy to see the SEC's court battles with Elon Musk as similar—he publicly flouted long-standing norms against insider trading, so they, in an equally public manner, go after him and signal to other corporate actors that there is a cop walking the beat, even if that cop is basically losing.

One final note. Toward the end of the conversation, Jeff makes use of the scanner to see whether there are trading opportunities for Tesla puts. The scanner is a robot; the scanner is an algorithm. It's a mechanical way that TradeCo identifies good trading opportunities according to how they are valuing particular stocks and who they think is trading against them. This is a much higher-touch, less automated system than, say, LINUS at Bradford. One interesting thing about the use of the scanner, given how committed to human trading TradeCo is, is not so much that it is being used but that it shows up in a relatively routine way. Recently, MacKenzie (2018a) has suggested that there is a thoroughgoing moral discourse entailed in the habits of high-frequency market makers—if you take quotes faster than others are able to, you are taking liquidity and doing something predatory. Conversely, if you make liquidity, you are doing the market a solid by creating more trading opportunities for others. Jeff and TradeCo observed to me that they basically didn't aggress in markets—they posted bids and made offers creating market liquidity. The scanner basically allows them to routinize this moral stance and carry on as liquidity-providing market makers.

Let's Own That Debt Payment

Up to this point, I've delivered on half of this chapter's promise. We've seen how the TradeCo traders' deliberations on how to price stocks or options have to do with multivariate weighing of different features of a company and the larger market environment. To simplify things a bit: Jeff (1) didn't quite know why other people on the market were trading Tesla the way they were, keeping its price either stable or bidding it up; (2) had big concerns about the fundamental analysis of Tesla's business;[22] and (3) noted the public actions of government actors and ultimately was trying to weigh whether or not Tesla's price would come down to earth and be subject to the laws of the market that so harshly discipline mere mortal companies (or, at least should—remember Jeff feels he is in an inflated market environment in which at the slightest sign of a downtick governments seem to take aggressive macroeconomic stimulating policy action). However, to understand why TradeCo would price Tesla options in any given way, to follow the money, we have to return to Jeff's long, lonely conversation and see how he and his traders weighed all these different factors and made a pricing and then buying decision:

[This exchange directly follows my "Long discussion about whether they should be trading Tesla" that ended the last exchange.]

Jeff. Really, this discussion shouldn't be confrontational.

Brandon. We're not confronting you. We just want to know what changed for you?

J. I just want a conversation: yay or nay?

Tony. I've had no opinion the last five months about Tesla, ever since the third quarter when they said they made money. I'm a lot less certain this thing is going to zero given that they actually reported earnings. I think we want to make a bet that something is going to happen around the time that their debt payment is due. We probably want to have that down.

B. The way I feel is that I have no reason to argue against your position. Your stuff checks out. If you want to short five thousand, go ahead and short five thousand. If that's how we feel about it, well, if we lose a bunch of money, that happens.

J. Let's talk more later.

T. I wouldn't mind having something on for the debt payment.

J. We could also move it to options.

B. The three-week-out-straddle is fifteen bucks. The vol is telling us that nothing is going to happen. Maybe that's the trade. I don't know.

T. I feel like owning that debt payment.

[*Jeff leaves for the pit. Silence descends.*]

Ultimately, they take an intermediate position. Instead of constantly speculating that Tesla is going to go bust right around the corner, they decide to take a bet on an options spread around the day of Tesla's upcoming debt payment. Tesla's volatility suggests that nothing is going to happen to the stock. So, they're going to short five thousand stock and hope to make money.

Tesla's stock was generally down in the months following my first visit on into the summer of 2019 and took a bit of a dive (around US$40) shortly after the bond payment came due on March 1. It's likely that Jeff and his group at TradeCo made money on their position, betting against Tesla (as Musk and others invested in Tesla lost money). So here, then, is an example of what I had hoped to elucidate: a concrete example of money moving around a financial market according to a local political economy. Jeff and his team weighed (1) their technological capabilities, (2) their fundamental analysis of Tesla, (3) the behavior of their unknowable market counterparties, (4) the government's public policy actions, and (5) their internal diversity of opinions to risk US$500,000 betting against Tesla via their options pricing decisions.

Their action, in turn, goes some small way to depressing Tesla's stock price and making it more difficult for Elon Musk to raise capital. Moreover, their specific action is only sensible given their specific market location. Different market participants (brokers, pensions funds, and so forth) would deliberate and express their market opinions according to the affordances and constraints of their specific nodal and functional points in market networks.

It's worth noting that running across every point in the traders' dialogue is a metaconversation about the larger arc of Tesla stories. Often, too, they're reflecting on Tesla around other conversations, such as those about retirement accounts and Jet Skis. I think this sort of reflective level of their conversation is important because it adds up to a sort of framing discourse they use to understand and perhaps even motivate some of their actions. In addition, once we see their conversations in this light, I think it invites us to consider some recent economic anthropology (e.g., Bear et al. 2015) that has said that, in the analysis of "capitalist" processes we should pay attention to the sorts of lifeworlds those capitalist processes can allow and not just make a reduced model of economic rationality or a reductive "economic" analysis.

Here, Jeff and co. offer explicit reflection in that regard. We hear about Elon Musk and the company he runs; we hear about other market actors, both political and financial; and we hear about retirees and how their wealth and livelihood is directly affected by Tesla's well-being. We also hear how skeptical the traders are of the validity of a number of those life projects and then see their actions accordingly.

However, the traders don't decide to go all in and presume Tesla will fail. The accumulated evidence and opinion of the group is too ambivalent to support that. As such, they take a middle path and peg what ended up being a more reasonable bet.

Put another way, Jeff and co. decided it was a bad idea to buy an electric car on Jet Ski Friday.

9

The Economy Will Be Open by Easter

Options markets are such a pimple on the elephant's ass.
Walt Bennett, partner supervising Jeff's group at TradeCo

In the grand scheme of things, when US GDP is around US$20 trillion per year, Tesla's market cap is around US$100 billion, and the market cap of firms listed on NYSE is around US$30 trillion, a US$500,000 bet on some Tesla options may not strike one as the most significant financial transaction, particularly if one has an eye for understanding grand things like the economy, capital markets, finance, and so on. But what I hope will be apparent by this point are two grounding assumptions I'm making about the study of financial markets and the people that work on them. First, markets can only really be understood from the ground up, taking seriously the perspective of different actors as they go about their lives. And second, work is increasingly characterized by digitization, automation, and the estrangement and alienation of human labor, specifically on the part of specialized traders.

The specific story about the US$500,000 bet on Tesla options was interesting for our purposes largely because it brought together the elements of the contemporary financial scene that make TradeCo's folks swear so much. To make this bet, Jeff and his team had to use their technology to read markets. They also had to speculate about the motivation of large political actors intervening in markets and wonder about the motivation of diehard, long-call Tesla enthusiasts bidding up Tesla's stock price no matter what. This is all in addition to a fundamental analysis of Tesla as a business that sat beneath all these other speculations. They then had to translate the result of this multivariate weighing into a directional bet about what Tesla would do with its debt and then translate that into an options position in the context of their larger, largely automated portfolio. The result of all of this was to bid Tesla's stock down just a little bit and make a bit of money.

I suggest that the aggregate of TradeCo's trading activity is simply hundreds of thousands of little bets, like that on Tesla, in the service of their market-making business—which, in their own estimation is profitable a bit over half the time. Many of these bets pass without explicit note, as they are (somewhat reliably) automated. But they are automated in such a way that the sort of management of their Tesla position can, could, and perhaps should apply to any of the names they trade, particularly those that strike them as acting funny.

Toward the beginning of this book, I suggested that the role Jeff and his team filled in markets—market making—was an essential function in capital markets and, probably, markets more generally that hope to have regular liquidity. After all, liquidity at root means having someone present to buy and someone available to sell (or maybe even just exchange) in whatever circumstances; liquidity is the quintessence of a market. Given that their function is essential, I suggested it was noteworthy that Jeff and his team spend a lot of their time frustrated, irritated, and angry. Moreover, I said parsing this irritation via the topics they repeatedly swore about would be a window into estranging changes that have happened on financial markets over the last few decades. As such, we've seen the way that automation has shifted the default assumptions of traders and trading firms on markets, substituting a supersocial kinetic risk-taking persona with that of a scientist who sees markets as just one more field of endeavor to be conquered.

We've also seen, sitting behind much of TradeCo's day-to-day work, a nagging suspicion that their larger market environment wasn't working as it should and that government actors, central bankers, or politicians were seeking to move markets for political or social ends with little regard for the sort of fundamental analysis on which Jeff and his team based their analysis of Tesla. Similarly, Jeff et al. couldn't ever be sure what exactly retail investors were up to or to what ends. The potential for this sort of intervention, manipulation, and rigging irritated Jeff and his team's sense of how a market should operate and how capitalism should work. In Jackson's (2002) language, this assumed market manipulation created a situation in which Jeff, Aaron, Tony, and all the rest could not be the sort of market actors they thought they should be. In turn, this alienated them. Anger then popped up as one doomed way to recapture their agency and their humanity. Anger often manifested in swearing.

All that said, it seems that history has vindicated (if not salved) the team at TradeCo. When I first drafted this manuscript, I found myself semiquarantined in an apartment in the middle of Copenhagen, Denmark, hiding (inadequately, as it turned out) from COVID-19 and its attendant viral assault on multiple organ systems, watching as various government actors intervened in unprecedented ways in financial markets and broader economies precisely along the lines and according to the priorities that Jeff and his team had been complaining about for years. In what remains of the conclusion, then, I'll show how government actors in the United States responded to the coronavirus pandemic, how that response matched up with TradeCo's irritation and rage, and, again emphasize the alienated view from the elephant's ass.

The Trolley Problem in a Pandemic

The "Trolley Problem" is an ethical thought experiment often credited to Phillipa Foot. At root it presents a dilemma in which taking a helpful action causes harm and ponders whether that harm is justified. Often this is manifested as a trolley, a train car approaching a switch. In one permutation of the problem, if the trolley proceeds without someone activating a switch, it will run over, say, five people strapped to the track. You can pull the switch and divert the trolley to its alternate heading, but, sorry to say, there are also people on that track, let's say only one person in this instance. If you take no action, five people die. If you take an action and pull the switch, one person will die and five people will live; and, *crucially*, you have taken an affirmative step to cause that outcome.

A philosopher concerned with outcomes, a utilitarian or a consequentialist, might say killing fewer people, reducing suffering, or maximizing utility takes precedent and that of course you should pull the switch. By contrast, a philosopher concerned with our obligations to one another, a deontologist, might say that there is no proper role for a human in society that has a human deliberately killing other humans, so doing nothing, not pulling the switch is the only defensible way through. There is no right answer to the trolley problem, and permutations of its circumstance help to probe different moral and

Figure I. Trolley comic, tweeted by Lily Simpson @LilySimpson1312, October 14, 2020

ethical schemas. Different versions of the trolley problem have also resulted in a subgenre of memes in which various scenarios are taken to satirical or absurd extremes.

About a month into the COVID-19 pandemic, a variation of the trolley problem, shown in figure 1, was floating around the internet. In this version of the problem, there is no diversion. There is simply one track, and one group of people about to be run over. There is one person at a switch who can stop the trolley at any time, should they choose to. However, as the lengthy comic text block points out, stopping the trolley and saving lives would entail the trolley company pausing or stopping its operation and thereby losing money. In miniature, this pandemic trolley problem was mocking many politicians' inclination to ignore the advice of medical professionals and forgo or cut short social and physical distancing measures meant to slow the spread of the virus. Sure, you could slow down or stop the economy to save lives, but then you'd lose money.[1]

As it became apparent how many people would need to stop working to arrest the spread of the pandemic and how many people would be sick or dying in any event, various US economic indicators responded. First, unemployment claims reached highs not seen since the Great Depression. Official figures, as represented in figure 2, show six million people filing for unemployment within a few weeks, a harbinger of what was to come over the rest of the pandemic. The graph is a good way to see what this looks like because it allows you to see that there is no other period that comes close to the concentrated nature of this level of job loss. The actual number of unemployed was probably much higher, as these statistics only represent people eligible for unemployment who were able to navigate overworked state-level bureaucracies.

This massive, immediate spike in unemployment represents the decimation of entire in-person service industries—travel, restaurants, sports, all shuttered practically overnight. The celebrity chef and restaurateur David Chang observed, "It's as if aliens came from outer space and decided to totally destroy restaurants" (in Marchese 2020). This devastation bled into financial markets too. Figure 3 illustrates the relative spike in the VIX index occurring as the pandemic hit the United States. Note that it gets up into the 80s. Following, logically, figure 4 illustrates losses in the S&P 500, tanking around 30 percent before public health policies designed to mitigate COVID-19 took place.

Recall that over the course of the book, I've suggested that Jeff and his team feel that politicians in the United States, particularly President Trump and his administration as well as the US Federal Reserve, identify a rising stock market with their continued electoral and governing success. Given that, the market effects of the pandemic terrified these politicians, which

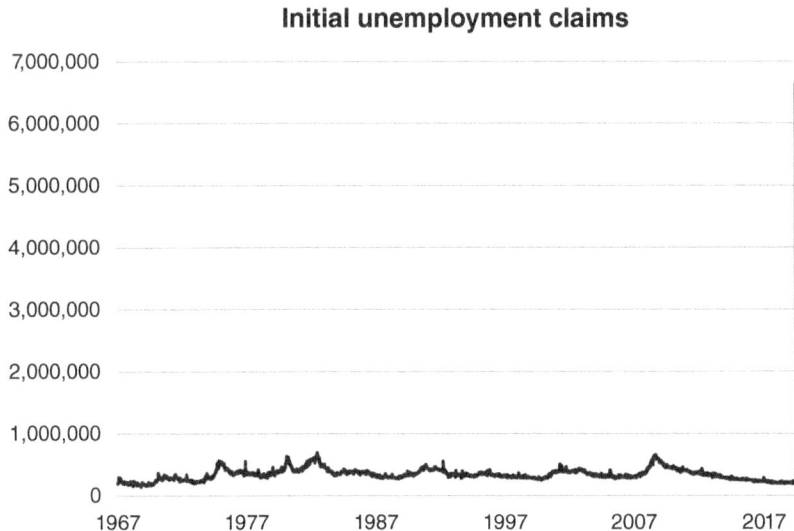

Initial unemployment claims

Source: US Employment and Training Administration via FRED

Figure 2. Initial coronavirus US unemployment claims from Reinecke 2020

Figure 3. Six-month VIX chart, November 13, 2019–April 9, 2020

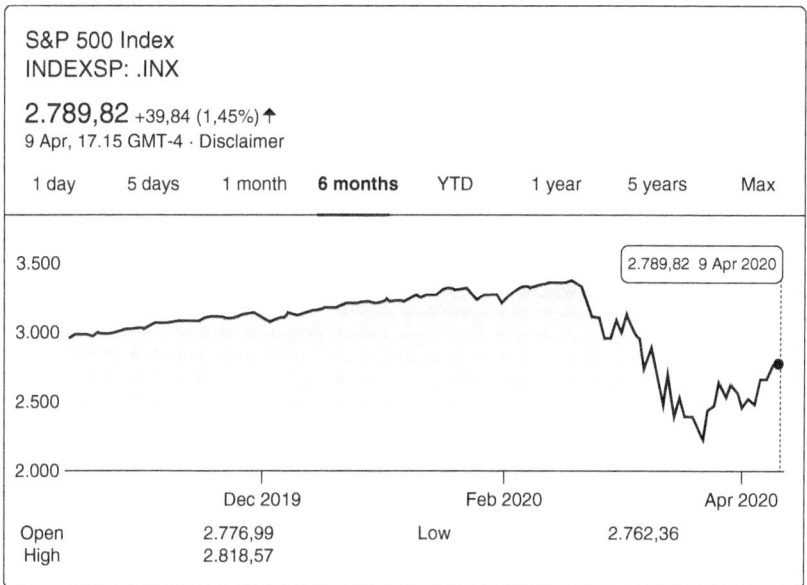

Figure 4. Six-month S&P 500 Index, November 13, 2019–April 9, 2020

led to an erratic pandemic response that suggested at various times people should be sacrificed so that "the market" or "the economy" would "open up" or "go up" again.

All this came into particularly sharp clarity shortly before Easter 2020. Epidemiologists and public health experts had been insistent that it would probably only be after a month or two of social and physical distancing that the public parts of society could *slowly* start to open again without risking huge new spikes in infection and death. President Trump, though, intimated several times, seemingly for no reason other than his own whims, that two weeks of distancing would be enough, and that the economy should open back up again, and quickly. At one point he picked up and accelerated a conservative talking point arguing that the cure for the virus shouldn't be worse than the virus itself (Associated Press 2020). This sort of indecision about the propriety of killing hundreds of thousands of people in the country he notionally ran, led him at one point to say, apropos of nothing, that the economy should be open by Easter, as "You'll have packed churches all over the country. It'll be a beautiful time" (Sevastopulo and Kuchler 2020).

In an article about another world leader, Boris Johnson, prime minister of the United Kingdom and Northern Ireland, waffling about keeping his society open at the expense of hundreds of thousands of lives, Stuart Heritage (2020), a journalist for the *Guardian*, notes the similarity between this style of leadership and that of the fictional mayor in the film *Jaws* (who is incidentally a hero of sorts to Johnson). Heritage sums up the mayor's roles as follows:

> Without [the mayor, Vaughn], Jaws would simply be about a policeman who spots a shark, imposes a stringent set of beachside social distancing and then kills the shark. But Vaughn is the necessary sand in the ointment. He can only see the potential economic losses caused by a beach closure, and pushes on against all arguments. "As you can see, it's a beautiful day," he tells the media at one point. "The beaches are opened, and people are having a wonderful time." Vaughn is the entire reason why Jaws became an enduring classic. (Heritage 2020)

All this was too much for the actor, writer, director, and producer Jordan Peele, whose tweet (fig. 5) has the mayor from *Jaws*, riffing on Trump, saying that "The beaches will be open by Easter." The dilemma here isn't how best to save lives and stop a pandemic but how many lives can we plausibly sac-

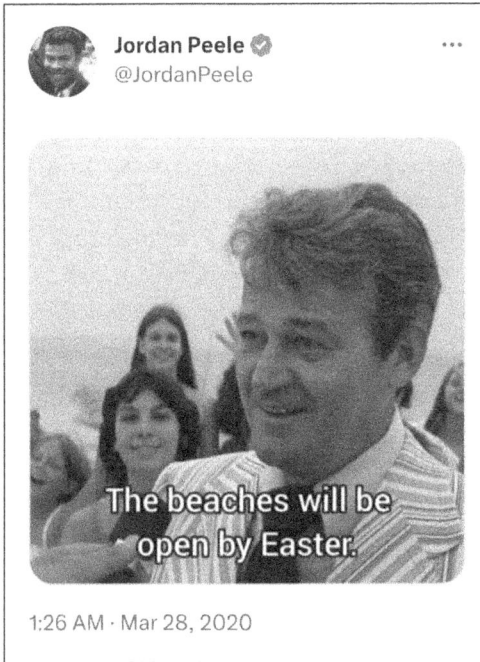

Figure 5. Jordan Peele, *Jaws* mayor tweet, March 28, 2020

rifice to the economy, or to the capital owners, to allow wealth to continue to multiply and to keep the stock market going up, economic or societal fundamentals be damned.

One result of the political discourse that pitted the health and lives of human beings against the health of an elaborate metaphor (the economy) was a US government response that prioritized business and financial health over expanding health care provisions and protections to all citizens. As a matter of first priority, the US federal government elected to bail out numerous corporate businesses to the tune of hundreds of billions of dollars in the context of a larger aid package that also benefited some hospital systems (to a lesser extent) and provided some direct cash payments and unemployment and poverty benefits to some American citizens (Serkez and Wu 2020). Note that at no point in the COVID-19 pandemic did the government of the United States extend (much less consider extending) health care to all of its citizens. Second, the US central bank, the Federal Reserve, dramatically expanded its loan facilities by trillions of dollars and began buying corporate debt and mortgage-backed securities to ensure that the financial system remained capitalized (Henderson and Wigglesworth 2020; Leonard 2020;

and Tett 2020). To reiterate this second point—the US central bank directly purchased corporate debt and thereby subsidized corporate business activity. Because the stock market went down so much, the Fed picked winners and gave them money.

All this intervention, too, resulted in a partial taming of the various market downturns. If you'll return to the VIX and SP 500 chart above, you'll note a bottoming out and a rebound in the weeks since these stimulus measures passed. In case you were wondering, at the time of writing there had been no parallel rebound in employment. So, the living economy diverged further from the plight of the financial economy.

Altogether, this is the world that Jeff, Tony, Brandon, Aaron, Rob, Kyle, and Lee insisted that we live in and that becomes visible and sensible in the context of their daily work. This is a world in which the priority of the federal government is to manipulate stock markets ever upward, since the stock market is both taken as a proxy of national health and electability and a network through which elite corporate and government actors, as well as swarming retail speculators and anyone with a retirement account, can continue to enrich themselves, business fundamentals be damned. All this, too, is a world in which intentionally designed markets live on a number of computer-mediated electronic exchanges with ever-shifting technological entailments and demands that connect all manner of investor, speculator, and market maker. All this is a world with an ebb tide of in-person trading and odds-making, risk-taking traders like those at TradeCo, and a flood tide of scientifically literate quantitative traders like Brad, Horace, and LINUS. One might say that this world is enough to make a trader cuss.

And, of course, all this keeps on happening no matter which horseman of the apocalypse comes galloping by.

Acknowledgments

Here, I'd like to walk through some of the material and social things that helped me write this book. Given that, a chronological ordering seems the right approach.

First, thanks are due to my parents, Dean and Sandy Souleles, who allowed me to stay in their basement in the spring of 2017 while I was teaching as an adjunct professor at Georgetown University, all to string along my academic "career" for one more semester. When the opportunity came to take up a job at the Copenhagen Business School, they gave me the money to pay for a move. Academia shouldn't work this way (and is broken because it does), but I'm endlessly grateful to my parents all the same.

Then, thanks are due to my wife, Amanda Lee Shapiro, who supported my move to Denmark and joined me in the fall of 2018. While we appreciate the benefits of the welfare state, it has been difficult to come to some sort of social modus vivendi in Denmark. Maybe this is just what it means to be foreign. Our being an ocean away from family and friends has helped nothing in this regard. Thank you for figuring out this new life with me.

Professionally, thanks are due to Christian Borch, who hired me onto his AlgoFinance research project. Thanks are also due to Henrik Hermansen, the department administrator at Management Politics and Philosophy (now Business Humanities and Law), who made me feel welcome and continues to help me navigate the volatile professional life that is the Copenhagen Business School. Thank you both for giving me a chance and helping me out.

Similarly, thanks are due to Lotte Jensen, my past department head, who both hired me at the assistant professor level and advocated for my promotion to associate professor, as well as to Mitchell Dean, my current department head, who also advocated for my promotion to associate professor. I really appreciate the promise Professors Jensen and Dean saw in my work.

Thanks then are due to Morten Sørensen Thaning, who was my immediate supervisor for much of this book's development. I really enjoyed working for Dr. Thaning and appreciate the help he's offered in making life at the Copenhagen Business School work. I'm happy, too, that we're friends, and look forward to future collaboration.

The European Research Council (ERC) funded work on the AlgoFinance project under the European Union's Horizon 2020 research and innovation program (grant agreement no. 725706). This was a large and competitive grant that Christian Borch won and then managed. While I appreciate the opportunity this grant provided, I've concluded that this is not how we should be supporting or managing academic research. Funding research via competitive grants makes it so that most people are unable to do the research that they are trained to do and creates a situation in which those who win grants have had to submit their research for preapproval (really, rejection most of the time) from a small clique of distant senior academics or administrators. Similarly, research by competitive block grant requires empire building atop a mostly permanent underclass of gig-working researchers with little possibility for promotion or stability, never mind the opportunity to conduct independent research. It's an unfair system that makes a mockery of academic freedom and care for junior colleagues. We can do better.

Thanks then are due to the AlgoFinance team. I'm grateful to have learned from Christian Borch, Bo Hee Min, Kristian Bondo Hansen, Nicholas Skar-Gislinge, Pankaj Kumar, and Zachary David. Professor Borch and Doctors Min and Hansen's ethnographic work on financial exchanges, trading firms, and regulators was helpful in my understanding of the significance of what I was learning in my own fieldwork. Similarly, Doctor Skar-Gislinge, Mr. David, and Mr. Kumar's simulation work helped me understand a bit of how financial exchanges, agent-based modeling, and various sorts of machine-learning work. Professor Borch and Dr. Hansen were kind enough to read and comment on early drafts of this book. My work is enriched through these collaborations. Thank you all.

Thanks are also due to my friends Bryan Haut, Matthew Shayefar, and Jonathan Calvin Weyant III, who put me up on various field trips. In the early years, part of what made immigration bearable were these frequent field trips home. Thanks, guys.

Thanks also go to the traders at TradeCo, who let me hang out with them. May all your whooshes be up.

Thanks are also due to my colleague Dr. Melissa Beresford, who read and commented on some of the methods and data analysis sections of this book. Similarly, thanks are also due to Dr. Steven Black, who read and commented on some of the sections in this book with linguistic arguments. I really appreciate the help.

Thanks also go to the anonymous reviewers from the University of Chicago Press and Hadas Weiss. Those anonymous reviewers pushed me to sharpen the theoretical argument of this book. In turn, Dr. Weiss's work helped me see my account as a story of automation and alienation.

An earlier version of chapter 8 appeared in the journal *Finance and Society* (Souleles 2021). Thank you to Leon Wansleben and the editorial collective for helping me work through my arguments.

While this book was in review, I had the opportunity to present its argument to audiences at Copenhagen University, the University of Southern Denmark, the University of Pennsylvania, the University of Massachusetts Boston, New York University, and Brandeis University. Thank you all for hosting me. It was fun seeing what worked, what didn't, and chatting about all this. Hopefully this book is every bit as exciting as those talks were.

If anyone would like me to come and present this argument at their school, college, or university, just drop me a line—it's always a good time!

APPENDIX A

Note-Taking Summary

Table A1. Note-taking summary

Day of observation	Pages of notes
February 4, 2019	13
February 4, 2019	15
February 6, 2019	51
February 7, 2019	30
February 8, 2019	52
February 11, 2019	37
February 12, 2019	44
February 13, 2019	39
February 14, 2019	39
February 15, 2019	56
May 6, 2019	63
May 7, 2019	67
May 8, 2019	46
May 9, 2019	52
May 10, 2019	56
May 13, 2019	52
May 14, 2019	58
May 15, 2019	59
May 16, 2019	70
May 17, 2019	72

Profanity Distribution

Fuck: The only fucking word that can be put everyfuckingwhere and still fucking make fucking sense.
Top definition of fuck on urbandictionary.com, January 31, 2020, with 9,192 upvotes and 718 downvotes

What follows is a chart meant to give some indication of the variety among TradeCo's use of the work *fuck*. As noted elsewhere, I created 387 conversation chunks from 694 instances of the word's appearance across just shy of one thousand pages of notes. I also categorized and counted different grammatical forms of *fuck*. Table B1, then, is a count of given uses of the word in each conversation chunk. It's worth noting that the table doesn't provide an absolute count of a given form of *fuck*; rather, it indicates in a binary way a given form's presence or absence in a conversation chunk. Put another way, in some conversation chunks the same form is used several times. This will not be reflected in table B1.

The distinctions I draw on come partially form the *Oxford English Dictionary*'s various entries on *fuck* in its different guises. Some of the terminology comes from there as well, as in the "phrasal" use of a word—that is, when a word appears in common phrases or in idiomatic use and not as a grammatical prescriptivist would expect—as well as the definitions of the verbs. I depart, though, from some of their categorization of the forms that *fuck* finds and toss a bit more into phrasal use than they would. Also, I've made instances in which *fucking* is modifying some other word its own category as it seems to serve a somewhat distinct purpose with the traders at TradeCo.

In any event, I hope table B1 gives some rough sense of the distribution of the word *fuck* among the traders at TradeCo.

Table B1. Profanity distribution

Grammatical form of fuck	Number of conversational chunks in which a given form appears
Nouns	
Noun with *the* (e.g., "what the fuck")	83
Noun, phrasal with *up* (e.g., "that's a fuck up")	3
Noun, phrasal with *give*	3
Noun, phrasal with "ton"	3
Total	93
Verbs	
Verb, transitive, literally having rough sex	3
Verb, transitive, metaphorical (as per the *OED*—to damage, ruin, spoil, botch, destroy, put an end to, put into a difficult or hopeless situation; *or* to cheat, to deceive, betray)	36
Verb, phrasal with a noun (e.g., "fuck brokers")	12
Verb, phrasal with *off* (the similar construction [*fuck* + a following word] follows with the remainder of the phrasal verbs)	2
Verb, phrasal with *up*	41
Verb, phrasal with *around*	4
Verb, phrasal with *you*	13
Verb, phrasal with *this*	9
Verb, phrasal with *that*	7
Verb, phrasal with *me*	5
Verb, phrasal with *it*	14
Verb, phrasal with *with*	4
Verb, phrasal with *him*	3
Verb, phrasal with *this guy*	1
Verb, phrasal with *down*	1
Verb, phrasal with *'em*	1
Verb, phrasal with *yourself*	10
Verb, phrasal with *us*	2
Total	129

Grammatical form of fuck	Number of conversational chunks in which a given form appears
Modifiers	
Modifier with noun (e.g., "look at that fucking market")	141
Modifier with verb (e.g., "I can't fucking trade faster")	43
Modifier with adjective (e.g., "he's fucking smart")	50
Modifier with "a" (e.g., "fucking 'a'")	2
Modifier, floating (e.g., "fucking . . .")	5
Total	241
Interjection (e.g., "fuck!")	42
Fucker	5
Motherfucker	5
Bumfuck nowhere	1
Fuck yeah	4
Fuckwads	1

AlgoFinance Project Informants

Table C1 lists the interviews the AlgoFinance team conducted as of the time of my writing as well as some descriptive information to characterize our informants. The reference number indicates who conducted the interview (see note to table C1) as well as what number interview it was for that person (e.g., d001 indicates Daniel Souleles conducted the interview, and this is his first interview).

Table C1. AlgoFinance informants

Index no.	Ref. no.	Gender	Type of firm	Position	Date of interview
1	b001	M	Technology company	Compliance solution engineer	2018 04
2	b002	M	European Exchange	President	2018 05
3	b003	M	European Exchange	CEO	2018 05
4	b004	M	American Exchange	President	2018 06
5	b005	M, F	Financial analysts	Chief compliance officers; business development	2018 06
6	b006	F	Broker	Managing director	2018 06
7	b007	M, F	American Exchange	Executive director, Rules and Regulatory Outreach, Market Regulation Department	2018 06
8	b008	M	American regulator	Senior futures trading investigator	2018 06
9	b009	M	Proprietary trading firm	CEO	2018 06
10	b010	M	American Stock Exchange	Former CTO	2018 06
11	b011	M	Technology company	President	2018 08
12	b012	M	American Exchange	(Former) senior vice president; chief economist	2018 08
13	b012b		American Exchange		2018 11
14	b013	M	Broker	(Former) vice chairman	2018 11
15	b014	F	Financial services corporation	Vice president	2018 11
16	b015	M	Proprietary trading firm	Trader (retired)	2018 11

Index no.	Ref. no.	Gender	Type of firm	Position	Date of interview
17	b016	M	American Exchange	Chief economist	2018 11
18	b018	M	American Exchange	Head of data products; (former) CEO European Exchange	2018 11
19	b017	M	Technology industry association	Member	2018 11
20	b019	M	European Exchange	President	2019 01
21	b020	M			2019 03
22	b021	F	American Exchange	Head of quantitative research	2019 03
23	b022	M	American Exchange	Business developer	2019 03
24	b023	M	American Exchange	Senior testing manager	2019 03
25	b024	M	American Exchange	Chief operations officer	2019 03
26	b025	M	Institutional investor	Senior quantitative analyst	2019 03
27	b026	M			2019 03
28			American Exchange	Head of global strategic relationship	
29	bnc001	M	European Exchange	President, VP cash equities product management	2019 04
30	c001	M	Proprietary trading firm	Senior analyst/quant developer	2017 11
31	c002	M	Financial services firm	Java developer	2017 11
32	c003	M	Proprietary trading firm	CEO	2017 11
33	c004	M		Quant trader	2017 11
34	c005	M	Proprietary trading firm	Senior quantitative/ML researcher	2017 11

(continued)

Table Cl. (*continued*)

Index no.	Ref. no.	Gender	Type of firm	Position	Date of interview
35	c006	M	Bradford Partners	Machine learning research engineer	2017 11
36	c007	M	Proprietary trading firm	CEO and partner	2018 01
37	c008	M	Bradford Partners	CTO and CEO	2018 01
38	c009	M	Financial services corporation	Head of FX quants	2018 01
39	c010	M	Proprietary trading firm	Quant trader	2018 01
40	c011	M	Financial services firm	Quant trader (vice president)	2018 01
41	c012	M	Financial services firm	Head of artificial intelligence credit	2018 02
42	c013	M	Proprietary trading firm	Head trader	2018 06
43	c014	M	Proprietary trading firm	Developer	2018 06
44	c015	M	Proprietary trading firm	Quantitative developer	2018 06
45	c016	M	Proprietary trading firm	Quantitative trading researcher	2018 06
46	c017	M	Think tank	CEO	2018 06
47	c018	M	Proprietary trading firm		2018 06
48	d001	M	Financial services firm	Head of big data trading analytics	2017 09
49	d002	M			2017 09
50	d003	M	Brokerage/ IT firm	Global data analyst	2017 12
51	d004	M	Financial services firm	Project manager	2017 12
52	d005	M	Proprietary trading firm	Technologist	2017 12

Index no.	Ref. no.	Gender	Type of firm	Position	Date of interview
53	d006	M	Proprietary trading firm	Senior research scientists	2017 12
54	d007	M	Brokerage/ IT firm	Global head of algorithmic trading	2017 12
55	d008	M	Financial services firm	Analyst, algorithmic trading	2017 12
56	d009	M	Proprietary trading firm	Analyst	2017 12
57	d010	M	Asset manager	Associate	2017 12
58	d011	M	Proprietary trading firm	Chief strategy officer	2017 12
59	d012	M	Proprietary trading firm	Former partner, current head of computer trading	2017 12
60	d013	M	Company that builds ETFs	Senior quantitative analyst	2017 12
61	d014	M	Financial services firm	Director (quant trading)	2017 12
62	d015	M	Proprietary trading firm	Quantitative research analyst	2017 12
63	d016	M	Financial Services Firm	Quantitative trading analyst	2017 12
64	d017	M	US government regulatory agency	Assistant director, division of economic and risk analysis	2017 11
65	d018	M	US government regulatory agency		2017 11
66	d019	M		HFT developer	2017 10
67	d020	M	Proprietary trading firm	Trade operations specialist	2017 10
68	d021	M		Software developer	2017 10
69	d022	M	Proprietary trading firm	Algorithmic trader	2017 10

(continued)

Table C1. (*continued*)

Index no.	Ref. no.	Gender	Type of firm	Position	Date of interview
70	d023	M	Proprietary trading firm	Software developer	2017 10
71	d024	M	Proprietary trading firm	Trading algorithm engineer	2017 10
72	d025	M	American University	Finance PhD student	2017 10
73	d026	M	Proprietary trading firm	Quant trader	2017 10
74	d027	M			2017 10
75	d028	M	Proprietary trading firm	Quantitative analyst	2017 10
76	d029	M	Proprietary trading firm		2017 10
77	d030	M	Proprietary trading firm	Options trader	2017 10
78	d031	M	Proprietary trading firm	Quant researcher	2017 10
79	d032	M	Investment manager	Founder/CEO	2017 10
80	d033	M	Proprietary trading firm	CEO	2018 01
81	d034	M	American Exchange	Software developer	2018 01
82	d035	M	American Exchange	Software developer	2018 01
83	d036	M	Industry lobbyist	Economist	2018 02
84	d037	M	American University	Director of a trading lab	2018 01
85	d038	M	Proprietary trading firm	Quantitative trading analyst	2018 01
86	d039	M	Investment manager	Vice president	2018 01

Index no.	Ref. no.	Gender	Type of firm	Position	Date of interview
87	d040	M	American Exchange	Former CEO	2018 01
88	d041	F	Senate office	Legislative aid	2018 02
89	d042	M	US executive branch department	Analyst	2018 02
90	d043	M, F	US government regulatory agency	Research and enforcement group interview	2018 02
91	d044	M	Proprietary trading firm	Financial engineer	2018 06
92	d045	M	Proprietary trading firm	Quant developer	2018 06
93	d046	M	Proprietary trading firm	Quant	2018 06
94	d047	M	Investment manager	Chief investment officer	2018 06
95	d048	M		Financial engineer	2018 06
96	d049	M	Proprietary trading firm	Quant	2018 06
97	d050	M	Technology company	Financial engineer	2018 06
98	d051	M	Proprietary trading firm	Managing director, options	2018 06
99	d052	M	Investment manager	Financial data engineer	2018 06
100	d053	M	Proprietary trading firm	Former partner, currently fintech investor	2018 06
101	d054	M	Proprietary trading firm	Financial engineer	2018 06
102	d055	M	Proprietary trading firm	Partner	2018 06
103	d056	M	Proprietary trading firm	Partner	2018 06

(continued)

Table C1. (*continued*)

Index no.	Ref. no.	Gender	Type of firm	Position	Date of interview
104	d057	M	American regulator	Compliance inspections exams	
105	d058	M	American regulator	Equity market structure policy	
106	d059	M	Financial services firm	Quant researcher	2018 07
107	d060	M	Financial services firm	MD, head of quantitative trading	2018 07
108	d061	M	Financial services firm	Algo/HFT quant modeling and strategy	2018 07
109	d062	M	Proprietary trading firm	Managing director	2018 08
110	d063	M	Financial services firm	Rates algo trading technology	2018 08
111	d064	M	Financial services firm	Partner and cofounder	2018 08
112	d065	M	Brokerage	Quantitative research analyst	2018 08
113	d066	M	Investment manager	Investment advisor	2018 07
114	d067	M	Proprietary trading firm	Corporate debt analyst and trader	2019 01
115	d068	M	TradeCo	Chief information officer	2019 03
116	d069	M	European Exchange	Executive board member	2019 02
117	g001	M	Proprietary trading firm	Former CTO	2018 04
118	g002	M	Proprietary trading firm		2018 05
119	bc001	M, M	Bradford Partners	Founder, CEO	2018 08
120	bc002	F	Bradford Partners	HR manager	2018 08

Index no.	Ref. no.	Gender	Type of firm	Position	Date of interview
121	bc003	M	Bradford Partners	Senior software engineer	2018 08
122	bc004	F, M	Bradford Partners	Delivery managers	2018 08
123	bc005	M	Bradford Partners	Head of market risk	2018 08
124	bc006	F, M, M	Bradford Partners	Delivery manager; senior software engineer; governance/compliance	2018 08
125	bc007	M	Bradford Partners	CTO	2018 08 & 11
126	bc008	M	Bradford Partners	Infrastructure engineer	2018 08
127	bc009	M	Bradford Partners	CEO	2019 02
128	bc010	M, M	Bradford Partners	CEO, CTO	2019 02
129	bc011	M, M, M, M	Bradford Partners	Production team	2019 03
130	bc012	M, M, M, M, M, M	Bradford Partners		2019 03
131	bc013	M, M, M, M	Bradford Partners	CEO, CTO, CRO, CFO	2019 03
132	bc014	M, M, M, M	Bradford Partners	CEO, CTO, production team	2019 08
133	bc015	M	Bradford Partners	CRO	2019 08
134	bc016		Bradford Partners	Trading team	2019 08
135	bc017	M, M	Bradford Partners	CEO, CTO	2019 08
136	k001	M	Proprietary trading firm	CEO and CIO	2017 10

(continued)

Table C1. (*continued*)

Index no.	Ref. no.	Gender	Type of firm	Position	Date of interview
137	k002	M	Proprietary trading firm	Senior VP and head of EMEA client business	2017 11
138	k003	M	Finance consultancy	Founder and CEO	2017 11
139	k004	F		data scientist	2017 12
140	k005	M	Asset manager	Trader	2017 12
141	k006	M	Investment manager	Chief scientist	2018 01
142	k007	M	Investment manager	Quantitative portfolio manager	2018 01
143	k008	M	Proprietary trading firm	Former CTO	2018 03
144	k009	M	Financial services firm	Quants	2018 04
145	k010	M	Proprietary trading firm	Developer and trader	2018 04
146	k011	M	Proprietary trading firm	Former CEO	2018 05
147	k012	M	Financial services firm	Machine learning expert	2018 05
148	k013	M	Independent	Consultant and trader	2018 05
149	k014	M	Financial technology firm	Chief data scientist	2018 06
150	k015	M	Proprietary trading firm	CTO	2018 06
151	k016	M	Proprietary trading firm	CEO	2018 06
152	k017	M	European university	Associate professor (former quant analyst)	2018 06
153	k018	M	Investment manager	Researcher	2018 06
154	k019	M	Technology firm	Head of research	2018 06

Index no.	Ref. no.	Gender	Type of firm	Position	Date of interview
155	k020	M	Financial services firm	quant strategy research	2018 06
156	k021	M	Proprietary trading firm	CEO and head of trading	2018 06
157	k022	M	Proprietary trading firm	Development process manager	2018 06
158	k023	M	Asset manager	Head of trading research	2018 07
159	k024	M	Broker dealer	Global head of product management	2018 09
160	k025	M	Financial services firm	Senior risk manager, head of quantitative risk and quantitative analysis	2018 09
161	k026	M	Proprietary trading firm	Director of investment strategies	2018 09
162	k027	M	Financial technology firm	CSO	2018 09
163	k028	M	Proprietary trading firm	Performance lead	2018 09
164	k029	M	Investment manager	Head of quant team	2018 10
165	k030	M	European Exchange	Model validation quant	2018 10
166	k031	M	Investment manager	Quantitative researcher	2018 11
167	k032	M	Financial services firm	Quant systematic investments	2018 11
168	k033	M	Financial consultancy	Data scientist and founder	2018 11
169	k034	M	Independent	Engineer	2018 11
170	k035	M	Investment manager	Quant	2018 11
171	k036	M	Simulation consultancy		2018 11

(continued)

Table C1. (*continued*)

Index no.	Ref. no.	Gender	Type of firm	Position	Date of interview
172	k037	M	Financial technology firm	Quant, founder	2018 11
173	k038	M	Financial consultancy	CEO and founder	2018 12
174	k039	M	Investment manager	Senior quantitative analyst	2018 12
175	k040	M		Quantitative trading/ hedge fund owner	2019 03
176	k041	M	Financial services firm	E-trading risk quant	2019 03
177	k042	M	Financial services consultancy	Head of quantitative strategies	2019 09
178	k043	M	Financial services consultancy	CEO	2019 09
179	bk001		Brokerage		2018 09
180	bk002	M			2019 06
181	bn001	M	European Exchange	Sales manager, global sales	2019 06
182	bn002	M	European Exchange	Head of core market, equities market analyst	2019 06
183	bn003	M	European Exchange	Head of market structure and UK business development	2019 06
184	bn004	M	European Exchange	Head of trading performance and changes	2019 06

Note: b = Bo Hee Min; c = Christian Borch; k = Kristian Bondo Hansen; n = Nichols Skar-Gislinge. Combinations of letters indicate a jointly conducted interview. Note that some interviews are with multiple informants.

How Exchange Professionals Use the Word *Market*

Despite being perfectly aware that people design markets according to a complex interplay of legal mandates, market competition, and aspirations about what capitalism should look like (e.g., Pardo-Guerra 2019), the traders at TradeCo often treat markets as factual entities with which they need to contend. To illustrate how much the traders at TradeCo's idea of markets differ from those of the people who design markets, I created a schema of the various ways exchange professionals and market designers use the word *market*. Below is the schema I generated, followed by a table of the informants (table D1) I used to generate the schema, and then the individual declarative statements about markets that I sorted into a schema.

Market Schema

- Markets as manipulable spaces (the things that exchanges see as mechanisms to shape markets) (34 total)
  - ◇ Umbrella concepts to understand markets (concepts through which practitioners understand manipulation)—m002, m0013, m017, m022, m025, m041, m042, m055, m063, m081, m082, m091, m093, m096 (14 subtotal)
  - ◇ Orders and speed (the mechanics of buying, selling, and accessing)—m004, m005, m010, m026, m028, m032, m046, m056, m057, m058, m059, m080, m083, m085, m086, m092 (16 subtotal)

- ◇ Data and information (the information that buying and selling generate and the way it is distributed [sold mostly])—m008, m015, m027, m030 (4 subtotal)
- Markets as made up of participants (the various people who are on markets)—m007, m021, m023, m031, m035, m039, m040, m047, m049, m050, m061, m065, m069, m071, m079, m088, m089 (17 total)
- Markets as exchanges that are competing and interacting entities and businesses—m011, m014, m043, m048, m051, m052, m054, m064, m068, m074, m076, m077, m078, m087, m090 (15 total)
- Markets as a thing that people do naughty stuff to—m001, m016, m033, m034, m036, m038, m060, m066, m067, m094 (10 total)
- MISC Market as a qualitatively described place (lot of overlap with traders here) (20 total)
  - ◇ Practical descriptions—m003, m006, m009, m019, m024, m029, m037, m045, m062, m070, m072, m073, m084 (13 subtotal)
  - ◇ Affective descriptions—m012, m018, m020, m044, m053, m075, m095 (7 subtotal)

Subsample of Informants Used to Generate Market Schema

The attentive reader will note that there are far more instances of the word *market*, even in this small subsample of informants, than there are declarative statements about markets, below. What I've done in the statements below is collapse repetitive uses of the word into distinct declarative statements for the purpose of analysis.

Table D1. Total instances of *market* in subsample of interviews

Informant ID	Number of instances of market in the interview
b010	120
b012	87
b023	41
b024	140
bN002	108
d034 and d035	57
Total	**553**

Declarative Statements about Markets

1. Market as a thing that can be manipulated (b012, m001)
2. Market as an arena for optimizing (b012, m002)
3. Market as factually different venues (b012, m003)
4. Market as a place that offers a rebate (b012, m004)
5. Market as a place to which you have relative latency (b012, m005)
6. Market as a place where you put risk (b012, m006)
7. Market as a place where engines trade (b012, m007)
8. Market as a place where you might identify yourself (b012, m008)
9. Market as a place of variable size (b012, m009)
10. Market as a place that can treat stocks similarly or differently (b012, m010)
11. Market as a place that can be national or not (b012, m011)
12. Market as a source from which you can buy data (b012, m012)
13. Market as a thing that is operated (b012, m013)
14. Market as a thing that has to comply with regulation (b012, m014)
15. Market as a thing that has variable data structures (which makes different algos possible) (b012, m015)
16. Market as a place to surveil (b012, m016)
17. Market as a place that should be fair and orderly (b012, m017)
18. Market as a thing you have an obligation to (b012, m018)
19. Market as a place that has a price (b012, m019)
20. Market as a place where you have no idea what is going on (b012, m020)
21. Market as a thing that is made by a market maker (b012, m021)
22. Market as a thing that has structure; and market as a thing that has microstructure (b012, m022)
23. Markets as a thing with participants (b012, m023)
24. Market as a thing with relative levels of liquidity (b012, m024)
25. Markets have the option of being electronic (b10, m025)
26. Markets have the option of being automated (b010, m026)
27. Markets are a place in which you can be anonymous (b010, m027)
28. Market as a venue with different types of orders (b010, m028)
29. Market as a place with bad information (b010, m029)
30. Market as a place where information leaks (b010, m030)
31. Market as a venue with increasing numbers of odd lots (b010, m031)
32. Market as a place that can be public (b010, m032)
33. Market as a thing that can be abused (b010, m033)
34. Market as a place to commit a crime (b010, m034)

35. Market as a place where people are different sized (b010, m035)
36. Market as a place to spoof (b010, m036)
37. Markets can be lopsided or asymmetric (b010, m037)
38. Markets are places where people can collude (b010, m038)
39. Markets are places that have common behavior (b010, m039)
40. Markets have exchanges that have their own rules (b010, m040)
41. Markets have operations people and have operations algorithms (b010, m041)
42. Markets are places where things evolve (like surveillance) (b010, m042)
43. Markets can be exchanges which have gone public and are for profit (b010, m043)
44. Markets can be clean (b010, m044)
45. Markets can have different levels of order flows (b010, m045)
46. Markets can cater to different people, like investors (b010, m046)
47. Market intermediaries can be a source of corruption (b010, m047)
48. Markets as a thing that can be disintermediated (b010, m048)
49. Markets can be dealer driven (b010, m049)
50. Markets are places where people can give false indications (b010, m050)
51. Markets are able to be influenced by other markets (e.g., e minis and SPY/equities) (b010, m051)
52. Markets can be under different jurisdictions (b010, m052)
53. Markets have frictions (b024, m053)
54. Markets can be part of a national market system (b024, m054)
55. Markets change and those changes can be predicted by models (b024, m055)
56. Markets can have fees around connectivity, membership, data, and trading (b024, m056)
57. Markets can sell speed advantages (b024, m057)
58. Markets have exchanges that can charge for colocation and connectivity (b024, m058)
59. Markets have traders with different resting times (b024, m059)
60. Markets can be profiled (b024, m060)
61. Markets can have natural interest (b024, m061)
62. Markets can imaginably have calamities due to speed bumps (b024, m062)
63. Markets have structure, and structure can be improved (b024, m063)
64. Markets have exchanges that compete in a free market (b024, m064)
65. Markets have participants that should not unduly try to influence the price of a security (b024, m065)

66. Markets have enforcement teams (b024, m066)
67. Markets can be surveilled, and that surveillance can be outsourced (b024, m067)
68. Markets have cross-market patterns (b024, m068)
69. Markets have exchanges that get orders and bring them to market (d034&035, m069)
70. Markets get hit by news (D034&035, m070)
71. Markets get orders that make market impact (D034&035, m071)
72. Markets have prices that they open at (D034&035, m072)
73. Markets have volatility that can then typify specific markets (D034&035, m073)
74. Markets have exchanges that compete and can squeeze each other out of existence (D034&035, m074)
75. Markets contain prices (D034&035, m075)
76. Markets exist in a marketplace and can become consolidated (D034&035, m076)
77. Markets can cover specific geographic locations (bn002, m077)
78. Markets exist in different nations, and different nations regulate them differently (bn002, m078)
79. Markets have vastly different trading participants on them (bn002, m079)
80. Markets can be lit or dark (bn002, m080)
81. Markets can be modeled (bn002, m081)
82. Markets can be transparent (bn002, m082)
83. Markets have matching engines, and they can be different (bn002, m083)
84. Markets have flows that people can get some percent of (bn002, m084)
85. Markets have technological specifications (bn002, m085)
86. Markets have different liquidity profiles (bn002, m086)
87. Markets can have consolidated tapes (bn002, m087)
88. Markets have different types of firms trading on them (bn002, m088)
89. Markets have brokers that have pipes that access the market (bn002, m089)
90. Markets exist in a hierarchy in which some are primary (bn002, m090)
91. Markets can behave or work the way they're designed to work (B023, m091)
92. Markets have hours and sessions (b023, m092)
93. Markets have a way that they're supposed to look (b023, m093)
94. Markets can be halted (b023, m094)
95. Markets have nuances that need to be understood (b023, m095)
96. Markets can be rationalized b023 (m096)

How Quants Use the Word Stem *Algo*

In order to illustrate the ways that quantitative traders think about their work differently from the traders at TradeCo, I went ahead and created a schema of the way they use the word *algorithm* (or, more specifically *algo*). The idea was that these quant traders interact with markets via algorithms. So, if you understand how they use algorithms, you'll understand how they see markets. Below is (1) a list of the schema I created noting the specific statements about algorithms from which I generated each element of the schema, (2) a list of the informants from whose interviews I generated statements about algorithms, and (3) the list of the algorithmic statements that are at the root of this schema analysis.

Algorithm Schema

- Generalizations about algorithms (30 total)
    - Algorithms have behaviors—a005, a006, a025, a030, a033, a045, a047, a048, a055, a056, a057, a058, a061, a064, a095, a101, a105, a106, a120 (19 subtotal)
    - Algorithms have limitations—a009, a018, a083, a100, a102, a110 (6 subtotal)
    - Algorithms do good and important things—a002, a008, a037, a043, a103 (5 subtotal)
- Algorithms conjure both specific people and specific arrangements of

people—a009, a017, a026, a028, a035, a052, a074, a082, a084, a087, a088, a089, a096, a099, a104, a107, a111 (17 total)
- On building algorithms (23 total)
  - ◇ Algorithm building has an aspirational, imprecise, often metaphoric component—a004, a015, a016, a019, a049, a050, a059, a067, a092, a114, a119 (11 subtotal)
  - ◇ Algorithm building has a precise, technically specific component—a001, a003, a010, a014, a031, a032, a038, a070, a075, a091, a094, a097 (12 subtotal)
- Algorithms have trading abilities and limitations (45 total)
  - ◇ Algorithms have specific trading abilities and features—a011, a012, a020, a021, a023, a024, a027, a029, a039, a040, a041, a044, a051, a053, a060, a062, a063, a066, a068, a071, a072, a073, a076, a078, a079, a080, a081, a084, a086, a090, a109, a113, a115, a117, a118, a121 (36 subtotal)
  - ◇ Algorithms create specific results and conditions in markets—a022, a036, a042, a054, a065, a069, a098, a108, a112 (9 subtotal)
- Algorithmic miscellany—a013, a034, a046, a077, a093, a116 (6 total)

Subsample of Informants Used to Generate Algorithm Schema

As in the market schema appendix, the attentive reader will note that there are far more instances of the word *algo* even in this small subsample of informants, than there are declarative statements about algorithms (table E1). What I've done, again, in the statements below is collapse repetitive uses of the word into distinct declarative statements for the purpose of analysis.

Declarative Statements about Algorithms

Each declarative statement has a parenthetical saying what informant interview the statement came from as well as an algorithmic identified number (e.g., a001) that can be used to correspond to the above schema. In some statements, I've broken form and started with the adjective *algorithmic* instead of the noun *algorithm*. This is a shorthand to make sorting and categorizing easier. Each instance of algorithmic could be expanded into a noun form along the lines of a105, which reads, "Algorithmic trading is the opposite of manual trading (c016, a105)." We could understand this as expandable

Table E1. Total Instances of *algo* in subsample of interviews

Informant ID	Number of instances of algo in the transcript
c001	19
c004	17
c010	27
c013	11
c016	25
d012	5
d014	2
d022	6
d026	5
d029	19
d033	49
d051	3
k002	4
k008	23
k026	13
k029	7
k039	1
Total	**235**

to "Algorithms are involved in some sorts of trading that might be called algorithmic, which is the opposite of manual trading." I hope the attentive among you will forgive this expediency.

1. Algorithms have parameters (d033, a001)
2. Algorithms solve problems (d033, a002)
3. Algorithms can be montecarlo or tree search (d033, a003)
4. Algorithms have ideas that were developed in the fifties (d033, a004)
5. Algorithms produce things that are unexpected (d033, a005)
6. Algorithms can produce things that are illegal (d033, a006)
7. Algorithms let you teach the machine to be the scientist (d033, a008)
8. Algorithms can contain the investment committee (d033, a009)
9. Algorithms can be overfit (d033, a009)

10. Algorithms can contain machine-learning algorithms on top of other algorithms (d033, a010)
11. Algorithms can figure out correlations (d033, a011)
12. Algorithms can make strategies (d033, a012)
13. Algorithms can predict how many calories you burn (d033, a013)
14. Algorithms can use feature generation, structural search, or common regressions (d033, a014)
15. Algorithms can be run on data (d033, a015)
16. Algorithms come from computer science and get better and better (d033, a016)
17. Algorithms let computers find strategies faster than humans can (d033, a017)
18. Algorithms have biases (d033, a018)
19. Algorithms can be precise (d033, a019)
20. Algorithms can be broker algos (d033, a020)
21. Algorithms can trade (d033, a021)
22. Algorithms can be broker algos and sell back to you at a higher price (d033, a022)
23. Algorithms can buy or sell (d033, a023)
24. Algorithms have difficulty assessing the permanence of price changes (d033, a024)
25. Algorithms can analyze other algorithms (d033, a025)
26. Algorithms are things that some people do not have (d033, a026)
27. Algorithms are able to trade (d033, a027)
28. Algorithms are written by some people (d033, a028)
29. Algorithms can be for strategy and are distinct from execution algorithms (d033, a029)
30. Algorithms can be supervised by humans (d033, a030)
31. Algorithms have source code that must remain secret in order to be profitable (K002, a031)
32. Algorithms can be based on machine learning and be completely random (K002, a032)
33. Algorithms ingest data and become automated (k008, a033)
34. Algorithms can be used in trading and it is a thing that you can believe is true or not (k008, a034)
35. Algorithms can be wickedly smart and support wickedly smart traders (k008, a035)

36. Algorithms can support trading, and that trading is a zero-sum endeavor (k008, a036)
37. Algorithms are far from the path pattern recognition of pigeon-brained humans (k008, a037)
38. Algorithms can be given heuristics and simulated (k008, a038)
39. Algorithms can lose shitloads of money (k008, a039)
40. Algorithms can be simple and market making (k008, a040)
41. Algorithms can be basic and used to hedge (k008, a041)
42. Algorithms and their application in trading have the potential to drive better pricing in the lower echelons of stocks and futures by making spreads small (k008, a042)
43. Algorithms can fix inefficiencies in complex, leaky, component-filled projects (C001, a043)
44. Algorithms can be momentum based (c001, a044)
45. Algorithms have their own world (c001, a045)
46. Algorithms can make up a purely algorithmic environment (c001, a046)
47. Algorithms are knowable by people (c001, a047)
48. Algorithms can be implemented (c001, a048)
49. Algorithms are made up of ideas from people about how they should work (c001, a049)
50. Algorithms can be run on data (c001, a050)
51. Algorithmic is a thing you can do on markets (c001, a051)
52. Algorithms can need high-level ideas people (c001, a052)
53. Algorithms can trade futures and options (c010, a053)
54. Algorithms, when they trade, smash volatility because they tend to follow each other (c010, a054)
55. Algorithms follow each other (c010, a055)
56. Algorithms try to detect what each other does (c010, a056)
57. Algorithms, some say, reduce volatility (c010, a057)
58. Algorithms look for statistical patterns (c010, a058)
59. Algorithms can be built for speed (c010, a059)
60. Algorithms are capable of being separated from all the practical details of trading (c010, a060)
61. Algorithms behave in ways other than how they are supposed to (c010, a061)
62. Algorithms can reduce trading inventory (c010, a062)
63. Algorithms and machines can run market making (c010, a063)

64. Algorithms can detect attacks (d012, a064)

65. Algorithms, specific algorithms in fact, may be used by competitors, but it's difficult or impossible to tell who is using what (d012, a065)

66. Algorithms in trading can be reduced to either trend following or mean reverting (d014, a066)

67. Algorithms can be data driven (d051, a067)

68. Algorithms can deliver investment results (d051, a068)

69. Algorithms allow traders to do thousands of orders a day, twenty-four hours a day, touching things by hand no more than a handful of times (d029, a069)

70. Algorithms can use conditional or Bayesian probability to determine whether markets are moving away or not (d029, a070)

71. Algorithms use market microstructure and microstructure theory to determine whether trades should be on the inside of the market or not (d029, a071)

72. Algorithms allow you to hold positions and hold risk for longer periods of time (d029, a072)

73. Algorithms allow you to avoid adverse selection risk (d029, a073)

74. Algorithms are employed by scientists (d029, a074)

75. Algorithms use strategies that employ scientific models (d029, a075)

76. Algorithms apply the scientific method to trading (d029, a076)

77. Algorithms in trading require you to understand your hypothesis (d029, a077)

78. Algorithms in trading require you to have a testable hypothesis (d029, a078)

79. Algorithms in trading have no secrets; you just need to put the pieces together (d029, a079)

80. Algorithmic strategies have a life cycle (d029, a080)

81. Algorithmic trading is distinct from stock picking (d029, a081)

82. Algorithms in trading have not been employed long enough for people's dads to have been in it (d029, a082)

83. Algorithms are important to understand before you use them (d026, a083)

84. Algorithms can determine the optimal place to put an order (d026, a084)

85. Algorithms allow you to not care about who is in the market save for whether they are informed or not (d026, a085)

86. Algorithms allow you to build in scale and edge (d026, a086)

87. Algorithms are used by people who are not the big swinging-dick banker bros (d026, a087)

88. Algorithms can be standardized by banks (d022, a088)

89. Algorithmic trading can coexist with nonalgorithmic trading in a firm (d022, a089)
90. Algorithms are inappropriate for some markets (d022, a090)
91. Algorithms cost a lot of time and money to develop (k026, a091)
92. Algorithms are important in the superliquid space (k026, a092)
93. Algorithms can be used internally (k029, a093)
94. Algorithms that use machine learning often use the same libraries as Google TensorFlow (k026, a094)
95. Algorithms can be tested against one another (k026, a095)
96. Algorithms can be developed by execution researchers who are separate from traders (k026, a096)
97. Algorithms that use machine learning benefit from high volumes of data from which you get more robust patterns (like in execution) (k026, a097)
98. Algorithms can make markets and grab as much value as possible from the order book (k039, a098)
99. Algorithms can drive hiring practices (k029, a099)
100. Algorithms in a series of automated processes can describe your daily life, leading you to question what makes you unique (k029, a100)
101. Algorithms need to be supervised to make sure they do what they say they're doing (k029, a101)
102. Algorithms for images, unless you specify that people have noses and eyes and mouths and ears, will follow rules for categorization that you will not be able to follow (k029, a102)
103. Algorithms create an incredibly fast society (k029, a103)
104. Algorithmic trading is the opposite of manual trading (c016, a104)
105. Algorithms can be made up of behaviors (c016, a105)
106. Algorithms can be turned on or off (c016, a106)
107. Algorithms require people who are in high demand to create and run them (c016, a107)
108. Algorithms make it hard for your orders to get filled; and this is difficult to understand why (c016, a108)
109. Algorithms are easier to model on futures than they are on options (c016, a109)
110. Algorithms making use of machine learning is a bit of a buzzword (c016, a110)
111. Algorithms presuppose an algo trader way of doing things that is more academic and cerebral than a pit trader way of doing things (c004, a111)

112. Algorithms and their use in financial markets and the resources that go into them could be good or bad for society (c004, a112)
113. Algorithms can be slightly different on different exchanges (c004, a113)
114. Algorithms can be generic (c004, a114)
115. Algorithms can be for the volume weighted average price (c004, a115)
116. Algorithms can be gorillas and algorithms can be snipers (c004, a116)
117. Algorithms are separable from trading algorithms (c013, a117)
118. Algorithmic trading in options is more complicated than algorithmic trading in underliers or deltas (c013, a118)
119. Algorithms take effort to get up and running (c013, a119)
120. Algorithms can be observed in the market (c013, a120)
121. Algorithms exist to look for bottoms in markets (c013, a121)

Glossary of Some Trading Words

Like any group of people, folks in, on, and around financial markets have specific words for what they do. These words are probably unfamiliar to those of us who don't make our living buying low and selling high. Given that, I'll provide here a brief, plain-language definition of some of the most common specialist terms that show up in this book. Don't worry, I'll also define these terms as they come up in the course of the chapters. Rather than read this outright, it's probably most useful to simply come back here if, while reading, you realize you're not quite sure what some word means.

Arca: Arca (pronounced "ark-uh") is an American financial exchange that is known for trading both stocks and exchange traded products (ETPs). Arca is owned by NYSE (the New York Stock Exchange). "Arca" is an abbreviation for "Archipelago."

bid/ask or bid/offer: The bid is the price at which someone will buy a stock. The ask/offer is the price at which someone will sell a stock. The bid is generally lower than the ask/offer (remember, buy low, sell high). The price space in between the highest bid and the lowest ask/offer is called the spread. If someone offers to buy at the ask/offer price, they've "crossed the spread," and the market is moving. Similarly, if people pull their bids to buy from a market, liquidity is going out of the market and prices are dropping.

broker: A broker is a person or institution that is a go-between for people that want to buy or sell investments. Brokers grant access to financial markets.

calls and puts: Calls and puts are the two basic types of options. Call options give the holder the option to buy a financial instrument at a given price over some period of time. Put options give the holder the option to sell a financial instrument at a given price over some period of time.

CBOE: CBOE (pronounced "see-bow") is short for the Chicago Board Options Exchange and is both a specific financial market, an exchange on which options are bought and sold, and a corporate umbrella group for a number of different financial exchanges.

CFTC: CFTC, or the Commodity Futures Trading Commission, is one of two American financial regulators (the other being the SEC). The CFTC has jurisdiction over futures and some options derivatives.

CME: CME stands for Chicago Mercantile Exchange and is both a corporate umbrella as well as the world's largest exchange for derivative financial products. The CME is particularly famous for its futures trading on everything from agricultural commodities to currencies to financial products.

dark pool: A dark pool is simply a nonpublic financial exchange. Many large banks and brokerages maintain their own dark pools. What makes a dark pool "dark" is the fact that whoever owns the dark pool need not publicly display the orders and prices on their dark pool (though they do report sales at a slight time delay). To outsiders, that market is dark. This is rhetorically contrasted with public exchanges (such as NYSE or NASDAQ) which are sometimes called "lit" markets or "lit exchanges."

delta: In order to price a stock option, traders use a modification of the Black Scholes Merton equation (which itself is derived from a physics equation used to measure Brownian particle motion). Various Greek letters stand for calculus manipulations (partial derivatives) of the Black Scholes Merton equation, which are meant to convey something of a relationship between an option and its underlying asset. Delta speaks to the relationship between an option's price and its underlying stock's price.

derivative: A derivative is an umbrella term for a sort of financial instrument or contract that gets its value from something else (an underlier). To take two examples, an oil future and a stock option are both derivatives in that their value only comes from some other thing that they're based on (in this case actual crude oil as a commodity, or the price of stock).

equity: Another word for a stock.

ETF/ETP: Often times an investor will want to be able to invest in something a bit more complicated than a single company, say in a specific industry, or a specific country's or region's economy. Usually this would be hard to do and would require that the investor buy a bunch of individual stocks in order to get to this broad sort of exposure. An ETF, or "exchange traded fund," is meant to be a solution to this problem. ETFs bundle a bunch of different but somehow related assets, put them in a single "fund," and then allow investors to buy shares in the fund. ETFs and ETPs ("exchange traded products") exist for all manner of assets (stocks, currencies, commodities, indexes [such as the S&P 500] and so on). Investors often feel that ETFs/ETPs provide natural diversification in their portfolio—meaning a variety of different investments. Having a variety of different investments ensures that if one particular investment goes down you don't lose the value of your whole portfolio.

exchange: An exchange is the place where buying and selling actually happen. Mostly exchanges are located on computer servers in the suburbs of financial centers (though there are still some in-person, open outcry trading at some exchanges). In addition to being the place where buying and selling actually happens, an exchange is also a specific, regulated, legal entity—the company and business that actually runs the servers and regulates the people and entities that buy and sell on financial markets.

financial instrument: Financial instrument is a generic term for the types of contracts, products, and legal claims having to do with some form of abstracted wealth and ownership of something in the world. Examples of financial instruments are stock (ownership shares of a business), bonds (debt contracts for a business or a government), or derivatives (contracts based on some underlying asset). If you owned a bar of gold, that would be a physical possession and perhaps a form of wealth but not a financial instrument. If, however, you owned a future contract for some quantity of gold at some price, that contract would be a level of abstraction away from real gold and would be a financial instrument. A few things that distinguish financial instruments: they involve some form of abstraction; people often buy and sell them; and they often circulate on markets that are also at some level of remove from that which they reference.

FINRA: The Financial Industry Regulatory Authority is a private, industry-run regulatory body that monitors, regulates, and sanctions its members. In the United States we might think of three layers of regulations: actual government regulation (the SEC and the CFTC), industry self-regulation (such as with FINRA), and then the regulation that happens at exchanges (such as CBOE or NYSE). Industry-organized self-regulators like FINRA sit between the government and the exchanges.

flow (or order flow): Flow is a loose way of talking about the orders coming and going from financial markets.

future: A future is a derivative financial product that requires you to buy something at a fixed price by a fixed date. For example, if you held a future contract to buy 100 barrels of oil at US$100 per barrel that expires on the first of the year, you would need to buy (and take possession of) that oil at that price on that expiration date. Some future contracts require you to take possession of an actual underlying commodity, whereas other futures allow you to settle in the cash equivalent value of that commodity.

gamma: In order to price a stock option, traders use a modification of the Black Scholes Merton equation (which itself is derived from a physics equation used to measure Brownian particle motion). Various Greek letters stand for calculus manipulations (partial derivatives) of the Black Scholes Merton equation, which are meant to convey something of a relationship between an option and its underlying asset. Gamma speaks to the rate of change in the relationship between the underlying stock's price and the option's price.

Greek letters (the Greeks): One thing that makes options trading so confusing to outsiders is the frequent, shorthand reference to a number of Greek letters (delta, gamma, theta, and vega). Each Greek letter refers to some calculus manipulations (partial derivatives) of the Black Scholes Merton equation, variations of which traders use to price options. The various Greek-named derivatives of the equation refer to specific features and behaviors of options, and they become shorthand for trading analyses and activities. To take one example—*theta* refers to the way an option's price changes as its expiration date approaches. A trader might say they have a "theta bomb," meaning that some portion of their portfolio is rapidly losing value because of the passage of time and the approach of an option contract's expiration date. Announcing a "theta bomb" would also implicitly gesture toward action that might mitigate this portfolio risk.

handle: *Handle* refers to whole number changes in the price of a financial instrument (as opposed to fractional or decimal changes). When things move in handles, they are moving in dollars as opposed to pennies. You can presume that when traders talk about handle moves, they are talking about big, quick moves in market prices.

hedge/hedging: Buying stocks, derivatives, or any sort of financial instrument is inherently risky because of the fact that the price of whatever you've bought can change. Hedging or a hedge is buying some sort of countervailing financial instrument to offer some insurance against your loss. To take an example, let's say you've bought some stock at US$100 per share and you hope the price goes up. If the price goes down you lose money on your investment. Hypothetically, if the company you bought stock in went bankrupt, you could lose all of your money (the stock price would go to US$0). One way to hedge against this loss would be to buy a put option (option to sell) at or below US$100 per share. Let's say you buy a put option with a strike price of US$90 per share. If the price of your original stock goes to US$0, you would still have a put option at US$90, which would let you sell your share for US$90 instead of zero. With your option hedge, you've only lost US$10 instead of US$100. Of course, you had to buy that put option and have spent a bit more for insurance. So, in the event that your stock went up, you would in aggregate make less money because you bought your hedge. The amount less that you would make, though, would have to do with the market price of your put option and how many people on markets think your stock is going to zero.

hedge fund: *Hedge fund* is a generic term for a company that exists to invest money according to some strategy or constraint. The huge variety of strategies that hedge funds employ make them hard to typify, though a few qualities are perhaps worth noting. Hedge funds generally don't take control over the things they invest in (as in, say, private equity investing). Hedge funds tend to make liquid investments, that is, investments that they can sell if they need to. Hedge funds also tend to have some sort of strategy, logic, or charismatic executive that allows them to brand themselves and drive their investing decisions. Hedge funds also tend to invest (mostly) other people's money.

implied volatility: Whereas how much a financial instrument's price has moved around in the past (its historic volatility) is measurable, present and future volatility are not. Given that present and future volatility are key variables in the pricing of options, market people often need to guess at present and future volatility of a financial instrument in order to come up with a defensible price. These guesses are called "implied volatility" and refer to a measure of volatility that is "implied" by other observable market features.

investor: An investor is someone who makes a bet on the direction of some financial instrument and hopes to profit from that bet. Within finance, people often make distinctions between different sorts of investors. Some examples: "Retail" investors are imagined as uninformed nonprofessional people investing their own money (sometimes derisively referred to as "dumb money"). "Institutional" investors, such as pension funds or sovereign wealth funds, are imagined as slow moving, big-position-taking investors who make educated though often conservative decisions imagining a long time horizon for returns to come in.

layering: See spoofing.

liquidity: On a market, liquidity means that people are freely able to buy and sell things. If there is no liquidity, you can't sell and there is no one to buy from. Many financial systems are set up around the idea that liquidity is a virtue and should be encouraged by all sorts of structural inducements (e.g., an exchange paying market makers rebates to trade) and market innovations (like high-frequency or high-speed trading).

long: A long position is a hope that some financial instrument will go up. If you are long on a stock, you hope its price will go up.

margin: Despite contemporary markets giving the appearance of near instant transactions between buyers and sellers, there is a whole infrastructure beyond the actual act of exchange that insures that people who buy financial instruments both pay for them and get them, and people who sell financial instruments dispatch them and receive money for them. This whole process is known as "clearing" or "market clearing"; it's extremely important (but a bit beyond the scope of this book). In order to ensure clearing, market participants post "margin" accounts, or ready piles of money to insure against problems in completing their obligations as market participants. Let's say you click a buy order on some exchange, but when clearing comes you don't have the money to buy the stock. That money could plausibly come from your margin account to ensure a smooth transaction. Also, if you have trouble paying for the things you buy, your margin requirements are likely to go up. Exchanges can change margin requirements often and quickly in response to their sense of market risk and the creditworthiness of given market participants.

market maker: A market maker is a special sort of market participant who seeks not to make bets on the direction of a given financial instrument but rather to always be present as both a buyer and seller to facilitate market liquidity. Their money, in theory, comes not from directional bets but rather from pocketing the monetary spread between bid and the ask/offer of a financial instrument. Put another way, if you buy low and then sell back slightly higher, that difference that you make is the "spread." Market makers also often collect fees from exchanges that encourage making specific types of trades ("rebates"). They collect wealth pennies and nickels at a time. Market-making firms are often highly specialized and have different margin requirements and regulatory requirements than other market participants. There is a distinction between designated or formal market makers, who are registered with exchanges and abide by rules and receive rewards for behaving a certain way, and informal market makers, who pursue market making as a strategy to make money but are not registered as such.

NASDAQ: Originally, NASDAQ stood for the National Association of Security Dealers Automated Quotations. It is an umbrella company for a number of public stock exchanges (many with some version of NASDAQ in their name). Historically, NASDAQ was the exchange for tech companies.

NYSE: NYSE (pronounced "nye-see") is short for the New York Stock Exchange and is owned by an umbrella company, the International Exchange. Historically, the NYSE was the dominant stock exchange and, as of this writing, it remains the largest stock exchange in the world in terms of the market capitalization of stocks originating and listed on the NYSE.

option: An option is a financial instrument that allows someone to buy or sell something at a set price by a fixed date. There are two basic types of options: "call options" that allow you to buy stock at a given strike price, and "put options" that allow you to sell options at a given strike price. Often traders simply refer to options as "calls" or "puts." American options can be exercised at any time up to their expiration date. European options can only be exercised on the expiration date. Much of the options talk in this book is about American options. Generally, options on a given financial instrument have a calendar of expiration dates that extends two years into the future at uneven intervals (more close expiration dates, fewer expiration dates as time recedes into the future).

order book: The order book is the way stock prices and quantities are displayed in present-day financial exchanges. An order book displays bids to buy and offers to sell (as well as quantities on offer) in descending price order. On markets, there never is a fixed price but rather a constant auction in which traders are offering various prices/quantities at a number of price levels. An order book is said to be deep when there are a lot of orders at each price level.

order stacking: See spoofing.

order type: When someone decides to buy or sell some sort of financial product on some manner of exchange, they generally have a choice in the attributes of the order they will send either directly to an exchange or to an exchange via their broker. The most basic types of orders are "market" orders and "limit" orders. Market orders instruct a broker to buy or sell something at whatever the "market" price is. "Limit" orders instruct brokers to buy or sell something given some manner of constraint on price. Often, limit orders can "rest" until their parameters are satisfied. Building on this basic logic are a myriad of order types that play with time, size, rate of delivery, relative hiddenness, relation to other prices, and so on, that exist across different brokerage platforms and at specific exchanges.

PnL/profit and loss: PnL (pronounced "pee-en-el") is short for profit and loss and is a method for analyzing a group's or individual's trading behavior by describing what they have bought and sold that made and lost money. PnL is also taken as a numerical shorthand for how some aggregate trading activity is going.

portfolio: A portfolio is the collection of investments an individual or group has.

position: Position is (1) a way to refer a specific financial instrument that someone owns and the hopes they have for it (e.g., what position they have on, say, Apple stock); (2) a more general way to refer to a set of related financial instruments that a trader or firm owns that add up to a general sense of how a sector, industry, market, or financial instrument will play out and a "positional" bet related to that general sense; and (3) an even more general way to refer to the lean of an entire portfolio in relation to some feature of financial markets. The metaphoric sense of position, as a specific role or place in a military campaign or in some sport, is helpful here, as a trader's or investor's position is always relative to markets, the other people they are interacting or competing with, and the trader's or investor's hope for the future. Finally, sometimes, position is simply a synonym for an opinion about a financial instrument.

publicly traded: A publicly traded company is one whose stock trades on some public stock exchange. By contrast, one wouldn't be able to buy shares in a private company on public exchanges. Publicly traded companies are regulated differently from private companies and have all manner of disclosure and accounting requirements. The idea is that investors are supposed to be able to know about how publicly traded companies are doing.

puts and calls: See "calls and puts."

rebate: A small fee for a trade that an exchange sends to some traders to encourage certain kinds of behavior. For example, if an exchange wanted to have more inventory on its order books, it might pay a rebate of one cent per posted order that a market maker offers for sale on their exchange.

S&P 500: The S&P 500 is a collection of five hundred large, publicly traded companies that tend to do a lot of business in the United States. The companies are currently chosen by the company S&P Dow Jones Indices. People often take this index as a proxy for the health of financial markets and/or the health of the US economy.

SEC: The Securities and Exchange Commission is one of two major government regulators of financial markets in the United States. The SEC has jurisdiction over the financial markets for stocks and options as well as publicly traded companies.

short: Metaphorically, a short position is a bet that some financial instrument will go down in price. "Short" also refers to a specific type of trade in which someone (1) borrows a financial instrument from someone for a nominal fee; (2) sells that financial instrument; (3) buys the financial instrument back when the price goes down; (4) returns the financial instrument to the original owner; and (5) pockets the difference in the price they sold the financial instrument for and the price at which they bought it back. This particular type of trade is risky and generally requires a large margin account. If the price of the financial instrument goes up between selling and buying back, the short seller could lose a lot of money.

spoofing: Spoofing is the general term for an illegal form of market manipulation in which someone makes an order on an exchange that they don't intend to fill. The point of sending an order that one does not wish to fill is to give the illusion of market activity and interest and then to exploit others when they chase these phantoms. Depending on how the spoof occurs, it might garner a more specialized term such as *layering* or *order stacking*, which refer to various sorts of accumulations of spoofed orders in an order book, meant, again, to give an impression of market activity and interest that ultimately don't exist. It's worth further noting that there are all sorts of legitimate reasons to cancel orders before they can be fulfilled. Given that, it can be difficult to distinguish between honest cancellations and nefarious spoofing. Insofar as regulators or prosecutors want to catch and punish would-be spoofers, they are faced with the often-daunting task of proving intent.

Spooz: *Spooz* is a slang term for futures based on the S&P 500 Index.

spread: On financial exchanges, the price and quantity of financial instruments are listed in descending order on an order book. One side of the order book (the top half) lists the asks/offers to sell; the bottom half lists the bids to buy (remember, always buy low and sell high, so the bids to buy will be lower than the asks/offers to sell). In between the highest bid and the lowest ask/offer is some amount of monetary space—this is the spread. In contemporary stock or equities exchanges, the minimum increment of price movement ("tick size") for a stock price is generally a penny. For options, the minimum increment of price movement is (usually) a nickel. Market makers collect the spread as profit for their market-making activity.

SPY: SPY is an ETF made up of S&P 500 company stock.

stock: A stock is a fractional ownership share of a business. Often stocks grant the holder some claim on company profits (in the form of dividends) as well as some form of voting or governance right in the company.

theta: In order to price a stock option, traders use a modification of the Black Scholes Merton equation (which itself is derived from a physics equation used to measure Brownian particle motion). Various Greek letters stand for calculus manipulations (partial derivatives) of the Black Scholes Merton equation, which are meant to convey something of a relationship between an option and its underlying asset. Theta refers to the time decay of an option contract. Put another way, theta refers to the tendency for an option to change in value over time as its expiration date approaches and uncertainty around pricing goes away.

trader: For the market makers in this book, a trader is distinct from an investor in that a trader simply seeks to make markets and not take investment positions.

vega: In order to price a stock option, traders use a modification of the Black Scholes Merton equation (which itself is derived from a physics equation used to measure Brownian particle motion). Various Greek letters stand for calculus manipulations (partial derivatives) of the Black Scholes Merton equation, which are meant to convey something of a relationship between an option and its underlying asset. Vega speaks to the relationship between an option's price and the volatility of its underlier.

VIX: The VIX (volatility index) is a number put out by the CBOE. It's meant to be a numerical heuristic for how turbulent equity markets are and is calculated using options on the S&P 500 Index. Financial service firms also have created financial products that change price depending on the VIX number. These products can function as portfolio insurance because they change price in predictable ways when markets are volatile and uncertain.

volatility: Volatility is some relative measurement for how much the price of a financial instrument moves around. See also "implied volatility."

Notes

Preface

1. All informant names are pseudonyms.
2. As this book was in peer review, the US Securities and Exchange Commission announced another series of potential rule changes that would require, among other things, a guarantee of "best execution" for retail traders and that might allow for fractional penny tick size (for reporting on these changes see FT Reporters 2022; for the proposed rules, see United States Securities and Exchange Commission 2022a and 2022b). What exactly "execution," and "tick size" mean as well as some possible effects of these changes will become apparent over the course of this book. That said, I can guarantee that these changes will shift the structure of the larger trading environment for the subjects of this book.
3. For a somewhat similar periodization of finance studies, though one that also offers a multitude of potential future directions of study, see Samman et al. (2022).

Chapter One

1. NB: This is the definition of "American"-style stock options. European-style stock options have an exclusive, fixed date on which they must be exercised.
2. As this book went through review, the CBOE announced that they would create a new version of the VIX index. Whereas historically the VIX had been a snapshot of volatility over a thirty-day period, CBOE felt that this relatively longer time horizon was not as useful for a new generation of retail day traders and the markets they were creating. Given that, CBOE now offers a one-day VIX volatility index. Nicholas Megaw (2023) reporting for the *Financial Times* explains the difference that the one-day VIX would make:

    > The Vix1d's short-term focus is expected to make it much more volatile than the 30-day original. In the days following Silicon Valley Bank's collapse last month, the Vix jumped from 19 to 26.5 — above its long-term average, but nowhere near the levels normally associated with panic. The Vix1d, in contrast, would have leapt from 15.3 to 40.2.

3. Common sense would have that the price of the underlying asset would lead or direct the price of a derivative such as a future or an option. If a stock's price changes, then we can imagine that its option price should change accordingly. In similar fashion, we might reasonably assume that there is no reason for an option's price to change if the price of an underlying stock has not changed. However, a number of my informants echoed academic research that suggests that at best this directional relationship is questionable, and more probably it's the case that speculation on, for example, futures markets often leads price movements in underlying assets (e.g., Chan 1992; Frino and West 2002; MacKenzie 2021).

4. This calculus-based transformation is also known as a "derivative equation."

5. It's worth noting that around the COVID-19 pandemic, the CME's clearing house switched from Black Scholes to a "Bachelier" options pricing model (CME Clearing 2020). The reason was that a number of futures had reached negative prices. Black Scholes assumes a log-normal distribution and as such doesn't go negative. Futures can go negative in the event that it costs more to store something (like oil) than it does to buy it. Essentially, the negative price is paying someone to store whatever commodity you're buying a future or an option on. Presumably, options or futures without physical delivery, that are settled in cash, like S&P 500 futures or options, wouldn't have this problem and wouldn't go negative.

6. As we've seen, one topic bleeds into another, and the conversations Jeff and his team have with each other have multiple overlapping topics and, often, no obvious start or stop. Given that, demarcation of conversational chunks by subject matter is tricky, and this sort of chunking should be taken basically as an expedient operationalization on my part: it gives me something to work with. The chunks don't necessarily indicate the start or stop of an exchange, just a rough boundary around a topic that someone is swearing about.

7. Given that I'm claiming that Jeff and his team swear "a lot," one may reasonably ask, what counts for "a lot"? Perhaps 694 instances of *fuck* across around one thousand pages are actually not that many. While I haven't found an absolute answer to this question of frequency, or some other spoken corpus to which I might compare my observations, I have found it is helpful to make a few internal comparisons to illustrate relative frequency. To give some sense of how often *fuck* comes up, I think it may be of use to compare its occurrence to that of some common modifying adjectives that also occur in the trading room. After all, we might argue that *fuck*, writ large and metaphorically, is one big, English-language conversational modifier that very quickly can come to typify a register of some language.

   Now, a few caveats are warranted. First, these words, as sampled here, function exclusively as adjectives. As noted elsewhere in the text, *fuck* functions as a verb, an interjection, and an idiomatic phrasal component, among other things, in addition to functioning as an adjective. If we're only counting *fuck* as a modifying adjective, we get only 241 occurrences, a distant seventh place to *good*, *right*, *little*, *new*, *only*, and *bad*. Second, modifiers don't show up exclusively. The appearance of a "non-fuck" modifier does not preclude the inclusion of a *fuck* in the same utterance or string of conversation. *Fuck* comes up so often that it does in fact co-occur in conversation with any number of these other adjectives. Third, other forms of compound modification are possible. For instance, if something is "not good," this sort of usage counts toward *good*'s stats. Given that *good* can be negatively modified in this way, we should not necessarily interpret *good*'s frequency as necessarily suggesting a subterranean vein of positivity in the trading room.

Non-*fuck* adjectives

Adjective	Frequency of occurrence
Good	583
Right	409
Little	322
New	294
Only	280
Bad	254
Sure	217
Better	146
Hard	145
Different	137
Small	128
Whole	123
Great	109
Best	100
Possible	78
Early	71
Clear	55
Easy	46
Strong	43
Worst	42
Free	37
Worse	34
Important	30
True	27
Large	26
Young	22
Recent	15

So, setting aside those caveats, *fuck* as a word comes up more frequently than any common adjective and far more frequently than most. It's telling that *fuck* is used more often than *good* or *bad, clear, possible,* or even *sure.* Imagine taking a politician's speech and editing it such that the word *fuck* has to occur more often than the use of any of these common adjectives. Or even more simply, imagine that for every time that a politician used the word *good* (say, "a good life," "a good home," "a good friend," or a "good country"), or whatever adjective they like most, that politician would also have to add a *fuck* of *any* variety to their speech. While it might be hard to quantify, we can be pretty sure that this sort of experiment in speech writing would switch the register of the politician's speech.

8. Anthropologists have noted elsewhere (e.g., Ho 2009; Fisher 2012; Souleles 2019b, 33–61) that many social norms in finance are white and male and exclude people of color and women. Language use is obviously part of this maintenance of white and male space and the exclusion of women. Given that, we might read the use of swearing in trading as an extension of this sort of boundary maintenance. Kiesling (2001) pointed out that white American college fraternity members repetitively use the way they describe and narrate their own actions as a means to aggressively assert forms of male dominance in a variety of social settings. Given that swearing allows for exceptional expressions of anger, frustration, and contempt, it's not much of a stretch to see an extension of Kiesling's observations in the trading room. However, as the following chapters on technology will point out, these verbal pyrotechnics don't always work to assert the sort of dominance traders might aspire to, as compared, to say, the way *fuck* might be part of a sort of an effective, feminist political rage (Wood 2019).

9. One further note: the swearing wasn't terribly artful either (as opposed to Cruz 2019). I noticed no premium put on linguistic innovation or creativity. All the instances of swearing that I heard I was familiar with as both a native speaker of English and someone familiar with most of the registers of English you would associate with male, college-educated, professional, urban-living, finance people.

Chapter Two

1. Incidentally, Zach actually started his career as a floor trader as well, although he didn't like it that much and transitioned to being a computer guy.

2. I came across this Jackson/Piipuu reference in a roundabout way that bears relating. At one point in the writing process I asked my colleague Matthew Archer whether he was aware of any literature on people being angry with technology. I poked around a bit and found stuff on new technology and technological adaptation, but nothing specifically on anger. Archer said no, but then a bit later he got back to me with two citations: the Jackson (2002) article and the master's thesis by Merilin Piipuu (2017) called "The Mobile Phone in the Hands of the Nepalese People: A Humanistic Perspective of Technology." Though anger is only one feature of the relationship that Piipuu describes, Piipuu makes use of Jackson's argument in a way that I found inspiring and followed in this chapter. Merilin Piipuu, if you read this—thank you!

Chapter Three

1. See Borch and Min (2022) for a generalized account of these different attitudes toward automated trading.

2. This is "first generation" algorithmic trading according to Borch and Min (2022, 1).

3. "Second generation" algorithmic trading in Borch and Min's typology (2022, 1).

4. Again, see Borch and Min (2022) for a typology and more thorough explanation of different sorts of machine-learning systems in finance.

5. Ted Chiang (2023a) suggests that while a computer system autonomously making itself smarter is a common aspiration for automated computer systems, it's unclear that this sort of machine "learning" can ever make a system "smarter." At stake is a basic interpretation of what learning computers are actually doing. Chiang suggests

that because computers are basing their future behavior and rules for conduct on an accumulation of past information, at best you'll receive something generic and conventional. In this way of reasoning, "thinking" machines are actually knowledge compressors, connection mappers, speedy actors, and plagiarism engines. It's worth noting, too, that LINUS functions by virtue of the extremely close maintenance of a large team of skilled workers.

6. The following picks up on a line of metaphorical observation that Borch and Min (n.d.) also analyzed, working independently and in parallel with the same project data set.

7. Remember, they're talking to Min and Borch, who are sociologists; I remain an anthropologist.

8. This observation of skilled traders supervising a machine-learning system parallels observations Borch and Min (n.d.) made and comes from work with a common data pool.

Chapter Four

I. The way traders describe a market is odd for an anthropologist, let alone an economic anthropologist. A bit of clarification might help the more specialized or just curious reader. Technically and comparatively, we might understand a market as *a place or occasion for the patterned redistribution of things, wealth, or people*. It's worth noting, too, that I am not defining a market exclusively as a price-finding technology—though price is one way we might understand how humans ascribe value. I am also not defining a market as an exclusively capitalist technology, as the last four hundred or so years of the rise of industrial capitalism is not the only context in which markets occur (take the Aztec empire as one spectacular noncapitalist example [Smith 2011, 5, "The Commercial Economy," 108–27]).

Given the broad and comparative definition of a market that I'm suggesting, we can find markets across numerous human societies, capitalist and otherwise, often at the place where different sorts of people meet. Given this sort of definition, too, ethnographers and social analysts have produced many closely observed accounts of markets, explaining the way that people gather, evaluate, and redistribute things, wealth, or people (Mauss's [2000] essay on the gift is one of anthropology's canonical theorizations of this process [see Graeber 2001]). Moreover, analysts have also observed the ways that markets often reinscribe and reinforce the values and priorities of particular groups of people in the larger society and can become a venue for this sort of valorization.

Theodore *Bestor's (2004) book *Tsukiji: The Fish Market at the Center of the World* is a canonical example of this sort of scholarship. Here *Bestor describes the operation of the fish market—how it consists of a wholesale auction market, as well as a large network of retail stalls. He also describes how *Tsukiji's* transactions and market operations are able to index a form of small-scale, urban capitalism that had become in other parts of Tokyo eclipsed by the glass skyscrapers of global capitalism. Beyond this he traces the way that the evaluation of fish and the curation of consumer taste that this evaluation entails shapes both local Japanese and global preferences for seafood. What's key to this analysis is that the market processes that *Bestor describes—the gathering, evaluation, and distribution of fish, people, and money—do all this social work. In this way markets are a process by which people both shape themselves and reenact specific values and possibilities for being people generally and being Japanese specifically in an ongoing way.

Ethnographic social scientists have done the sort of work that *Bestor did in a variety of contexts, from Texas livestock auctions (Boeck 1990) to French public grocery markets (de la Pradelle 1995) to the computerized networked auction market eBay (Hillis, Petit, and Epley 2006). By my definition, too, the various financial markets and exchanges that TradeCo and Bradford operate on are clearly markets (see also Hertz 1998 or Zaloom 2006). Contemporary financial markets all gather wealth and companies, or wealth and derivatives, evaluate them, and redistribute them according to various trader and investor desires and knowledge. Take a stock exchange (say NASDAQ) as a specific example of one of these financial markets: in a stock market like NASDAQ, wealth in the form of money/capital meets ownership stakes in firms. Via an auction process mediated by traders like those at TradeCo and machines like LINUS, some ascription of value emerges (an ever-shifting price) on a server in a suburb of New York City. People on these markets redistribute wealth and ownership and keep the whole financial capitalist system going.

So, technically, financial markets are just one of a class of human phenomena that anthropologists like me have no problem studying comparatively and calling a "market." This specialist definition of a market, though, is at odds with how traders use the exact same word. Their "markets" can be one type of my markets. They use the word *market* to describe a much more specific entity—the marketscape of financial capitalism on which capital, companies, and risk all churn. In turn, this is what I'll spend my time describing—markets from their point of view. But I'll draw on larger insights from the anthropology of markets as I go, specifically, when I talk about the sort of people and ideas that markets create and allow.

Two further notes—one problem in anthropology and the social sciences more generally is that we often take our theoretical terms of analysis from the people we study or our own cultural contexts. Here, the market becomes both a specific entity that traders act on and try to understand as well as a generic human activity attested in multiple times and at multiple places. I don't know that there is much to do about this—plenty of other words can mean two things, after all, and we seem to cope just fine. But it is important to acknowledge the bias that comes with importing terms in this way. Still, it's worth acknowledging, and perhaps working a bit to allay confusion, particularly of the more specialist reader.

Finally, readers may have noted that I put an asterisk in front of Theodore Bestor's name. That's intentional because it's not clear what to do with him as an academic source, despite the depth, quality, and reach of his work. While writing this book, James S. Bikales in the *Harvard Crimson* (2020) reported on years of sexual harassment allegations against a number of senior anthropologists, one of whom was Bestor. Bikales notes, "In 2018, a Harvard investigation found Bestor committed two counts of sexual misconduct during an interaction with a female professor at a 2017 conference at UCLA. Harvard's Faculty of Arts and Sciences disciplined Bestor for the incident, but allowed him to return to work before completing required sanctions." The gist of the article is that not only had some senior academics abused their authority to sexually coerce and harass people but their elite status protected them. Given all this, what to do with Bestor? One way to deal with the disjuncture between work that feels foundational and the dubious moral standing of the author is to, well, to not bury the bad stuff. Bestor both made contributions to the field and seems to have abused his power, power that, circularly and neatly, allowed him to make his contributions. These asterisks and this aside are an attempt to not bury the bad stuff (see also Souleles 2020c).

2. Unicorns are venture capital-funded companies that have at least a US$1 billion valuation.
3. Strikes mean the numerical value of the VIX on a given contract.

Chapter Five

1. When I say cultural or relational or human meaning data, I am referring to a very specific operationalization of the culture concept. Most simply this understanding of culture sees culture as shared knowledge, metaphors, or symbols that a group of people use to communicate with each other and understand the world. Alternately, shared knowledge, metaphors, or symbols might also be understood as the common ground of friction and politics that characterize a society. Either way, culture understood as this type of shared knowledge/meaning has specific knowable attributes for the people who study it. Moreover, these attributes are distinct from more commonly encountered statistical or individual case-based knowledge. For an excellent explanation of the use of this sort of distinction, see Handwerker and Wozniak (1997).

It's a bit beyond the scope of this modest note to write a primer on the distinction between relational data and individual case data (the first few chapters of Russ Bernard's 2017 textbook *Research Methods in Anthropology* are a good start, though), or to harmonize this operationalization of the culture concept with all the other ways that anthropologists understand social meaning. That said, an example might help.

If I were curious about why high schoolers started smoking, I could ask a sophomore to name all the reasons people generally start smoking. We could imagine them saying: "to fit in," "to look cool," "to help with anxiety," "to lose weight," "because someone important in my life does it," "people were doing it at a party," "boredom," and so on (perhaps you can come up with a few more). Now, imagine that we went on to ask another student at the same high school the same question. And we did this a few more times. It's easy to imagine that we would exhaust the inventory of interpretive scenarios or explanations that people have in their head for explaining why people start smoking, given that people at this high school probably exist in some sort of a shared cultural scene. Moreover, it probably doesn't matter where we start interviewing in the high school or how we pick the next person with whom to talk. These explanations only work because people, in some odd cultural way, agree that they're plausible and collectively and tacitly maintain their validity. This is cultural, shared, relational, meaning data.

Now, if we took that same question, that question about the onset of smoking, and asked an individual, "When did you start smoking?" or if we wanted to know whether high schoolers smoke or not, we would need to randomly sample whatever we defined as our population, and our responses would be subject to the rules of statistical estimation. This data would be unique to the individual's biography and life course and would only make patterned sense in the context of an adequate random sample of the population we have decided that individual comes from (say, smokers of high school age). This is individual or case-based data (and, incidentally, if gathered in the context of a survey or interview is subject to all sorts of recall biases; Bernard et al. 1984). Appreciating this distinction allows for sharper research questions when people study people.

One further note—often when people talk about research on humans, they talk about data being either "qualitative" or "quantitative." "Qualitative" data is meant to be interpretive data with which one does not use numbers or counting, and "quantitative" data is meant to be enumerated and involve math. Within the university (and perhaps society at large), quantitative data has prestige, gets listened to, receives grants, and serves to calcify disciplinary distinctions that exclude messy and unreliable qualitative data. In turn, qualitative data has a monopoly on truth, beauty, and the things that matter. Qualitative data allows researchers the self-satisfaction that they are doing something important even if the jerks with the grants and the prestige don't think so. Given the above distinction between meaning and case data I've presented, I suspect you may have picked up that I think this "qual-quant" distinction is counterproductive nonsense. Both forms of data involve quantification (just according to different sampling norms), and both forms of data involve moments of the interpretive evaluation of significance (some level of acceptable saturation in one case or hitting an arbitrary, disciplinarily agreed on "p value" in another). Perpetuating this distinction stands in the way of doing good research and keeps academics pitted against one another when we all know the real enemies are racism; misogyny; settler colonialism; capitalist exploitation; inaction in the face of climate change; resurgent, politically viable ethnofascism; and the University of Chicago economics department.

2. Exchanges even compete with each other for market share (see Asgari 2023).

3. Those interested in auction and game mechanics will be pleased to hear that there is a lively economics and game theory literature on auction design, and how different designs lead to different allocative outcomes. Milgrom's (2004) *Putting Auction Theory to Work* is both a nice primer on game theory and auction and a good catalog of the various ways that auctions have been put to applied use. Closer to home, Haim Bodek and Stanislaw Dolgopolov (2015) have self-published a selection of critical essays about market design and the fragmentation of the exchange environment with special attention to how this privileges some market actors and hinders and taxes others. I cite them not necessarily to endorse their conclusions but to provide an example where this sort of conversation about auction structure and design meets up with financial markets and exchanges. And, within financial academia, Budish, Cramton, and Shim (2015) have suggested an auction mechanism to mitigate some of the excessed of the technological arms race costs in high-frequency trading.

4. Whatever you do, don't count your money when you're sitting at the table. There'll be time enough for counting, when the dealing's done.

5. David Pinzur (2016) offers another comparative case of market design. He compares commodity exchanges—nineteenth-century cotton markets in New Orleans and wheat futures markets in Chicago. He notes that one of the reasons that Chicago was able to survive and thrive is that it put in place mechanisms for standardizing the grading of wheat for futures contracts. By contrast, New Orleans relied on specialists to examine each lot and slowed down potential trading. Pinzur suggests that this sort of distinction is part of the reason that Chicago commodity trading still exists today.

6. An anonymous reviewer was kind enough to point out that this characterization may verge on a sort of sales pitch for the Shanghai stock exchange that overstates its differences between it and, say, US stock exchanges. To take one example, while stock exchanges in the US do not clear trades in-house, there is a congressionally mandated, single national clearing and settlement systems operated by the Depository Trust and Clearing Corporation. Given that, it's not entirely clear what difference it would make to have either clearing in-house at an exchange or managed for all exchanges by a single independent organization. The larger point, though, still stands, namely, that

market design is not innocent and structures the financial arena in such a way as to privilege some, disadvantage others, and advance normative, often moral agendas.

7. An anonymous reviewer has pointed out to me that it's difficult to know why exactly an order gets pulled from an order book and that there are all sorts of legitimate reasons to pull orders that don't necessarily have to with latency arbitrage or other high-speed trading strategies.

8. Even this lack of control is historically specific. Not too long ago, most stock exchanges were collectively owned and governed by member traders and not, as they are today, publicly traded companies in their own right (Pardo-Guerra 2019).

Chapter Six

1. Target is a large, nationwide, American big-box store that sells relatively affordable food, clothing, home goods, electronics, and sporting goods.

2. Another way to look at this might just be that someone is making use of VIX as portfolio insurance like it was more or less designed for—something else happened somewhere in their investments, and now they need the benefit of the value of their VIX contracts. This sort of charitable framing, though, did not come up in our conversation.

3. Shorting stocks is a little complicated. Let me explain it by a hypothetical example—let's say a hedge fund is convinced that GameStop's stock is going to go down and they want to make some money on this decline. First, our hedge fund will borrow some GameStop stock for a nominal fee. Let's say that GameStop is trading at US$10 per share. GameStop will then pay US$1 to Citadel to borrow a share, sell it at the market price of US$10, and wait for the price to go down. Now, because our hedge fund borrowed a share, they have to give it back at some point, and to do so, they need to buy another share. Let's say the hedge fund has a month to return the share. If at the end of that month GameStop stock has indeed declined to US$5 per share, the hedge fund could buy the share at that price, return the share to Citadel and make a US$4 dollar profit on shorting (remember the fee for borrowing). If, however, the price of the stock goes up, our hedge fund has the potential to be extremely screwed. If they borrowed a stock at US$10 per share, sold it, and then had to buy it back at US$350 per share, they will have to pay US$340 more than what they borrowed it for. And the thing about short selling is our hedge fund has to buy the stock so that they can return to whomever they borrowed it from. In the same way that creating an option contract forces TradeCo to hedge, opening a short position forces the hedge fund to buy the stock back.

4. This trading maneuver, buying equity options to force market makers to buy stock in order to hedge their options position, is also known as a "gamma squeeze."

5. On YouTube there is a hip-hop song produced by a trader who died young and used to work in one of the CBOE pits. Periodically the traders would play the song in their rotation of music they would put on at different market moments in memory of their fallen colleague. Here is the song: https://www.youtube.com/watch?v=0mWFluQHVlE.

Chapter Eight

1. https://www.tesla.com/about.

2. In their minds the 2007/2008 financial crisis was one potential watershed in which markets seem to function qualitatively different on either side of that event. The exact

cause of this, though, was not quite clear. It could be due to some combination of central bank action, increasing electrification and automation, shifting bank risk parameters, changes in the form of regulation, or some combination of all of the above. Some traders will refer to the market precipitate of all these inputs as a "market regime" in which markets start to exist in a specific historic era according to some relatively predictable patterns.

3. Upon review of a draft of this chapter, Walt corrected me, noting that in the short run there is no aggregate bias in market direction, whereas, yes, in the long run there seems to be documented upward bias to equity markets. This is an important distinction for a market maker to note because they're not interested in the direction of markets per se, they're interested in trading in such a way as to provide liquidity and, again, collect the spread.

4. A more thorough, systematic treatment of this sort of market weirdness can be found in a *Financial Times* article written by Robin Wigglesworth called "Are Markets Somehow 'Broken'?" (2019).

5. Though some other traders maintained it was more widespread, to my knowledge only the central banks of Israel, Sweden, and Japan have acknowledged equity purchases as part of their balance sheets (Powell 2019; Kennedy 2019; see also Kremmidas 2019).

6. Jeff actually gave me one of the shirts and suggested I wear it on Fridays as it would bring good luck, market rallies, and profits. Of course, I did my part to help the American dream.

7. A Norwegian colleague of mine told me that, back in 2012, his then twenty-four-year-old brother spent six months on a study abroad in the US in San Diego. Upon arrival and in pursuit of the American dream, my colleague's brother rented a house on the beach, bought a jeep, and then two Jet Skis, one pink and the other teal.

8. In this sense, *normality* has a specific resonance: options pricing, as noted elsewhere, is governed by the Black Scholes Merton equation—an equation, derived from physics, designed to give an option's price. The Black Scholes Merton equation assumes a lognormal, that is, a regular distribution or prices. Prices are not normally distributed in the real world, and a lot of the value that TradeCo's traders bring to their work is the ability to price "nonlognormal" events.

9. The group generally has a pit trader (Lee Foster) in one of the exchanges on which they trade. However, Lee was away on his honeymoon, so Jeff was covering for him. Not everyone in the firm was certified to trade in the pit.

10. Walt is asking about a debt payment that Tesla has coming due. While I was there, there was speculation that Tesla wouldn't be able to make its payment and, therefore, no longer have access to capital. In turn, its stock price would plummet as it would no longer be able to function without credit. Tesla ended up making the payment but did so using a large amount of its cash reserve.

11. Again, options traders' conversations are peppered with Greek symbols that come from the Black Scholes Merton equation and its derivatives, which are all used to price options. When they make a trade that is a bet on a specific aspect of an option's characteristics, they will often refer to the Greek letter referring to that characteristic. Collectively, these are referred to as "The Greeks." In this case, Vega is referring to a stock's sensitivity to price changes given some change in a stock's volatility. Carrying 1,200 Vega means carrying some quantity of options that are reliant on a bet on Vega.

12. Again, Tesla made the payment but dipped into its own cash reserves to do so.

13. Still talking about Tesla: when they talk about individual stock, they will refer to them as a "symbol" or a "name."

14. "Short players" here means investors who are betting on Tesla's stock going down.

15. US$500,000.

16. Elon Musk.

17. Oh boy. In a series of tweets, Elon Musk said that he was going to take Tesla private and buy it out at US$420 per share, which sent the stock soaring. This is a pot reference—either the time of day (4:20 p.m.) or the day of the year (April 20) when you're supposed to get high—"four-twenty." Musk picked 4-20, allegedly, because he had just "gotten into" marijuana and thought his girlfriend, the pop singer Grimes, would find it funny. Partially as a consequence, the SEC wanted to bar Musk from running a publicly traded company (Taylor 2018).

18. One of the features of options and holding options as investments is that their value often degrades over time as a given option price becomes increasingly unlikely over a shorter and shorter time to expiration.

19. BATS is a group of stock exchanges owned by the Chicago Board Options Exchange (CBOE, pronounced "see-boe").

20. The "scanner" is the name of one of TradeCo's proprietary technologies that literally scans options markets for potential trading opportunities.

21. One CNBC analyst claimed that Tesla stock would go up 1,800 percent and was therefore a strong buy. This led Aaron to wonder, "Where do you even get that number?"

22. In a conversation following a draft of this article, Jeff summed up his theory of Tesla around chronic lying. He observed the following: Tesla had never made money in over a decade; lied about its margins; lied about its new products and when they would come to market; lied about being taken over; lied about its waiting lists for products. This doesn't even get to their bizarre accounting practices. One lying example he noted was that in midsummer 2019 Tesla said that there would be full autopilot at the end of the year. He said that they said basically the same thing in 2016, that you would be able to call your car to come and get you. All this added up to a company and a CEO that Jeff saw as compulsive liars. So much of Jeff's frustration came from a belief that these lies should catch up with Tesla and Musk via fundamental business analysis and that markets should be the ones to bring this sort of justice.

Chapter Nine

1. Not two weeks after I wrote this, anthropologist Webb Keane (2020) made similar observations about the pandemic and the Trolley Problem.

References

Abolafia, Mitchel. 1996. *Making Markets: Opportunism and Restraint on Wall Street*. Cambridge, MA: Harvard University Press.

Adams, Michael. 2016. *In Praise of Profanity*. Oxford: Oxford University Press.

Agha, Asif. 2000. "Register." *Journal of Linguistic Anthropology* 9 (1/2): 216–19.

Agha, Asif. 2015a. "Tropes of Slang." *Signs and Society* 3 (2): 306–30.

Agha, Asif. 2015b. "Voice, Footing, Enregisterment." *Journal of Linguistic Anthropology* 15 (1): 38–59.

Anderson, Benedict. 1983. *Imagined Communities: Reflections on the Origin and Spread of Nationalism*. New York: Verso.

Appel, Hannah. 2017. "Toward an Ethnography of the National Economy." *Cultural Anthropology* 32 (2): 294–322.

Asgari, Nikou. 2023. "CBOE Prepares for European Stock Market Listings Grab." *Financial Times*, May 24. https://www.ft.com/content/a491ebd6-d7ce-475f-b80d-8a695f12277d.

Associated Press. 2020. "Trump Says He Intends to Reopen Country in Weeks, Not Months." *New York Times*, March 23. https://nyti.ms/2QHdnGv (no longer posted; accessed, March 27, 2020).

Baker, Wayne E. 1984. "The Social Structure of a National Securities Market." *American Journal of Sociology* 89 (4): 775–811.

Bakhtin, M. M. 1981. *The Dialogic Imagination: Four Essays*. Edited by Michael Holquist and translated by Caryl Emerson and Michael Holquist. Austin: University of Texas Press.

Barley, Stephen R. 1986. "Technology as an Occasion for Structuring: Evidence from Observations of CT Scanners and the Social Order of Radiology Departments." *Administrative Science Quarterly* 31 (1): 78–108.

Bauman, Richard. 2000. "Genre." *Journal of Linguistic Anthropology* 9 (1/2): 84–87.

Bear, Laura, Karen Ho, Anna Tsing, and Sylvia Yanagisako. 2015. "Gens: A Feminist Manifesto for the Study of Capitalism." *Cultural Anthropology*, March 30. https://culanth.org/fieldsights/652-gens-a-feminist-manifesto-for-the-study-of-capitalism/.

Beckert, Jens. 2016. *Imagined Futures: Fictional Expectations and Capitalist Dynamics*. Cambridge, MA: Harvard University Press.

Benanav, Aaron. 2020. *Automation and the End of Work*. London: Verso.

Bernard, H. Russell. 2017. *Research Methods in Anthropology: Qualitative and Quantitative Approaches*. 6th ed. Lanham, MD: Rowman and Littlefield.

Bernard, H. Russell, Peter Killworth, David Kronenfeld, and Lee Sailer. 1984. "The Problem of Informant Accuracy: The Validity of Retrospective Data." *Annual Review of Anthropology* 13: 495–517.

*Bestor, Theodore C. 2004. *Tsukiji: The Fish Market at the Center of the World*. Berkeley: University of California Press.

Beunza, Daniel. 2019. *Taking the Floor: Models, Morals, and Management in a Wall Street Trading Room*. Princeton, NJ: Princeton University Press.

Beunza, Daniel, and David Stark. 2004. "Tools of the Trade: The Socio-technology of Arbitrage in a Wall Street Trading Room." *Industrial and Corporate Change* 13 (2): 369–400.

Beunza, Daniel, and David Stark. 2012. "From Dissonance to Resonance: Cognitive Interdependence in Quantitative Finance." *Economy and Society* 41 (3): 383–417.

Bhupathi, Tara. 2010. "Technology's Latest Market Manipulator? High Frequency Trading: The Strategies, Tools, Risks, and Response." *North Carolina Journal of Law and Technology* 11 (2): 377–400.

Bikales, James S. 2020. "Protected by Decades-Old Power Structures, Three Renowned Harvard Anthropologists Face Allegations of Sexual Harassment." *Harvard Crimson*, May 29. https://www.thecrimson.com/article/2020/5/29/harvard-anthropology-gender-issues/.

Bjerg, Ole. 2011. *Poker: The Parody of Capitalism*. Ann Arbor: University of Michigan Press.

Blythe, Bruce. 2018. "The Electronic Platform That Took Markets Global." *OpenMarkets*, CME group (blog), December 19. https://www.thestreet.com/markets/the-electronic-platform-that-took-markets-global-14815383.

Bodek, Haim, and Stanislaw Dolgopolov. 2015. *The Market Structure Crisis: Electronic Markets, High Frequency Trading, and Dark Pools*. Self-published.

Boeck, George A. 1990. *Texas Livestock Auctions: A Folklife Ethnography*. New York: AMS Press.

Borch, Christian. 2016. "High Frequency Trading, Algorithmic Finance and the Flash Crash: Reflections on Eventalization." *Economy and Society* 45 (3/4): 350–78.

Borch, Christian. 2022. "Machine Learning, Knowledge Risk, and Principal-Agent Problems in Automated Trading." *Technology in Society* 68. https://doi.org/10.1016/j.techsoc.2021.101852.

Borch, Christian, Kristian Bondo Hansen, and Ann-Christina Lange. 2015. "Markets, Bodies, and Rhythms: A Rhythmanalysis of Financial Markets from Open-Outcry Trading to High-Frequency Trading." *Environment and Planning D: Society and Space* 33 (6): 1080–97.

Borch, Christian, and Bo Hee Min. 2022. "Machine Learning and Social Action in Markets: From First- to Second-Generation Automated Trading." *Economy and Society*. https://doi.org/10.1080/03085147.2022.2050088.

Borch, Christian, and Bo Hee Min. N.d. "Socially Explainable AI: Knowledge and Risk in Machine Learning-Based Finance." Unpublished paper.

Borg, Kevin. 1999. "The 'Chauffeur Problem' in the Early Auto Era: Structuration Theory and the Users of Technology." *Technology and Culture* 40 (4): 797–832.

Boyd, Danah, and Kate Crawford. 2011. "Six Provocations for Big Data." Paper presented at the Oxford Internet Institute's A Decade in Internet Time: Symposium on the Dynamics of the Internet and Society, September 21. https://papers.ssrn.com/sol3/papers.cfm?abstract_id=1926431.

Broussard, Meredith. 2018. *Artificial Unintelligence*. Cambridge, MA: MIT Press.

Budish, Eric, Peter Cramton, and John Shim. 2015. "The High-Frequency Trading Arms Race: Frequent Batch Auctions as a Market Design Response." *Quarterly Journal of Economics* 130 (4): 1547–621.

Burrell, Jenna. 2016. "How the Machine 'Thinks': Understanding Opacity in Machine Learning Algorithms." *Big Data and Society* 3 (1): 1–12.

Byrne, Emma. 2018. *Swearing Is Good for You*. New York: W. W. Norton.

Cetina, Karin Knorr, and Urs Bruegger. 2002. "Traders' Engagement with Markets." *Theory, Culture and Society* 19 (5/6): 161–85.

Cetina, Karin Knorr, and Alex Preda. 2007. "The Temporalization of Financial Markets: From Network to Flow." *Theory, Culture and Society* 24 (7/8): 116–38.

Chan, Kalok. 1992. "A Further Analysis of the Lead-Lag Relationship between the Cash Market and Stock Index Futures Market." *Review of Financial Studies* 5 (1): 123–52.

Chiang, Ted. 2023a. "ChatGPT Is a Blurry Jpeg of the Web." *New Yorker*, February 9. https://www.newyorker.com/tech/annals-of-technology/chatgpt-is-a-blurry-jpeg-of-the-web.

Chiang, Ted. 2023b. "Will A.I. Become the New McKinsey?" *New Yorker*, May 4. https://www.newyorker.com/science/annals-of-artificial-intelligence/will-ai-become-the-new-mckinsey.

Chong, Kimberly. 2018. *Best Practice: Management Consulting and the Ethics of Financialization in China*. Durham, NC: Duke University Press.

CME Clearing. 2020. "Switch to Bachelier Options Pricing Model—Effective April 22, 2020." CME Group, advisory 20-171. https://www.cmegroup.com/notices/clearing/2020/04/Chadv20-171.html#pageNumber=1.

Coombs, Nathan. 2016. "What Is an Algorithm? Financial Regulation in the Era of High-Frequency Trading." *Economy and Society* 45 (2): 278–302.

Coyle, Diane. 2015. *GDP: A Brief but Affectionate History*. Rev. and expanded ed. Princeton, NJ: Princeton University Press.

Cruz, Emiliana. 2019. "Swearing and Cursing in San Juan Quiahije Chatino." *Journal of Linguistic Anthropology* 29 (2): 181–87.

de la Merced, Michael J., and Kate Conger. 2019. "Uber I.P.O. Values Ride-Hailing Giant at $82.4 Billion." *New York Times*, May 9. https://www.nytimes.com/2019/05/09/technology/uber-ipo-stock-price.html?auth=login-email&login=email.

de la Pradelle, Michèle. 1995. "Market Exchange and the Social Construction of a Public Space." *French Cultural Studies* 6: 359–71.

Derman, Emanuel. 2004. *My Life as a Quant*. Hoboken, NJ: John Wiley and Sons.

DiFruscia, Kim. 2012. "Work Rage: The Invention of a Human Resource Management Anti-Conflictual Fable." *Anthropology of Work Review* 33 (2): 89–100.

Douglas, Mary. 1966. *Purity and Danger: An Analysis of the Concepts of Pollution and Taboo*. London: Routledge.

Ehrenreich, Barbara. 1989. *Fear of Falling: The Inner Life of the Middle Class*. New York: Twelve.

Fisher, Melissa. 2012. *Wall Street Women*. Durham, NC: Duke University Press.

Frino, Alex, and Andrew West. 2002. "The Lead-Lag Relationship between Stock Indexes and Stock Index Futures Contracts: Further Australian Evidence." *Abacus* 35 (3): 333–41.

FT Reporters. 2022. "Brokers Braced for Big Overhaul of US Stock Trading Rules." *Financial Times*, FT Trading Room, December 16. https://www.ft.com/content/66bb47cb-ab02-4764-90da-6cbc05c53672?shareType=nongift.

Graeber, David. 2001. *Toward and Anthropological Theory of Value: The False Coin of Our Own Dreams*. New York: Palgrave Macmillian.

Guest, Greg, Arwen Bunce, and Laura Johnson. 2006. "How Many Interviews Are Enough? An Experiment with Data Saturation and Variability." *Field Methods* 18 (1): 59–82.

Guyer, Jane. 2007. "Prophecy and the Near Future: Thoughts on Macroeconomic, Evangelical, and Punctuated Time." *American Ethnologist* 34 (3): 409–21.

Handwerker, W. Penn, and Danielle F. Wozniak. 1997. "Sampling Strategies for the Collection of Cultural Data: An Extension of Boas's Answer to Galton's Problem." *Current Anthropology* 38 (5): 869–75.

Hansen, Kristian Bondo. 2021. "Model Talk: Calculative Cultures in Quantitative Finance." *Science, Technology, and Human Values* 46 (3): 600–27.

Hansen, Kristian Bondo, and Christian Borch. 2021. "The Absorption and Multiplication of Uncertainty in Machine-Learning-Driven Finance." *British Journal of Sociology* 72 (4): 1015–29. https://doi.org/10.1111/1468-4446.12880.

Hart, Keith, and Horacio Ortiz. 2014. "The Anthropology of Money and Finance: Between Ethnography and World History." *Annual Review of Anthropology* 43: 465–82.

Harwell, Drew. 2019a. "SEC's Fight with Musk over His Tweets Seems Likely to Go a Few More Rounds." *Washington Post*, March 20, A16.

Harwell, Drew. 2019b. "Tesla's Model Y Is a Car Elon Musk Hopes Will Distract from Everything Else." *Washington Post*, March 15, A19.

Heath, C., M. Jirotka, P. Luff, and J. Hindmarsh. 1994. "Unpacking Collaboration: The Interactional Organization of Trading in a City Dealing Room." *Computer Supported Cooperative Work* 3 (2): 147–65.

Henderson, Richard, and Robin Wigglesworth. 2020. "Fed's Big Boost for BlackRock Raises Eyebrows on Wall Street." *Financial Times*, March 27. https://www.ft.com/content/08b897a5-aadb-40d7-922c-431154ed968a?shareType=nongift.

Heritage, Stuart. 2020. "Boris Johnson's Hero Is the Mayor Who Kept the Beaches Open in *Jaws*: That's Fine by Me." *Guardian*, March 13. https://www.theguardian.com/film/2020/mar/13/boris-johnson-coronavirus-hero-mayor-larry-vaughn-jaws.

Hertz, Ellen. 1998. *The Trading Crowd: An Ethnography of the Shanghai Stock Market.* Cambridge: Cambridge University Press.

Hillis, Ken, Michael Petit, and Nathan Scott Epley. 2006. *Everyday eBay: Culture, Collecting and Desire.* London: Routledge.

Ho, Karen. 2009. *Liquidated: An Ethnography of Wall Street.* Durham, NC: Duke University Press.

Holmes, Douglas. 2014. *An Economy of Words: Communicative Imperatives in Central Banks.* Chicago: University of Chicago Press.

Hughes, Jennifer, and Chris Flood. 2022. "Tesla Shares Lose $85bn in Market Value over Brutal Week." *Financial Times*, December 23. https://www.ft.com/content/c0cb1126-1842-45f2-ad94-2cd75fdbc6bf?shareType=nongift.

Hull, John C. 2018. *Options, Futures, and Other Derivatives.* 10th ed. New York: Pearson.

Hutchins, Edwin. 1995. *Cognition in the Wild.* Cambridge: MIT Press.

Intercontinental Exchange. 2020. "NYSE ARCA Trading Information: Order Types." NYSE spreadsheet. https://www.nyse.com/markets/nyse-arca/trading-info#equities-order-types.

Jackson, Michael. 2002. "Familiar and Foreign Bodies: A Phenomenological Exploration of the Human-Technology Interface." *Journal of the Royal Anthropological Institute*, n.s., 8: 333–46.

Keane, Webb. 2020. "Your Money or Your Life: The Virus, the Economy, and the Trolley Problem." In "Pandemic Diaries," edited by Gabriela Manley, Bryan M. Dougan, and Carole McGranahan. Special issue, *American Ethnologist*, April 21, 2020.

https://www.rebuildingmacroeconomics.ac.uk/post/your-money-or-your-life-the
-virus-the-economy-and-the-trolley-problem.

Kennedy, Robert F. 1968. "Remarks at the University of Kansas, March 18, 1968." John F. Kennedy Presidential Library and Museum. https://www.jfklibrary.org/learn/about -jfk/the-kennedy-family/robert-f-kennedy/robert-f-kennedy-speeches/remarks-at-the -university-of-kansas-march-18-1968.

Kennedy, Simon. 2019. "Central Banks Boost Holdings of Equities beyond $1 Trillion." *Bloomberg*, June 11. https://www.bloomberg.com/news/articles/2019-06-11/central -banks-boostholdings-of-equities-beyond-1-trillion/.

Kiesling, Scott Fabius. 2001. "'Now I Gotta Watch What I Say': Shifting Discourses of Masculinity in Discourse." *Journal of Linguistic Anthropology* 11 (2): 250–73.

Kolhatkar, Sheelah. 2021. "The Big Gamble: Is Robinhood Democratizing Finance or Encouraging Risk?" *New Yorker*, May 17, 30–41.

Kolodny, Lora. 2022. "Tesla Stock Set for 3-for-1 Split after Market Close." CNBC Tech, August 24. https://www.cnbc.com/2022/08/24/tesla-stock-set-for-3-for-1-split-after -market-close.html.

Kremmidas, Tina. 2019. "Central Banks Invest in Equities as Foreign Exchange Reserves Swell." *Canadian Business Journal*, August 14. https://www.cbj.ca/central_banks_invest _in_equities_as_foreign_exchange_reserves_sw/.

Kuiper, Koenraad. 1996. *Smooth Talkers: The Linguistic Performance of Auctioneers and Sportscasters*. Mahwah, NJ: L. Erlbaum Associates.

Lange, Ann-Christina. 2016. "Organizational Ignorance: An Ethnography of High-Frequency Trading." *Economy and Society* 45 (2): 230–50.

Lange, Ann-Christina, Marc Lenglet, and Robert Seyfert. 2019. "On Studying Algorithms Ethnographically: Making Sense of Objects of Ignorance." *Organization* 26 (4): 598–617.

Langlois, Shawn. 2018. "Former Target Manager Aims to Bounce Back with $600,000 Bet against Volatility." *Market Watch*, February 7. https://www.marketwatch.com/story/ former-target-manager-doubles-down-600000-bet-against-volatility-2018-02-07.

Leins, Stefan. 2018. *Stories of Capitalism: Inside the Role of Financial Analysts*. Chicago: University of Chicago Press.

Leonard, Christopher. 2020. "How Jay Powell's Coronavirus Response Is Changing the Fed Forever." *Time*, June 11. https://time.com/5851870/federal-reserve-coronavirus/.

Lewis, Michael. 2015. *Flash Boys: A Wall Street Revolt*. New York: W. W. Norton.

Loder, Asjylyn, and Gunjan Banerji. 2017. "The Snowballing Power of the VIX, Wall Street's Fear Index: Created to Track Expectations of Volatility, It Has Spawned a Giant Trading Ecosystem That Could Magnify Losses When Turbulence Hits." *Wall Street Journal*, June 12.

Lowrie, Ian. 2017. "Algorithmic Rationality: Epistemology and Efficiency in the Data Sciences." *Big Data and Society* 4 (1): 1–13.

MacKenzie, Donald. 2006. *An Engine, Not a Camera: How Financial Models Shape Markets*. Cambridge, MA: MIT Press.

MacKenzie, Donald. 2018a. "'Making,' 'Taking' and the Material Political Economy of Algorithmic Trading." *Economy and Society* 47 (4): 501–23.

MacKenzie, Donald. 2018b. "Material Signals: A Historical Sociology of High-Frequency Trading." *American Journal of Sociology* 123 (6): 1635–83.

MacKenzie, Donald. 2018c. "Short Cuts." *London Review of Books*, January 24.

MacKenzie, Donald. 2019. "Market Devices and Structural Dependency: The Origins and Development of 'Dark Pools.'" *Finance and Society* 5 (1): 1–19.

MacKenzie, Donald. 2021. *Trading at the Speed of Light: How Ultrafast Algorithms Are Transforming Financial Markets*. Princeton, NJ: Princeton University Press.

MacKenzie, Donald, Daniel Beunza, Yuval Millo, and Juan Pablo-Guerra. 2012. "Drilling through the Allegheny Mountains." *Journal of Cultural Economy* 5 (3): 279–96.

Marchese, David. 2020. "David Chang Isn't Sure the Restaurant Industry Will Survive Covid-19." *New York Times Magazine*, Talk, April 5. https://www.nytimes.com/interactive/2020/03/27/magazine/david-chang-restaurants-covid19.html.

Marx, Karl. (1867) 1992. *Capital*, vol. 1, *A Critique of Political Economy*. Translated by Ben Fowkes. New York: Penguin.

Marx, Karl. 1978. "Estranged Labor." In *The Marx Engels Reader*, 2nd ed., edited by Robert C. Tucker, 70–81. New York: W. W. Norton.

Mauss, Marcell. 2000. *The Gift: The Form and Reason for Exchange in Archaic Societies*. Translated by W. D. Halls. New York: W. W. Norton.

McIntosh, Janet. 2021. "Maledictive Language: Obscenity and Taboo Words." In *International Encyclopedia of Linguistic Anthropology*, edited by James Stanlaw. Hoboken, NJ: Wiley Blackwell.

Megaw, Nicholas. 2023. "New Wall Street 'Fear Gauge' to Track Short-Term Market Swings." *Financial Times*, April 23. https://www.ft.com/content/566cd60f-1189-4aee-9333-f665d8ff7a2e.

Mendoza-Denton, Norma. 2008. *Homegirls: Language and Cultural Practice among Latina Youth Gangs*. Malden, MA: Blackwell.

Milgrom, Paul. 2004. *Putting Auction Theory to Work*. Cambridge: Cambridge University Press.

Min, Bo Hee, and Christian Borch. 2022. "Systematic Failures and Organizational Risk Management in Algorithmic Trading: Normal Accidents and High Reliability in Financial Markets." *Social Studies of Science* 52 (2): 277–302.

Mohr, Melissa. 2013. *Holy Shit: A Brief History of Swearing*. Oxford: Oxford University Press.

Molla, Rani. 2021. "When Elon Musk Tweets, Crypto Prices Move." *Vox*, May 18. https://www.vox.com/recode/2021/5/18/22441831/elon-musk-bitcoin-dogecoin-crypto-prices-tesla.

Ortiz, Horacio. 2020. "A Political Anthropology of Finance: Studying the Distribution of Money in the Financial Industry as a Political Process." *Anthropological Theory* 21 (1). https://doi.org/10.1177/1463499620951374.

Ortiz, Horacio. 2021. *The Everyday Practice of Valuation and Investment*. New York: Columbia University Press.

Pardo-Guerra, Juan Pablo. 2010. "Creating Flows of Interpersonal Bits: The Automation of the London Stock Exchange, c. 1955–90." *Economy and Society* 39 (1): 84–109.

Pardo-Guerra, Juan Pablo. 2019. *Automating Finance: Infrastructures, Engineers, and the Making of Electronic Markets*. Cambridge: Cambridge University Press.

Petry, Johannes. 2020. "Financialization with Chinese characteristics? Exchanges, Control and Capital Markets in Authoritarian Capitalism." *Economy and Society* 49 (2): 1–26. https://doi.org/10.1080/03085147.2020.1718913.

Piipuu, Merilin. 2017. "The Mobile Phone in the Hands of the Nepalese People: A Humanistic Perspective of Technology." MA thesis, University of Tartu.

Pinzur, Alex. 2016. "Making the Grade: Infrastructural Semiotics and Derivative Market Outcomes on the Chicago Board of Trade and New Orleans Cotton Exchange, 1856–1909." *Economy and Society* 45 (3/4): 431–53.

Powell, Jamie. 2019. "The ECB Buying Equities: SNORE." *Financial Times*, July 29. https:// ftalphaville.ft.com/2019/07/29/1564403005000/The-ECB-buying-equities-SNORE.

Preda, Alex. 2012. "Interaction and Decisions in Trading." In *The Oxford Handbook of the Sociology of Finance*, edited by Karin Knorr-Cetina and Alex Preda, 152–68. Oxford: Oxford University Press.

Preda, Alex. 2017. *Noise: Living and Trading in Electronic Finance*. Chicago: University of Chicago Press.

Reinicke, Carmen. 2020. "US Jobless Claims Skyrocket to 6.6 Million, Doubling Last Week's Record, as Coronavirus Layoffs Persist." *Business Insider*, April 2. https://www .businessinsider.com/us-weekly-jobless-claims-unemployment-filings-record-labor -market-coronavirus-2020-4?r=US&IR=T.

Riles, Annelise. 2018. *Financial Citizenship: Experts, Publics, and The Politics of Central Banks*. Ithaca, NY: Cornell University Press.

Samman, Amin, Nina Boy, Nathan Coombs, Sandy Hager, Adam Hayes, Emily Rosamond, Leon Wansleben, and Carola Westermeier. 2022. "After the Boom: Finance and Society Studies in the 2020s and Beyond." *Finance and Society* 8 (2): 93–109.

Sample, Tax. 2018. *Working Class Rage: A Field Guide to White Anger and Pain*. Nashville, TN: Abingdon Press.

Schiffrin, Deborah. 1987. *Discourse Markers*. Cambridge: Cambridge University Press.

Schleifer, Theodore. 2019. "Uber Lost an Eye-Popping $5 Billion in a Single Quarter: Wall Street Isn't Happy." *Vox*, August 8. https://www.vox.com/2019/8/8/20793935/uber-q2 -earnings-5-billion-loss.

Seaver, Nick. 2017. "Algorithms as Culture: Some Tactics for the Ethnography of Algorithmic Systems." *Big Data and Society* 4 (2): 1–12.

Seizer, Susan. 2011. "On the Uses of Obscenity in Live Stand-Up Comedy." *Anthropological Quarterly* 84 (1): 209–34.

Serkez, Yaryna, and Tim Wu. 2020. "These Companies Enriched Themselves: Now They're Getting a Bailout." *New York Times*, March 27. https://nyti.ms/2QPP09M.

Sevastopulo, Demetri, and Hannah Kuchler. 2020. "Donald Trump's Chaotic Coronavirus Crisis." *Financial Times*, March 27. https://www.ft.com/content/80aa0b58-7010-11ea -9bca-bf503995cd6f.

Seyfert, Robert. 2016. "Bugs, Predations or Manipulations? Incompatible Epistemic Regimes of High-Frequency Trading." *Economy and Society* 45 (2): 251–77.

Sinclair, Euan. 2010. *Option Trading: Pricing and Volatility Strategies and Techniques*. Hoboken, NJ: Wiley.

Smith, Michael E. 2011. *The Aztecs*. 3rd ed. Hoboken, NJ: Wiley.

Souleles, Daniel. 2019a. "The Distribution of Ignorance on Financial Markets." *Economy and Society* 48 (4): 510–31.

Souleles, Daniel. 2019b. *Songs of Profit, Songs of Loss: Private Equity, Wealth, and Inequality*. Lincoln: University of Nebraska Press.

Souleles, Daniel. 2020a. "Knotty Financiers: A Comparative Take on Finance, Value, and Inequality." *Journal of Anthropological Archaeology* 59 (September). https://doi.org/10 .1016/j.jaa.2020.101205.

Souleles, Daniel. 2020b. "Trading Options and the Unattainable Dream: Some Reflections on Semiotic Ideologies." *Signs and Society* 8 (2): 243–61.

Souleles, Daniel. 2020c. "What to Do with the Predator in Your Bibliography?" Allegra Lab: Anthropology for Radical Optimism (blog), September. https://allegralaboratory.net/ what-to-do-with-the-predator-in-your-bibliography/.

Souleles, Daniel. 2021. "Why Would You Buy an Electric Car on Jetski Friday? Or, a Critique of Financial Markets from an Options Trading Room." *Finance and Society* 7 (2): 113–29.

Stein, Felix. 2017. *Work, Sleep, Repeat: The Abstract Labour of German Management Consultants.* London: Bloomsbury.

Stein, Felix. 2018. "Selling Speed: Management Consultants, Acceleration, and Temporal Angst." *Political and Legal Anthropology Review* 41 (S1): 103–17.

Taussig, Michael. 1977. "The Genesis of Capitalism amongst a South American Peasantry: Devil's Labor and the Baptism of Money." *Comparative Studies in Society and History* 19 (2): 130–55.

Taylor, Kate. 2018. "The SEC Alleges That Elon Musk's $420 Price Point Was a Weed Reference to Amuse His Girlfriend." *Business Insider*, September 27. https://nordic.businessinsider .com/sec-says-elon-musks-420-price-point-was-a-weed-reference-2018-9?r=US&IR=T.

Tett, Gillian. 2020. "Why the US Federal Reserve Turned Again to BlackRock for Help." *Financial Times*, March 26. https://www.ft.com/content/f3ea07b0-6f5e-11ea-89df -41bea055720b?shareType=nongift.

Thomas, Landon, Jr. 2017. "Day Trading in Wall Street's Complex 'Fear Gauge' Proliferates." *New York Times*, August 28. https://www.nytimes.com/2017/08/28/business/dealbook/ vix-trading.html?auth=login-email&login=email.

Thompson, E. P. 1967. "Time, Work-Discipline, and Industrial Capitalism." *Past and Present* 38: 56–97.

United States Department of Justice, U.S. Attorney's Office, Middle District of Florida. 2017. "Marion County Convicted Felon Charged with Possession of Destructive Devices." Press release, February 16. https://www.justice.gov/usao-mdfl/pr/marion-county-convicted -felon-charged-possession-destructive-devices.

United States Securities and Exchange Commission. 2022a. "SEC Proposes Regulation Best Execution." Press release. https://www.sec.gov/news/press-release/2022-226.

United States Securities and Exchange Commission. 2022b. "SEC Proposes Rules to Amend Minimum Pricing Increments and Access Fee Caps and to Enhance the Transparency of Better Priced Orders." Press release. https://www.sec.gov/news/press-release/2022 -224.

United States Securities and Exchange Commission. N.d.a. "Fast Answers: National Securities Exchanges." https://www.sec.gov/fast-answers/divisionsmarketregmrexchangesshtml .html (accessed February 14, 2020; no longer posted).

United States Securities and Exchange Commission. N.d.b. "Form ATS-N Filings and Infor- mation." https://www.sec.gov/divisions/marketreg/form-ats-n-filings.htm.

Waters, Richard. 2022. "Musk Breaks the Spell He Had Woven around Tesla." *Financial Times*, December 30. https://www.ft.com/content/cf81ea51-d1bb-4145-8157-e514025c63ef ?shareType=nongift.

Waterston, Alisse. 1999. *Love, Sorrow, and Rage: Destitute Women in a Manhattan Residence.* Philadelphia: Temple University Press.

Weiss, Hadas. 2019. *We Have Never Been Middle Class.* London: Verso.

Weiss, Hadas. 2021. "Elusive Adulthood and Surplus Life-Time in Spain." *Critique of Anthro- pology.* https://doi.org/10.1177/0308275X211004717.

Weller, Susan C., Ben Vickers, H. Russell Bernard, Alyssa M. Blackburn, Stephen Borgatti, Clarence C. Gravlee, and Jeffrey C. Johnson. 2018. "Open-Ended Interview Questions and Saturation." *PLoS One* 13 (6): e0198606. https://doi.org/10.1371/journal.pone.0198606.

Wigglesworth, Robin. 2018. "How a Volatility Virus Infected Wall Street." *Financial Times*, April 12. https://www.ft.com/content/be68aac6-3d13-11e8-b9f9-de94fa33a81e.

Wigglesworth, Robin. 2019. "Are Markets Somehow 'Broken'?" *Financial Times*, June 14. https://www.ft.com/content/af043692-8d4c-11e9-a24d-b42f641eca37.

Wigglesworth, Robin. 2021. "'Weaponised' Options Trading Turbocharges GameStop's Dizzying Rally." *Financial Times*, January 27. https://www.ft.com/content/ae1ecff4-9019 -4a2a-97ea-55a3cd15c36a?shareType=nongift.

Wood, Helen. 2019. "Fuck the Patriarchy: Towards an Intersectional Politics of Irreverent Rage." *Feminist Media Studies* 19 (4): 609–15.

Zaloom, Caitlin. 2006. *Out of the Pits*. Chicago: University of Chicago Press.

Zaloom, Caitlin. 2009. "How to Read the Future: The Yield Curve, Affect, and Financial Prediction." *Public Culture* 21 (2): 245–68.

Zuckerman, Gregory. 2019. *The Man Who Solved the Market: How Jim Simons Launched the Quant Revolution*. London: Penguin Business.

Index

Page numbers in italics refer to illustrations.

adverse selection, 111-12
agent-based modeling simulation, 14
Agha, Asif, and slang, 9, 10
Agile (Scrum), 29-30
AlgoFinance project, and effects of computerized and algorithmic trading on markets, 13-14
algorithms, and automated trading: ability to reduce volatility and cause price swings, 106-7; as application of scientific model to trading strategies, 110-11, 128; broker algorithms, 106, 168; capabilities for trading on markets, 105-8; and changing reality for market traders, 95; complex relation with one another, 104; difficulty of defining, 101-2; execution and strategy, 105, 168; "first generation," 37, 186n2; inappropriateness for some markets, 106; limitations of, 104-5; as more academic and cerebral than pit trading, 107; need for supervision, 104; and order book, 106, 107, 171; require people in high demand to run them, 107; scanner, 123-24; "second generation," 39, 186n3; and solving problems, 104; and "techno-chauvinism," 97, 112; usage of word by quant traders, 102-5

algorithms, data analysis from interviews with exchange workers and quant traders: declarative statements about algorithms, 166-72; declarative statements about markets, 161-63; differences between exchange workers and TradeCo options traders in use of *market*, 67-68, 159-60; informants table, 147, 148-58; interviews with exchange workers, 65-66; interviews with people specialized in algorithmic or quantitative finance and trading, 102-3; schema of use of *algorithm* across subsample of quant traders, 165-66; schema of use of *market* across subsample of interviews, 65-68, 159-60; total instances of *algo* in subsample of quant interviews, 167; understanding of algorithms by quant traders, 103-5; understanding of what algorithms can do on markets by quant traders, 105-8
alienation and estrangement: of options market group in response to irrational market conditions, xi, xvii-xviii, xx, 62-63, 64, 128; technological, 23, 32, 33-35, 42, 50, 113; of workers in capitalist system, xiv-xx, 43, 113
Amazon, 52

American Depository Receipt (ADR), 17–19, 21

Appel, Hannah, and "national economy," 57–58

Arca. *See* NYSE Arca

Archer, Matthew, 186n2

ask/offer, 173, 178, 181

auction design, 69, 101, 190n3

automated computer algorithms. *See* algorithms, and automated trading

automation: and declining factory work in North Atlantic countries, xvi–xvii; and diminished role of specialized traders, 37

Banning, Horace (pseud.), and quant trader team, 108–12, 135; avoidance of "adverse selection," 111–12; and distinctions from pit traders, 109–10

Barnett, Mark Charles, 83–84

BATS, 122, 193n19

Bauer, Zach (pseud.): demographic characteristics, viii; early career as floor trader, 186n1; as head of TradeCo market group development team, 26–32, 33–34, 43, 50, 64

Bauman, Richard, 8

Benanav, Aaron, xvii

Bennett, Walt (pseud.), manager of group, viii, 31, 59–60, 118–20, 127, 192n3, 192n10

Bernanke, Ben S., 61, 62

Bernard, Russ, *Research Methods in Anthropology*, 189n1

"best execution," 183n2

*Bestor, Theodore, *Tsukiji*, 187n1

Beunza, Daniel, 7, 61, 87

Bhatt, Baiju, 88

bid/ask or bid/offer, defined, 173

Bikales, James S., 187n1

Bitcoin, 98

BlackRock, 117

Black Scholes Merton equation (or derivative equation), 3, 184n4; and the Greeks, 22, 91, 174, 176, 182, 192n11; lognormal distribution, 184n5, 192n8

Bodek, Haim, 190n3

bond, defined, 175

Borch, Christian, 13–14, 36, 38, 40, 187nn6–8

Borg, Kevin, "The 'Chauffeur Problem' in the Early Auto Era," 29–30, 35

Bradford Partners (pseud.): creation of adaptive machine-learning system with firm built around it, 36–37, 39–42, 50, 96, 113 (*see also* LINUS (pseud.)); firm as symbiotic environment for computerized trading system, 42, 46; and regenerative manufacturing, 47–48; subordination of individual traders to collaborative management of system, 36–37, 40–41, 43–44, 45, 50; trader of interest rate products and currency and commodity futures, 36; as traders adapting to new market conditions, 96

broker: defined, 173, 179; and TradeCo team, 80, 85, 86, 87–88

broker algorithms, 106, 168

Broussard, Meredith, 97

Brownian particle motion, 3, 182

Budish, Eric, 190n3

Burrell, Jenna, and automated computer algorithms, 95

calls and puts (options), 2, 174, 179

capitalism: accumulation by workers' generation of more wealth than they are paid, xv–xvi; uncoordinated accumulation of surplus wealth, xv, xvii

capitalist wage labor, and alienation and estrangement, xiv–xvi, 113; scholarship on, xvii–xx; worker creation of technology that allows increased production with less human labor, xvi–xvii, 43

CAP X (capital expenditure), 120, 122

CBOE. *See* Chicago Board Options Exchange (CBOE)

central banks, and equity purchases, 116, 192n5

CFTC. *See* Commodity Futures Trading Commission (CFTC)

Chang, David, 131

Chauffeur Problem, 28–35, 43

Cheatin' Chuck (Chuck Mark, pseud.), 85–88, 92

Chiang, Ted, 186n5

Chicago Board of Trade (CBOT), 62–63

Chicago Board Options Exchange (CBOE), 64; BATS, 122, 193n19; defined, 174, 175; volatility index (VIX), 183n2

Chicago Mercantile Exchange (CME): defined, 174; Globex electronic trading platform, xii; switch to "Bachelier" options pricing model, 184n5

Citadel, as large volume, fully automated firm, xi, xii–xiii, xiv, xvii, 4, 15, 92–93, 96

clearing or market clearing, 178

click trading, 37

CME. *See* Chicago Mercantile Exchange (CME)

colocation, 76, 162

commentary genre of speech, 8, 10

commodity exchanges, nineteenth-century, differences in design, 190n5

Commodity Futures Trading Commission (CFTC), 174, 175

COVID-19 pandemic, US response: drop in S&P 500, 131, *132*; government failure to extend health care to all citizens, 134; government response suggesting that human lives be sacrificed to improve economy, 131, 133–34, 193n1; and market crash, 53, 79; and spike in unemployment claims, 130–31, *131*; and spike in VIX, 131, *132*, 135

Cramton, Peter, 190n3

cryptocurrency, 98, 120

cultural or relational data, as shared knowledge, metaphors, or symbols used by group to communicate and understand the world, 189n1

dark pools, xii, 174

David, Zachary, 14

delta, 22, 91; defined, 174

$Delta, 22

"delta hedging," 6

Depository Trust and Clearing Corporation, 190n6

derivative: defined, 3, 174, 175; and price of underlying asset, 184n3

Derman, Emanuel, *My Life as a Quant*, 29

Discord, 88

"dissonance" in trader deliberations, 61

DMK, 22

Dolgopolov, Stanislaw, 190n3

DTheoPnL, 22

"dumb" money, 82, 177

Ebbtide (pseud.), 89–90, 92

economic anthropology, 126

Ellis, Tony (pseud.), 54, 92–93; and algorithmic traders, 102; commentary and formulaic talk, 7, 8; computer systems as "math and algorithms," 35, 42, 50; contempt for other traders, 89–91; demographic characteristics, viii; estrangement from market activities, 61, 62; and ITG, 26–27; and market villains, 55–56; and scanner, 25–26; and Tesla stock, 118–19, 121–22, 124–25; and trade tape, 24–25; and trading with the devil, 85, 86–87

equity, defined, 174

ETF (exchange traded fund), 15, 175

ETP (exchange traded product), 175

European Research Council, 13–14

exchanges: alternative ("dark pools"), xii; competition for market share, 190n2; defined, 175; electronic access to, xii; forms that orders can take on the exchange, 69–70; "matching engine" governed by auction rules, 69; people designing and working at (*see* market engineers)

"execution," 183n2

EXP (expiration date), 22

Federal Reserve: effects of actions on market, 116; response to COVID-19 pandemic, 134–35

financial crisis: defined, x; of 2007/2008, 191n2

financial instrument, defined, 175

financial markets: ability to make money in given period time period, 58; as defined by sample of market engineers, 65–68 (*see also* financial markets, described by market engineers); effects of government actions on, 4–5, 54–56, 61, 115–16; effects of highly automated

financial markets (*continued*)
market makers on, xii, 61–62, 92–95, 123–24; history of last half century, xviii–xix; as increasingly characterized by digitization and automation, xviii–xix, 4, 13–14, 28–29, 44, 50 (*see also* algorithms, and automated trading); as increasingly complex, politically managed, and confusingly regulated, xii, xx; largest way that society allocates wealth, 68–69; metaphoric use of *market*, 52; reversal of traditional distinction between "front office" and "back office," 29; stock exchange as example of, 187n1; takeover by people with backgrounds in physics, mathematics, data science, and engineering, xix; "the market," 51. *See also* exchanges; financial markets, design

financial markets, described by market engineers: affective or metaphorical descriptions of markets, 66–67; comparison with markets as decried by Trade-Co options group, 67–68; markets as places to be designed and manipulated, 68; markets as qualitatively described places, 66–67; practical descriptions of markets, 67

financial markets, design: commodity exchanges, differences between markets in New Orleans and Chicago, 190n5; dimensions affecting trader control over order behavior, 70–73; IEX, 76–78; "matching" servers, 69; and normative agendas, 78, 190n6; order forms, 69–70; Shanghai Stock Exchange (SSE), 73–75

FINRA (Financial Industry Regulatory Authority), 175

first in, first out (FIFO) matching, 69

Fitbit, 97

flashboyed, 4, 92, 95, 101

flow (or order flow), defined, 176

"flow whores" (momentum traders), 55

formulaic play-by-play speech, 7–8, 9, 24

Foster, Lee (pseud.), viii, 192n9

fuck, urbandictionary.com definition, 143. *See also* TradeCo (pseud.) options market group, language use

futures: defined, 176; negative prices, 184n5; Spooz (S&P 500 futures contracts), 7, 59–60, 86, 181; traders of, 62–63

GameStop stocks, 88–89, 119–20

gamma, defined, 22, 176

"gamma squeeze," 191n4

Golden, Seth M., 81, 82–83

Goldman Sachs, 29

Google, 52

Greek letters ("the Greeks"), 22, 91, 174, 176, 182, 192n11

Greenspan, Alan, 62

handle: defined, 6, 176; whooshes, 6–7

Hansen, Kristian Bondo, 13

Hart, Keith, xx, 114

hedge fund, defined, 177

hedge/hedging, 15, 88–89, 191n4; defined, 176

Heritage, Stuart, 133

Hertz, Ellen, *The Trading Crowd*, 73–75, 78

Holmes, Douglas, 123

Hughes, Kyle (pseud.), viii, 24, 26–27, 31, 61, 90–91

Hunsader, Eric, 77

ICE chat, 23–24, 85, 92

IEX, and neutralization of high-speed advantages to trading, 76–78

implied volatility, defined, 177

individual, or case-based data, 189n1

industrial time clock, and displacement of local notions of time, xvii

initial public offering (IPO), Uber, 7, 52–53

in-person traders. *See* pit traders

institutional investors: defined, 177; and Tesla stock, 117

interest rate products, and chain of expiration dates, 36

International Exchange, 179

investor, defined, 177

Invisible Scalp, 77

ishares.com, 18, 21

ITG, 26–27, 64

Jackson, Michael, "Familiar and Foreign Bodies," 33, 34, 37, 44, 128–29, 186n2

Jaws, character of mayor, 133–34

Jeff Miller (pseud.) and group. *See* TradeCo (pseud.) options market group

"Jet Ski Fridays," 26, 117, 126, 192n6

Johnson, Boris, and COVID-19 pandemic, 133

Keane, Webb, 193n1

Kolhatkar, Sheelah, 88

Kudlow, Larry, 81

Kuiper, Koenraad, 7, 10

Kumar, Pankaj, 14

latency, defined, 23

layering. *See* spoofing

lean manufacturing, 47

leverage costs, 100, 101

Lewis, Michael, *Flash Boys*, 4, 75–78, 94

limit orders, 69, 179

LINUS (pseud.), 96, 123, 135, 187n1; advantage of in trading, 92; increased managerial control over trading and reduced role of traders, 36–37, 42–43; limitations, 106, 186n5; personification of, 44–46; as personified embodiment of all who work at company, 42, 44, 50, 187n6; production system, 46–48; supervision by skilled market analysts, 48–50, 186n5, 187n8; understanding of human intention and ability to learn, 44–46

liquidity, 100, 124; defined, 178; and role of market makers or middlemen, ix–x, 192n3

live stand-up comedy, "dirty" or "clean," 10–11

London Stock Exchange, 64

long, defined, 178

Lyft, 7

machine learning: algorithms, 97; limitations, 186n5; philosophical idea of, 41–42. *See also* Bradford Partners (pseud.); LINUS (pseud.)

MacKenzie, Donald, 123–24

margin, defined, 178

"market": broadly defined, 187n1; use of *market* in interviews with market engineers, 65–68. *See also* financial markets;

TradeCo (pseud.) options market group, view of "the market"

market design. *See* financial markets, design

market engineers, 64–65; use of *market* across subsample of interviews, 65–68

market makers or middlemen: defined, 178; high-speed traders, xii; interest in trading to provide liquidity and collect spread, ix–x, 192n3; and options, xiii; transition to screen trading, xii. *See also* TradeCo (pseud.) options market group

market orders, 69, 179

"market sentiment," 51–52

Marx, Karl, and dynamics of estranged labor, xvi, 95

matching: first in, first out (FIFO), 69; pro rata, 69

"matching" servers, 69

Mauss, Marcell, *The Gift*, 187n1

Megaw, Nicholas, 183n2

"meme stocks," 88

Meyers, Aaron (pseud.): anxiety over future of group, x–xi, xiii–xiv; demographic characteristics, viii; estrangement from market, 31–32, 50, 53, 62; and other traders, 53–55, 80, 83, 87, 89, 91; and technology failures, 31–32, 50; and Tesla stock, 193n21

Milgrom, Paul, *Putting Auction Theory to Work*, 190n3

Miller, Jason, 81–82

Miller, Jeff (pseud.): background as in-person pit trader, xii, 23, 30–31, 192n9; commentary and formulaic talk, 7–8; contempt for people seeking to trade with group, 85–91; demographic characteristics, viii; and Ebbtide, 89–90; estrangement from market activities, 60–61; and large mechanical markets, 94–95; and market villains, 55–56; metaphoric use of *market*, 51, 52; speculation on group's future, xiii–xiv; swearing, 11–12; and Tesla stock, 118–26, 193n22; on trade tape, scanner, and ITG, 25–27; on Uber's overpriced stock, 53

Min, Bo Hee, 13, 36, 38, 187nn6–8

Mktpnl, 22

Mnuchin, Steven T., 54, 56

multilegged trades, 84–85

Musk, Elon, 114, 115, 125, 126, 193n22; and 4-20 reference, 122, 193n17; influence on Tesla and other stocks, 119–20; investigation by SEC, 123; largest shareholder of Tesla stock, 117; selling of Tesla stock to purchase Twitter, 123

NASDAQ, 7, 64, 187n1; automated brokerage network, xii; defined, 179

national economy, as metaphor for understanding countries, 57–58, 135

National Market System, 94; defined, xi–xii; orders designed not to route to other exchanges, 70; SIP (Securities Information Processor), aggregated data feed, 4, 76

National Securities Exchanges, xii

New Jersey Division of Investment, 117

New York Times, profile of Seth Golden, 82–83

Nguyen, Michael, 51

note-taking summary, and observations of TradeCo options market group, x, 141

NYSE (New York Stock Exchange), xii, 7, 64; defined, 179

NYSE Arca: defined, 173; dimension along which traders can control order behaviors, 70; order types, 69–70; TradeCo group difficulty in communicating with, 15–16, 23

Olin, Brad (pseud.): application of computer programming techniques to various businesses and hedge fund, 98; overcoming ignorance of finance and markets, 98–101; surveillance and tracking algorithms in personal health monitoring, 96–97; "technochauvinism," 97, 102, 135

OmktPnL, 22

open outcry trading, 175

options: "American"-style, 183n1; calls and puts, 2, 174, 179; defined, 1–2, 179; differing prices and times of expiration,

2; option chains, 3–4; value degradation over time, 193n18

options, pricing, 3, 184n5, 192n8, 192n11. *See also* Black Scholes Merton equation (or derivative equation)

order books, 68, 71, 80, 101, 111; accessible only through computer intermediation, 28–29; and algorithms, 106, 107, 171; defined, 179; orders pulled from, 191n7; and pay-for-play schemes, 76; and rebates, 180; and spoofed orders, 181; and spread, 181

orders: complexity of types, 69–70; limited, 69; market, 69; order type, defined, 179

order stacking, defined, 181. *See also* spoofing

Organisation for Economic Co-operation and Development (OECD), 38

Ortiz, Horacio, xx, 114

Ortiz, Rob (pseud.), viii, 7, 60, 61, 87

OtheoPnL, 22

Pardo-Guerra, Juan Pablo, 64–65

partial derivatives, 182

pay-for-play and pay-for-data schemes, 76

Peele, Jordan, and *Jaws* mayor tweet, 133–34, *134*

penny pilot, 93–94

Piipuu, Merilin, "The Mobile Phone in the Hands of the Nepalese People," 33, 186n2

Pinzur, David, 190n5

pit traders: certified, on TradeCo team, 192n9; distinction from quant traders, 107, 109–10; pushed out by electronic access, xii

PnL (profit and loss), 22–23, 180; ledger, 43, 44

portfolio, defined, 180

position, defined, 180

Powell, Jerome, 87

PremovrPty, 22

Price, Brandon (pseud.): and advantages of automated traders, 92–94; background as in-person pit trader, xii, 23, 30–31; demographic characteristics, viii; on future in trading, x, xi; and

market time period as "over," 58–59; and other traders, 85, 86, 87, 89–90; and technology failures, 31–32; and Tesla stock, 121–22, 124–25
profanity distribution of *fuck*, in TradeCo options market group conversations, 143, 144–45
pro rata matching, 69
publicly traded, defined, 180
puking, 80, 81, 84, 89
put option, 2, 174, 177
puts and calls. *See* calls and puts (options)

qualitative versus quantitative data, false distinction between, 189n1
quant traders: commentary on what algorithms can do on markets, 105–8; concern with mathematical formalism, raw data, and theories and predictions, 108, 112; distinctions between themselves and older style traders, 107–8, 113, 128, 135; understanding of algorithms, 101, 102–5. *See also* Banning, Horace (pseud.), and quant trader team

rebate, 178, 180
Reddit, 88
registers: categorized as slang, 9, 10; distinct ways of talking, 9; of professional "trader," 9, 11
Renaissance Technologies, 107–8
"resonance" in trader deliberations, 61
"retail traders" or "dumb" money, 82, 177
Robinhood, smartphone-based retail trading platform, 87–88
Robinhood traders, 87, 92, 94; and "meme stocks," 88–89, 119
r/wallstreetbets, 88

S&P Dow Jones Indices, 180
S&P 500 stock index: defined, 180; futures based on (Spooz), 7, 59–60, 86, 181; and VIX, 2
saturation, defined, 65–66
scalps, 5, 6
scanner, 25–26, 31, 122, 123–24, 193n20
Scrum (Agile), 29–30, 51
Seaver, Nick, 102

Securities and Exchange Act of 1934, 1975 amendment, xi
Securities and Exchange Commission (SEC): defined, 174, 175, 181; investigation of Musk for manipulating Tesla stock, 119–20, 123; Reg NMS, xi, 4, 76; rule changes, 183n2
Seizer, Susan, and live stand-up comedy, 10–11
Seyfert, Robert, 102
Shanghai Stock Exchange (SSE), ability to accumulate foreign capital and preserve government control, 73–75, 190n6
Shim, John, 190n3
shorting, 88–89, 181, 191n3, 193n14
Simons, Jim, 107–8, 112
SIP (Securities Information Processor), aggregated data feed, 4, 76
Skar-Gislinge, Nicholas, 14
"skew" strategies, 91
slang, 9, 10
"sodomites," as manipulators of market's accurate pricing of stocks, 55
SpaceX, 115
spoofing, 73, 181
Spooz (S&P 500 futures contracts), 7, 59–60, 86, 181
spread, 178, 181, 192n3
"sprint lists," 26, 32
SPY, ETF made up of S&P 500 stock, 55, 182
Stark, David, 61
Starlink, 115
stock, defined, 175, 182
stock exchange, as example of financial market, 187n1
stock market, as proxy of national health and politicians' electability, 57–58, 135
stock price inflation, 52
strike, 56, 189n3
swearing: as part of professional speech register, 11; as taboo behavior in US, 11. *See also* TradeCo (pseud.) options market group, language use

Target, 191n1
Target traders, 81–84; and "retail traders" or "dumb" money, 82, 177

Taussig, Michael, xvii
"technochauvinism," 97, 102, 112, 135
technological alienation, 23, 32, 33–35, 42, 50, 113
tech stocks, 6
Tenev, Vlad, 88
Tesla Inc., 114, 192n12
Tesla stock: and institutional investors, 117; Musk's influence on price of, 119–20; options traders and, 114–15; TradeCo options market group investment decision on, 114–24
Theo (theoretical), 23
TheoPnL, 22
theta, 90, 91; defined, 22, 176, 182
"theta bomb," 176
Thomas, Landon, 82–83
Thompson, E. P., xvii
tick size, 93–94, 181, 183n2
Toyota production system, 47
TradeCo (pseud.) options market group: certified pit traders among, 192n9; critical of structure and governance of markets, xix; demographic characteristics of members, viii; essential function in capital markets through provision of liquidity, ix–x, 192n3; individualization in relation to markets, xviii; liminal status, xvii–xviii; options "market makers" or middlemen, ix–x, 114–15; pit and phone trading and conventional trading backgrounds, xii, xix, 23, 30–31, 84, 108; pricing in unusual events and market-making, 118–24; pricing of "nonlognormal" events, 192n8; purchase of equities to hedge risk of options positions, 15, 88–89; real-time analysis and action within never-ending conversation, 5–8, 184n6; surprise at survival against more profitable company, x–xi, xiii–xiv; tradable names and options calendars, 16, 17–21, 22; trading activity as small bets, 128; view of themselves as in-control traders, 36, 43, 108
TradeCo (pseud.) options market group, and other market traders: adjustment of trading behavior based on that of other market traders, 79–81, 84–85,

191n2; and "adverse selection," 111; big movers who are out of their depth, 91–92; brokers on ICE chat or who call, 92; Cheatin' Chuck, 85–88, 92, 111; contempt for people seeking to trade with them, 85–91, 111; Ebbtide, 89–90, 92; mechanical or automated actors, 92–95, 112; personification of others they are trading against, 80–84, 91–92, 112, 128; Robinhood traders, 87–89, 92; Target traders, 80–84
TradeCo (pseud.) options market group, and Tesla options: conversations about abnormal risk, pricing, and motivation of political and other actors, 114–26, 192n3, 192n5; evaluation of stock price and how investors will trade it, 114–15; example of money moving around financial market according to local political economy, 125; intermediate position on Tesla stock, 125–26; and "Jet Ski Fridays," 117; use of scanner to read markets, 122, 123–24, 127, 193n20
TradeCo (pseud.) options market group, language use: epithets for women, 10; formulaic language of statistics, 23; formulaic play-by-play reporting and commentary genres, 7–8, 9, 24; *fuck* morphological distribution, 9, 12, 13; *fucks*, as discourse markers, affective tags, and emphases of importance, 11–12, 128; *fucks*, more frequent occurrence than other common adjectives, 184n7; profanity distribution of *fuck* among traders by grammatical form and number of appearances, 143, 144–45; swearing as lacking in innovation or creativity, 186n9; swearing as part of professional speech register, 8–13, 129; and white male social norms, 186n8
TradeCo (pseud.) options market group, technology problems: bugs across system, 27, 32; frustration and rage with technical system, 23, 32, 33–35, 42, 50; ICE chat, 23–24; inability to fix problems, 28, 29; ITG, 26–27, 64; and latency, 23; and need for capability to receive and interpret data feed and

send and receive messages to and from all exchanges, 16; reliance on market access from third-party brokers, 26–27; reliance on off-site development team, 16, 26, 27, 28, 29, 31–32; "sprint list," 26, 32; systemwide freezes, 28; trade tape, 24–25. *See also* TradeCo (pseud.) options market group, view of "the market"

TradeCo (pseud.) options market group, view of "the market": differences between traders and exchange workers in use of *market*, 67–68, 159–60; estrangement and alienation, xi, xvii–xviii, xx, 62–63, 64, 128; frustration with high-speed and highly automated market makers, xii–xv, xx–xxi, 61–62, 92–95, 112, 135; identification with market, 63; and imagining of different possible futures for markets, 59–62, 111; on manipulation of stocks as result of acts of governments, central bankers, and politicians, 54–56, 59–63, 64, 74, 84, 87, 115–18, 123, 125, 128, 135, 191n2; market as possible universe of moneymaking opportunities, 52; *market* as reference to both actual stock exchanges and metaphorical totality, 56–57; and possibility for making money within specific units of time, 58–59; on "sodomites" and "flow whores," 55; on stocks as overpriced, 52, 53, 55

traders: defined, 182; diminished role of with automation, 37; futures of, 62–63; high-speed, xii; in-person, pushed out by electronic access, xii; momentum, or "flow whores," 55; pit versus quant, 109–10; "retail," 82, 177. *See also* market makers or middlemen; quant traders; TradeCo (pseud.) options market group

trade tape, unreliability of, 24–25

Trolley comic, pandemic meme variation of trolley problem, 130

"Trolley Problem," 129–30, 193n1

Trump, Donald: COVID-19 pandemic response that economy reopen "by Easter," 133; trade war with China, 54, 59

Twitter (now X), 115, 123

Uber: basic business model, 52; initial public offering (IPO), 7, 52–53

underwriting, 53

unicorns, 189n2; "unicorn" cycle, 53, 55

valuation analysis of companies, 122

Vanguard, 117

vega, 22, 182, 192n11

Virtu, 93, 96

VIX (volatility index): defined, 182; as numerical abstraction of stability or volatility, 2–3; one-day, 183n2; spike during COVID-19 pandemic, 2

VIX (volatility index) contracts, xii; bought by fund managers as portfolio insurance, 1, 3; derivatives, 3, 79, 82; determining price of, 3–4; and option chains, 3–4

volatility, defined, 2, 182. *See also* implied volatility, defined

Weiss, Hadas, "Elusive Adulthood and Surplus Life-Time in Spain," xv, xviii

"whooshing" up, 5, 6, 59

Wigglesworth, Robin: "Are Markets Somehow 'Broken'?," 192n4; "'Weaponised' Options Trading Turbocharges GameStop's Dizzying Rally," 88–89

Yellen, Janet, 61, 62

Zuckerman, Gregory, 107–8